Double Eagle

Double Eagle

The Epic Story of the World's
Most Valuable Coin

Alison Frankel

W. W. Norton & Company

New York London

For information about permission to reproduce selections from this book, write to Permissions, W. W. Norton & Company Inc., 500 Fifth Avenue, New York, NY 10110

Manufacturing: The Courier Companies, Inc.
Book design: Lovedog Studio
Production manager: Amanda Morrison

LIBRARY OF CONGRESS CATALOGING-IN-PUBLICATION DATA
Frankel, Alison.
Double eagle : the epic story of the world's most valuable coin / Alison Frankel. — 1st ed.
p.m.
Includes bibliographical references and index.
ISBN-13: 978-0-393-05949-6 (hardcover)
ISBN-10: 0-393-05949-9 (hardcover)
1. Double eagle (Coin)—History. I. Title.
CJ1834.F73 2006
737.497309—dc22
2005030676

W. W. Norton & Company Inc., 500 Fifth Avenue, New York, N.Y. 10110
www.wwnorton.com

W. W. Norton & Company Ltd., Castle House, 75/76 Wells Street, London W1T 3QT

1 2 3 4 5 6 7 8 9 0

For Dan, Anna, and Lily:
My life's treasures

Contents

Double Eagle

Prologue

WHEN HE AWOKE AT the New York Hilton on the day he was supposed to complete the biggest deal of his career, Stephen Fenton put on a brand-new black cashmere sweater. He wasn't dressing up for the occasion—Fenton is a coin dealer, a breed for whom the rule is sartorial indifference—and he paid no more attention to his clothing on February 8, 1996, than he usually did. He would only remember the sweater because he never wore it again. For years he couldn't bring himself to throw it out—it was still a perfectly good cashmere sweater, worn just one time—but after what happened that day, Fenton could hardly stand the sight of it.

That was later, though. On the morning of February 8, Fenton was trying not to think about everything that might go wrong with his deal. He finished dressing, left his hotel room, and took the elevator down to the Hilton's lobby. There he retrieved from the hotel safe a small object in a square plastic envelope. It was a coin, a one-of-a-kind $20 gold piece, and it was the most valuable ounce of gold the forty-three-year-old Fenton, a coin dealer for more than twenty-five years, had ever held. If his deal went through—and even after six weeks of negotiation, Fenton wasn't sure that it would—he'd trade the coin later that morning for $850,000.

Fenton, a Londoner, had flown into New York City the night before on the Concorde. He always flew the Concorde to New York; he hated flying and the Concorde was the quickest way to end the misery. Besides, he liked the luxury, and he could afford it. An unassuming man with a rubbery bulldog face and a fringe of brown hair, Fenton was one of the most successful coin dealers in England. Coins had been his salvation. Fenton had been a quirky, insular child, in the habit of skipping school for solitary restaurant lunches. His mother, a casual coin collector herself, suggested that he take up the hobby. The boy began by looking through pocket change. Then he started reading coin books and magazines, discovering that he had an effortless recall of dates, denominations, and mintage figures. He also had a good eye. He could look at a coin, assess its quality, and store its image in his memory. Most important, he learned that he had the one talent indispensable to a dealer: Even as a kid, Fenton knew what buyers wanted. At fifteen, he had quit school and, after aborted training at Harrod's, talked his way into the employ of a coin shop across the street from the menswear store his father managed. Seven years later, with a £1,000 loan from his parents, he'd opened his own coin business.

By the morning of his big deal, Fenton had owned his own shop for fifteen years. He'd bought and sold most of the great coin rarities of Britain, and many of the United States as well. None had had the effect on him of the 1933 Double Eagle, the coin that he slipped into his shirt pocket in the lobby of the New York Hilton. The 1933 Double Eagle was a hallowed coin. It was surpassingly rare—so rare, in fact, that until Fenton first saw it in September 1995, he wasn't sure the coin really existed. It was beautiful, a mint-condition specimen of America's most gorgeous coin design. It was also, at least for Fenton, a bit of a problem. The 1933 Double Eagle was illegal to own in the United States.

Almost half a million $20 gold Double Eagles had been minted in Philadelphia at the beginning of 1933, but none had been officially released from U.S. Mint vaults before President Franklin Roosevelt banned Americans from owning gold later that year. Two 1933 Double

Eagles were sent to the Smithsonian Institution to be preserved as part of the National Numismatic Collection. All the rest, on orders of the Treasury Department, were supposed to have been melted down into gold bricks. Yet somehow, a handful had slipped out of the Mint in Philadelphia. Of those, only one 1933 Double Eagle was known to have survived beyond the 1950s. Its story—a tale that included a conspiracy at the Mint, a bloated Egyptian prince, and forty years of mystery and rumor—seemed too bizarre to be true.

But true it was. And now Stephen Fenton had the coin. Just seeing it gave him a jolt. Like most coin dealers, Fenton didn't like to talk much about how he acquired his coins or how much he'd paid for them. In the weeks of negotiation to sell the 1933 Double Eagle, he never disclosed the coin's provenance. He didn't need to. All that mattered was the date, that tiny, magical 1933 on the face of the gold piece. For anyone who cared about coins, handling a 1933 Double Eagle was like catching a ride on a unicorn.

Fenton's sale of the coin was to take place at the Waldorf-Astoria, a few blocks across town from the Hilton. It was an easy twenty-minute walk, but not for someone carrying an $850,000 coin in his pocket. In the Hilton's lobby, Fenton met up with his cousin, Barry Castelete, who would be accompanying him to the Waldorf, just in case the deal went bad. The two men took a cab to the hotel's grand Park Avenue entrance. They walked up a short flight of stairs and into the paneled Art Deco lobby. Fenton unbuttoned his coat. Castelete took off his black knit cap and stuffed it in his back pocket. The Waldorf's lobby was crowded, so it took a couple of minutes for the two men to find Jasper Parrino, the Kansas City coin dealer who had arranged the sale of Fenton's 1933 Double Eagle. Fenton had never been introduced to Parrino, but he knew what Parrino looked like. Everyone in the coin business knew. Parrino had burst into the rare-coin market in the 1980s, arriving from obscurity with piles of money to spend on coins. He bought and sold only the rarest and most expensive pieces, and was a tireless self-promoter, running flashy advertisements in coin magazines and buying the most prominent tables at the big coin shows.

Parrino, a small man with a square face dominated by heavy black eyebrows and sharp eyes, was standing next to one of the glass display cases in the Waldorf lobby. The case was filled with equipment from a store in the hotel's shopping arcade that sold spy gear. "Look at the stuff they've got," Parrino said to Fenton after handshakes and introductions. "Isn't this stuff neat?" Fenton agreed that it was, but he wasn't really paying attention to Parrino's small talk. He just wanted to sell his coin and collect his money.

Parrino told Fenton that the buyer was staying in a suite in the Waldorf Towers section of the hotel. He'd already talked to him that morning, and everything was all set. They'd complete the trade up in the buyer's room. As Fenton, Castelete, and Parrino headed for the elevator bank, Fenton finally began to relax. "It's going to be a wonderful deal," Parrino said.

He was wrong. The story of the 1933 Double Eagle was about to swerve, yet again, in a weird and unexpected direction.

Chapter One

"Give Us a Coinage That Has Some Beauty!"

A COIN—EVEN A COIN as beautiful as the 1933 Double Eagle—is nothing more than a small, round piece of metal, cold and hard to the touch. A coin does not change. The figure of Liberty caught in mid-stride on the front of the 1933 Double Eagle will never complete her step. Her face, frozen in determination, will never break into a smile, a grimace, a sneer. A coin feels nothing. It has no heart and no soul.

But it does have a story. Every coin has one, even the humblest penny lying forgotten on the pavement. Whose pockets carried that coin? How long is the chain of people who touched that particular bit of metal? And what fleeting moments in their lives does it commemorate? Coins are the tokens of destiny, hard evidence of millions of random, ephemeral intersections between otherwise-unconnected existences. Coins' stories are our stories, their changeless faces the silent witnesses to our engagement with the world.

And those are just the stories of ordinary coins. The 1933 Double Eagle is anything but ordinary. For most coins, the chain of history is a flimsy construction of pure caprice. Not so for the 1933 Double

Eagle, which was special from the moment it was minted and has become even more extraordinary with every addition to its story. The 1933 Double Eagle doesn't merely reflect emotions, it inspires them—outsize passion, greed, and yearning. It's just a coin, just one cold ounce of gold fashioned into a small disk worth twenty dollars on its face. But its grand, sprawling opera of a story is priceless.

THAT STORY begins a hundred years ago, with the dazzle of a Gilded Age banquet at the Arlington Hotel in Washington, DC. The January 11, 1905, dinner was a celebration of the American Academy in Rome, a festive alliance of politics and art in an age of exuberant American empire-building. The toast list alternated between artists and Washington eminences. John LaFarge was to represent painters. Nicholas Murray Butler, the president of Columbia University, was to speak on the topic of art in civilization. Elihu Root, the distinguished former secretary of war, was to speak for the government, as was Justice John Harlan of the United States Supreme Court. George McClellan, the mayor of New York, was to give the final toast, "The Making of a Beautiful City."[1]

Poor Augustus Saint-Gaudens. The artist—fifty-six years old, reedy, and redheaded—was to give the toast celebrating sculpture, and, in such silver-tongued company, he dreaded it. "Ten lines of oratorical idiocy," he grumbled in a letter to his wife, Augusta.[2] It wasn't that Saint-Gaudens was unaccustomed to grandeur. In his thirty-five-year rise to fame, this son of an immigrant French shoemaker had learned to cultivate men and women of influence. Saint-Gaudens created monumental public statuary—he was renowned for his sculptures of Admiral David Farragut, President Abraham Lincoln, and General William Tecumseh Sherman—and to win those commissions, he had to have connections as well as talent. Saint-Gaudens had both, in abundance. People who met the sculptor were inevitably attracted to his diffident manner and sly flashes of humor; Saint-Gaudens never pretended an intellectualism he didn't possess, but he counted great minds of the time among his good friends. He made such an impression on Robert Louis Stevenson, who sat for a Saint-Gaudens bas relief in 1888, that Stevenson addressed him as "God-like sculptor" in the correspondence the writer maintained with Saint-Gaudens until he died.[3] Nor was the artist intimidated by wealth; Saint-Gaudens was perfectly comfortable writing a personal letter of solicitation to Henry Clay Frick on behalf of the academy.[4]

Yet for all his native charm, Saint-Gaudens hated making speeches. Henry Adams—for whom the sculptor created his masterpiece, an enigmatic memorial to Adams's wife that stands in Washington's Rock Creek Park—called him, "the most sympathetic, but certainly the most inarticulate" of American artists.[5] Adams believed that it was, in fact, Saint-Gaudens's directness, his lack of artifice, that made him a genius. "He required no incense; he was no egoist; his simplicity of thought was excessive; he could not imitate, or give any form but his own to the creations of his hand," wrote Adams. "No one felt more strongly than he the strength of other men, but the idea that they could affect him never stirred an image in his mind."

Saint-Gaudens got through his toast at the American Academy dinner, saying nothing so memorable that he bothered to save it. Relieved, he took his seat at the head table, next to his dear old friend John Hay, the secretary of state. He had managed to hide his nervousness, Saint-Gaudens later wrote to Augusta,[6] and the speech had been a success. "Decidedly the best because it was the briefest!" he crowed. The night, he told his wife, turned out to be exhilarating. Justice Harlan had praised Saint-Gaudens in his toast, and the tables were crowded with friends of the sculptor, among them Whitelaw Reid of *The New York Herald*, the architectural giants Stanford White and Charles McKim, and a protégé, Daniel Chester French. Not until one-thirty in the morning did Saint-Gaudens crowd into a two-person taxi with Henry James, John LaFarge, and LaFarge's butler, all of them still laughing about the toastmaster's drunken efforts.

Saint-Gaudens had another reason to be exultant about the affair, though he didn't mention it in his first report to his wife. President Theodore Roosevelt had made an appearance at the banquet and had sought out Saint-Gaudens. The president and the artist held each other in high regard. After Saint-Gaudens's statue of General Sherman was unveiled in New York in 1903, Roosevelt had sent his congratulations. "Thrice over for the good fortune of our countrymen," he wrote, "it was given you to strike this highest note."[7] Saint-Gaudens had responded in kind: "Your letter will be set aside and treasured for those who come after me."[8] At the American Academy feast, Roosevelt made the sculptor a flattering proposition. He was dissatisfied with the inaugural medal the U.S. Mint had created to mark his 1904 election, Roosevelt told Saint-Gaudens. Would the sculptor care to design an alternate inaugural medal?[9]

Saint-Gaudens hesitated. As gratified as he was by Roosevelt's request, he was overwhelmed with work; a notorious perfectionist, he was chronically late in completing commissions. But Roosevelt was, as always, irrepressible in pursuit of what he wanted. The night after the American Academy banquet, Saint-Gaudens dined at the White House with the president and Henry Adams, Henry James, and John LaFarge. Again, Roosevelt raised the prospect of Saint-Gaudens designing his inaugural medal, suggesting a visit to the director of the U.S. Mint to discuss it. Saint-Gaudens, LaFarge noticed, was quiet that night, studying the contours of Roosevelt's face as if he were already envisioning the president's portrait in clay.[10]

By the time Saint-Gaudens left Washington to return to his retreat in New Hampshire, Roosevelt had prevailed. Saint-Gaudens had agreed to design the medal. How could he refuse? Not only would he be creating a historic image of Roosevelt, a man he admired enormously, he'd also be supplanting the work of a man he could not abide: the Mint's longtime chief engraver, Charles Barber.

SAINT-GAUDENS WAS not alone in his disdain for Charles Barber, a haughty, peevish man who guarded his ground at the U.S. Mint with the yapping ferocity of a terrier. Barber came from a line of engravers that extended back to the family's roots in Germany. In 1879, he succeeded his father, William Barber, as the chief engraver of the United States Mint—not because he was the most talented candidate but because he was expert at squelching competitors. By 1905, when Saint-Gaudens agreed to design Roosevelt's inaugural medal, he and Barber had already tangled twice. In 1891, the Department of the

Treasury decided to hold a competition to remake three silver coins—a signal of discontent with Barber, since coinage design had always been the province of the chief engraver.[11] The department at first invited ten prominent artists, including Saint-Gaudens, to submit designs, but that scheme ended when the artists responded with their fee requests. Then Treasury officials announced that members of the public could compete for the honor of redesigning the coins. Three judges would evaluate submissions: a Boston gem engraver and medalist named Henry Mitchell, Augustus Saint-Gaudens, and Charles Barber.

Barber and Saint-Gaudens were quickly at odds, not over the designs that had been submitted—none of which, the judges all agreed, was remotely acceptable—but over who was qualified to undertake the redesign. Saint-Gaudens told Mint Director Edward O. Leech that only four men in the world were capable of creating coins of beauty and inspiration—he and three French artists. Barber, particularly after observing Saint-Gaudens's penchant for high-relief designs, informed Leech that he knew of no artist competent even to *assist* him in preparing models for new coins.[12] The contest, needless to say, limped to a close without an announcement of a winner. That result was fine for Barber, who proceeded with his plans for new silver dollars and quarter-dollars, but not as felicitous for the nation's coinage. Barber's designs debuted in 1892 with a thud, leading a number of numismatic organizations to begin agitating for more artistic U.S. coins.

By then, Saint-Gaudens and Barber were back at it. The sculptor had been asked to design the official medal of the Columbian Exposition of 1893, the national extravaganza known as the Chicago World's Fair. Saint-Gaudens was a supporter of the exposition, advising on the selection of the young artists who created statuary for the "White City." But twice he declined the $5,000 commission to design the Columbian Exposition medal. Only when the medal's patroness, Chicago society doyenne Bertha Palmer, prevailed upon him did Saint-Gaudens finally accept. His design was an artistic triumph. On its face was a depiction of Christopher Columbus that "breathes mastery of the human figure over a limited area made interesting by variations in surface planes," wrote Cornelius Vermeule in *Numismatic Art in America*.[13] The medal's reverse showed a Greek-inspired young man and a small eagle, a design that Vermeule pronounced, "an essay in patriotic idealism." The Treasury secretary pronounced it obscene. Saint-Gaudens's youth was nude, and, despite two attempts by the sculptor to cover up the offending anatomy, the image was deemed unacceptable. Barber was called upon to design a new reverse side for the medal. He produced a busy tableau, crowding together Columbus's ship the *Santa Maria*; a pair of crouching Greek goddesses and a globe; and two torches flanking an inscription. "Prosaic in the extreme," was Vermeule's assessment. The Saint-Gaudens family was appalled at the final medal, which paired Saint-Gaudens's sublime Columbus with the uninspired work of Barber, a man whom Saint-Gaudens considered a hack.

But with the commission Roosevelt urged upon him in January 1905, Saint-Gaudens would have a chance to put Charles Barber in his place. For the president didn't just ask the sculptor to design a new inaugural medal for him. Roosevelt also wanted Saint-Gaudens to redesign the nation's coins.

It's HARD to remember now, in an age of electronic money, that for almost three thousand years coins were the very emblems of civilization. Before coins, commerce was chaos. Ancient trade meant barter, whose drawbacks were so quickly evident that before the people of long-ago China, Africa, India, and Europe learned to produce metal coins, they were using everything from cattle to cowrie shells to serve as currency.[14] Given the manifest inconvenience of using a cow as a marker of value, it's quite lucky that the Lydians of Asia Minor (present-day Turkey), in around 700 BC, hit upon the idea of producing irregular disks of electrum, a naturally occurring alloy of gold and silver, to simplify trade. Those first coins weren't much—just lumps of metal heated over a fire and stamped on one side with their owner's design—and they fell into disfavor because of variations in electrum's proportions of gold and silver.[15] King Croesus, the famously wealthy Lydian, solved that problem with the minting of coins of pure gold and silver whose value could be more reliably determined. Croesus's coins were carried west along trade routes to Ionia, which in turn spread coinage across the sea to the city-states of Greece.

The Greeks improved upon the crude Lydian manufacturing techniques, carving high-relief cameo dies and using them to strike working dies for mass production.[16] By 400 BC, Greek city-states were turning out gloriously detailed specimens stamped with designs of gods and goddesses and marked with the symbol of the state of origin. Coins—designed to be of consistent size and weight from state to state—established such a degree of order on the ancient marketplace that even war between city-states didn't mean an interruption of trade.

A few centuries later, Julius Caesar had the genius to see that in their ubiquity, coins were invaluable vehicles for propaganda. Most Roman coins, like their Greek predecessors, were stamped with mythological images. But in 48 BC, Caesar ordered the production of a series of coins to commemorate his historic victory over Pompey.[17] The coins featured his image and were issued in his name. Successive emperors followed his example, using their coinage "much like a tabloid newspaper of their tenure."[18] Brutus, for instance, celebrated his elimination of Caesar with a minting of silver coins in 44 BC. The general's profile appeared on one side; on the other were a pair of daggers, a liberty cap, and an inscription, *EID MAR*, marking the date of Caesar's death. (As if to warn his subjects not to question the legitimacy of his rule, Brutus used the coins to pay his army.)[19] Roman currency, in other words, was history writ small.

The Romans, like the Greeks before them, also understood that the greatness of a culture could be conveyed to the world by the artistry of its coins. Coins, as the Roman emperors used them, advertised their accomplishments not only to the people they governed but also to their trading partners. Coins were a point of pride, designed as miniature bas-relief sculptures. They were the cheapest art on the market—available at face value—and thus the most visible. From Greek and Roman times onward, coins carried a heavy responsibility: Those metal disks were their nations' most effective emissaries of might and beauty.

In the ensuing centuries, any government that desired international legitimacy produced its own currency. The United States was no exception, though it got off to what can most charitably be described as a bumbling start in the money business. The earliest indigenous currency in the New World was *wampum*, money the Native Americans made from shells. In its two denominations—the valuable blue or black and the more common white—wampum was so widely used in the 1600s that the Massachusetts Bay Colony legislature established official exchange rates between the shells and colonial pennies.[20] Wampum was fatally devalued, however, when some industrious Dutch settlers perfected methods of manufacturing it, flooding the market and rendering the shell-money obsolete.

In the eighteenth century, the colonies permitted a hodgepodge of coins and tokens. Colonists relied on silver and gold from England, Spain, Holland, France, and Germany. New Jersey and Massachusetts produced their own crude coppers. Connecticut and New York minted tokens. So many currencies were afloat that counterfeiting was rampant, as was the practice of clipping and filing precious metal from coins.[21] Colonists could never be sure of the true worth of their money.

In 1776, Congress (or some congressional committee) authorized the first American coin. A New York engraver named Elisha Gallaudet designed a crowded one-dollar coin, squeezing onto its two sides a sundial, a sun, thirteen linked circles containing the names of each colony, the date 1776, and the phrases *MIND YOUR BUSINESS, CONTINENTAL CURRENCY, FUGIO, AMERICAN CONGRESS,* and *WE ARE ONE*. In Philadelphia, experimental pieces of the Gallaudet design were struck in brass, tin, copper, silver, and pewter.[22] Some of the coins apparently reached circulation, but they were never officially declared currency,[23] leaving the colonies, through the end of the Revolutionary War, with no choice but to rely on foreign coins and colonial coppers.

The next attempt at a national coinage was an unqualified fiasco. In 1787, the Continental Congress issued a contract to produce 300 tons of official American one-cent copper coins to a New England businessman named James Jarvis, who promptly took possession of about thirty-five tons of federally owned copper. Jarvis bought a controlling interest in the mint that produced Connecticut's pennies, placed his father-in-law in charge of production, and sailed to Europe to obtain more copper. His mission was a failure, on both sides of the Atlantic. Jarvis returned empty-handed from Europe to find that his father-in-law had made only one delivery of cents to the U.S. Treasury, having diverted most of the copper Jarvis had been given to the more profitable minting of Connecticut cents. Moreover, the U.S. cents he had produced were so underweight as to be unusable. The Treasury sold the whole lot of them to a New York merchant, who defaulted on payment and went to debtor's prison. Nor did Jarvis and his father-in-law ever repay the government for the raw copper they'd received. The older man fled to Europe, and Jarvis ended up so broke that a court judgment against him was never collected.

If Jarvis rendered any service to the country, it was to give impetus to the notion of establishing a federal mint to produce United States coins. Alexander Hamilton's famous 1791 report to Congress was the decisive document. In it, Hamilton advocated that the dollar be named the official unit of U.S. currency, and that the nation issue both gold and silver coins, setting a fixed ratio between the values of the two metals. Hamilton proposed several denominations: a $10 gold piece, a $1 gold piece, a $1 silver piece, a copper cent, and a copper half-cent.

He suggested calling the $10 piece an eagle, after the bald eagles that had already appeared on colonial coins and in the seal of the United States. (He had thought hard, he said in a letter to Congress, but nothing better occurred to him.) Congress liked the eagle designation and subsequently authorized the minting of half-eagles and quarter-eagles of gold. Congress also added half-dollars, quarter-dollars, dimes, and half-dimes of silver to Hamilton's list of coinage denominations. By Congress's Mint Act of 1792, the U.S. Mint was authorized to make coins from government bullion reserves and from deposits by private citizens, who could have their gold and silver converted to United States coins at no cost.

Construction of the U.S. Mint was underway in Philadelphia, the nation's capital, by mid-September 1792. George Washington took great interest in its progress, visiting frequently. Martha Washington herself, according to an oft-repeated and unverifiable legend of numismatics, donated her silver tea service for the minting of the nation's first silver coins, 1,500 half-dismes (the ten-cent piece was then spelled *disme*, and five-cent pieces were called *half-dismes*).[24] Martha was also rumored to have sat for the bust portrait of Liberty that appeared on the half-disme of 1792, but that story wasn't true.[25]

It would have been no compliment to Martha if it were. The 1792 half-disme was one of several design clunkers among the early coins of the United States. The figure of Lady Liberty on the half-disme and other coins, intended to fill Americans with pride in the beauty of their new independence, bore as much resemblance to George as to Martha Washington. She was positively radiant, however, in comparison to the woman who appeared on the 1793 cent, an amateurishly executed, wild-haired creature who looks not proud but downright terrified. The wild-haired cent was roundly rejected by the public.[26]

The nation's gold coins were equally uninspiring—once the U.S. Mint finally began issuing them. Congress had mandated that before the production of gold coins could begin, top Mint officials had to produce $10,000 surety bonds to guarantee their honesty. No one could afford to post the requisite money, so no gold coins were produced until 1795. They were hardly worth the wait, artistically. The $10 eagles and $5 half-eagles featured a depiction of Liberty on the front and an eagle on the back. The first gold-coin Liberty, designed by a Mint employee named Robert Scot, was a hearty, buxom woman whose long hair was covered by a cap fashionable in those days. The eagle, though modeled after a Roman cameo,[27] was notably scrawny, hardly a symbol of might.

Liberty's look changed slightly over the next forty years—a Mint engraver's "fat mistress"[28] inspired one makeover—and the scrawny eagle of 1795 was fattened up. The $10 gold piece underwent a wholesale redesign in 1838: The new Liberty was more attractive, better coifed, and more elegantly hatted than her predecessors, and the spread-winged eagle on the reverse side of the coin now clutched not only a heraldic shield but also a quiver of arrows in its talons. The coin was still pedestrian, but it remained essentially unchanged for the next sixty years.

The $20 double eagle only came into existence in 1849, a year after the California gold rush began with the discovery of gold at Sutter's Mill. There had been no need for $20 coins before then; even $10 eagles were infrequently circulated before 1850. But with a river of gold streaming east from California, the new double eagles were necessary to convert raw gold into currency as quickly as possible, ending the chaotic private minting out West.

As was usual in the history of U.S. coinage, the double eagle's introduction was fraught with conflict. The chief engraver at the time was James Longacre, who had secured his appointment by reaching over the head of Mint Director Robert Patterson and appealing to U.S. Senator John C. Calhoun. Patterson and his cronies, particularly chief coiner Franklin Peale, resented Longacre, and they made his attempts to design the double eagle almost unendurable. Peale taunted Longacre to produce a design, conspired to destroy his first model, then rejected subsequent attempts and threatened to hire an outside engraver.[29] Finally, in 1850, the U.S. Mint began the regular production of double eagles, with a design that satisfied neither Longacre nor Mint Director Patterson. The coins featured a portrait of Liberty that was a simple head topped by a coronet, very similar to the portrait that appeared on gold dollars. On the reverse was the familiar eagle, shield, and ornaments.

Congress added the motto, *In God We Trust*, in 1866, but as of 1905, when President Roosevelt approached Saint-Gaudens, no other significant changes had been made to Longacre's double-eagle design. At the turn of the twentieth century, the best that could be said of America's gold coins—the coins that represented the country in international trade—was that they were workmanlike.

WORKMANLIKE WAS not good enough for Theodore Roosevelt—not good enough at all. More than any president before him, Roosevelt appreciated the power of art. As the United States unfurled its imperialist ambitions, Roosevelt wanted America's coins to match his vision of the country. That meant getting a proper artist to remake them, not a mere Mint engraver like Charles Barber. Roosevelt began plotting the coinage redesign soon after his election, even before he mentioned it to Saint-Gaudens. "I think our coinage is artistically of atrocious hideousness," he wrote to Secretary of the Treasury Leslie Mortimer Shaw on December 27, 1904. "Would it be possible, without asking permission of Congress, to employ a man like Saint-Gaudens to give us a coinage that would have some beauty?"[30]

Roosevelt had in mind the coins of ancient Greece and Rome, he told Saint-Gaudens in late 1905, as he nudged the sculptor—behind in his work, as usual—to get started on the redesign. "How is that gold coinage design getting on?" he wrote to Saint-Gaudens on November 6, 1905.[31] "I was looking at some gold coins of Alexander the Great today, and I was struck by their high relief. Would not it be well to have our coins in high relief . . . like the figures on the old Greek coins?" Roosevelt was eager to launch the project he called, "my pet baby," though in the November 6 letter to Saint-Gaudens, he blithely predicted, "I suppose there will be a revolt about it!" (Saint-Gaudens, more wary of reaction at the tradition-bound Mint, called the coinage redesign Roosevelt's "pet crime.")

Up at his retreat in Cornish, New Hampshire, Saint-Gaudens caught the president's enthusiasm. Roosevelt had appealed to the artist's own deepest instincts: Saint-Gaudens, whose long face and red beard gave him the look of a Greek or Roman god, was a student of classical sculpture, and he often decorated letters to friends with cartoons of himself wearing a toga and laurel wreath. "You have hit the nail on the head," he wrote back to Roosevelt on November 11, 1905. "Nothing would please me more than to make the attempt in the direction of the heads of Alexander. . . . Up to the present I have done no work on the actual models for the coins, but have made sketches, and the matter is constantly in my mind. . . . My idea is to make it a living thing and typical of progress."

For the next few months, excited letters, as well as books with photographs of Greek coins, traveled between the White House and the tiny village in New Hampshire. Cornish had been the sculptor's retreat for more than ten years. At first it had seemed a strange fit for

Saint-Gaudens, who had lived in cities for most of his life. He grew up in New York, where he proved his talent early as an apprentice to a cameo cutter. He spent his student days in Paris, enrolled at the prestigious École des Beaux-Arts, and in Rome, where he won his first commissions. After his marriage 1877 to Augusta Homer, known as "Gussie," Saint-Gaudens maintained studios in Paris and New York. His greatest work was linked to cities: the statue of Diana (modeled by his mistress, the mother of his illegitimate son) atop Madison Square Garden in New York; the Robert Gould Shaw Memorial in Boston; the standing Lincoln in Chicago. Especially as he and his wife grew estranged in the 1880s, Saint-Gaudens depended on the diversions of Manhattan. He taught at the Art Students League, he caroused with Stanford White and other artist friends, and he dined at his club, the Century Association, whose membership consisted of "some five-hundred of the city's eminent men in art, architecture, literature and science."[32]

When he and Augusta first went to Cornish, a tiny village across the Connecticut River from Windsor, Vermont, to visit a friend, Saint-Gaudens hated the abandoned old tavern their friend offered to rent to them. The artist described the place as "so forbidding and relentless that one might have imagined a skeleton half-hanging out the window, shrieking and dangling in the gale."[33] But Augusta, envisioning the garden she would eventually plant, liked the place, so Saint-Gaudens agreed to try it. That summer, he found a New Englander to pose for a Lincoln statue with which he had struggled, and he surprised himself with his productivity. The sculptor agreed to continue summering in New Hampshire.

Over the years, and with counsel from Stanford White, he and Augusta remodeled the old brick tavern. Augusta planted her garden. Saint-Gaudens added a wide porch from which he could look out at Mount Ascutney, sticking up from the trees and foothills of Vermont like Saint-Gaudens's own long nose from his profile. As the funny little house—which they named Aspet, after Saint-Gaudens's ancestral village in France—expanded with white pillars and Italianate pergolas, one family friend said it "looked like an elderly New Hampshire farmer with a new set of false teeth." Another friend improved on the simile, calling the place a "New England old maid struggling in the arms of a satyr."[34]

In 1900, while living in Paris, Saint-Gaudens was diagnosed with cancer. He and Augusta returned to the United States and made Aspet their full-time home. Saint-Gaudens's doctors had instructed him to spend more time out of the studio after his cancer surgery, so Aspet's twenty-two acres became his playground. "His slogan now that he had become ill was that everyone must take time out to play,"[35] recalled James Earle Fraser, a Saint-Gaudens assistant who later became famous for his own coinage design, the buffalo nickel. Saint-Gaudens built a nine-hole golf course for use during the summer and a toboggan run for winter exercise with his assistants. When he was in the studio, the young sculptors who came up to Cornish to assist him would hear Saint-Gaudens booming out French folk songs, competing in volume with his studiomate, Gaetan Ardisson, a French craftsman who for fifteen years had transferred Saint-Gaudens's clay models to plaster.[36]

Saint-Gaudens presided over a studio filled with assistants, as many as thirty at a time. "He had an extraordinary ability to use other sculptors to carry out his designs," recalled Frances Grimes, who joined the studio in 1901. Saint-Gaudens functioned as the chief executive officer, creating sketches and supervising their execution in marble or bronze. The young artists were grateful for the opportunity to learn from him. "Of course we complained, we found the Saint unreasonable and mysterious and sometimes expecting the impossible, but I never heard any one there say he wished he were somewhere else," Grimes wrote. "Always there was the appreciation that we were fortunate to be in that beautiful country, associated with this artist whose greatness as an artist we never lost sight of, whose authority in art we never questioned, who dominated us by the power and beauty of his designs."[37]

With Roosevelt waiting impatiently for new designs in the fall of 1905, Saint-Gaudens concentrated first on the eagle that would appear on the reverse side of the gold coins. For Roosevelt's inaugural medal, he had reprised an eagle he'd originally designed for the rejected World's Fair medal. The bird was standing rather than flying, broad-chested and noble-beaked. Saint-Gaudens made some seventy plaster sketches of the eagle and selected two of them for more extensive modeling.

For Liberty, Saint-Gaudens drew inspiration from his statue of General Sherman, which included a winged Nike, the angel of victory. He described his vision to Roosevelt in the November 11, 1905, letter: "Some kind of a (possibly winged) figure of Liberty striding forward as if on a mountain top, holding aloft on one arm a shield bearing the stars and stripes with the word Liberty marked across the field; in the other hand, perhaps a flaming torch, the drapery would be flowing in the breeze."

Roosevelt, meanwhile, had ideas of his own. He wanted to settle the issue of Liberty's headgear, that always-troublesome item of apparel. "If we get down to bedrock facts, would the feather headdress be any more out of keeping with the rest of Liberty than the canonical Phrygian cap which never is worn and never has been worn by any free people in the world?" he wrote to Saint-Gaudens on November 14, 1905. Saint-Gaudens agreed to try a feather headdress on Liberty. The sculptor wrote to Adolph Weinman, a former student who'd worked with him on Roosevelt's inaugural medal, asking Weinman to find a chief's war bonnet. Saint-Gaudens also asked Weinman, whose studio was in New York, to pass along a letter to a New York artists' model, Hettie Anderson, whom Saint-Gaudens considered "certainly the handsomest model I have ever seen of either sex." The evidence isn't entirely conclusive, but it's likely that Anderson traveled to New Hampshire to pose for Liberty.[38]

"The models are both well in hand," Saint-Gaudens was able to report to Roosevelt in January 1906. "I assure you I feel mighty cheeky so to speak, in attempting to line up with the Greek things."

TWO MONTHS later, however, there was trouble in Cornish. Saint-Gaudens was sick again. After his cancer surgery in 1900, the sculptor suffered from chronic digestive problems. In the winter of 1905, he'd been to New York for x-ray and electrical treatments, but the pain steadily worsened, forcing Saint-Gaudens to resort occasionally to morphine. In March 1906, Saint-Gaudens suffered a vicious attack of abdominal pain. He traveled to a hospital in Massachusetts,[39] and a week later underwent surgery. Doctors removed a large, cancerous tumor from Saint-Gaudens's colon. One doctor told Augusta that the cancer would be back in five years. Another said it would return much sooner. Saint-Gaudens's first cancer diagnosis had thrown him into black despair,[40] so this time, his wife and son resolved to keep the news from him, telling the sculptor instead that he had tuberculosis of the lower intestine and would recover.[41]

Whether Saint-Gaudens believed them, he never said. He returned to Cornish in the spring of 1906 and attempted to resume his work. Within a few weeks of the operation, he was dictating his memoirs and visiting the studio. He was too ill, however, to continue modeling coin sketches.

Saint-Gaudens chose Henry Hering, one of the assistants living at Cornish, to translate his clay and plaster sketches into three dimensions. Hering, like Saint-Gaudens, had grown up poor in New York City, receiving his early training at the tuition-free Cooper Union. After studying with Saint-Gaudens at the Art Students League in Manhattan, Hering had become a fixture at the studio in Cornish, living with Frances Grimes, James Earle Fraser, and his future wife, Elsie Ward, in a farmhouse up the hill from Aspet. Saint-Gaudens considered Hering "an admirable workman who can understand and execute what you explain most intelligently." He was no genius in his own right—Saint-Gaudens said Hering was "sadly at sea when I am away"[42]—but Saint-Gaudens planned to supervise the coinage project closely.

Under Saint-Gaudens's guidance, and with President Roosevelt contributing design suggestions from the White House, Hering worked on a series of models. The standing eagle Saint-Gaudens had first contemplated for the $20 coin, the sculptor decided, would work best on the back of the $10 piece. The double eagle would instead depict a flying bird, recalling an eagle that had first appeared on a one-cent piece designed by James Longacre, the Mint engraver who'd produced the first double eagles. The double eagle's Liberty would be a full figure caught in midstride. Saint-Gaudens and Hering tried to portray her wearing the Indian headdress to which Roosevelt was so attached, but they ultimately simplified the design, eliminating both the headdress and a pair of feathered wings attached to Liberty's back. (The headdress wasn't abandoned entirely; it became the centerpiece of the Liberty-in-profile design that appeared on Saint-Gaudens's $10 coin.) Whatever his shortcomings of imagination, Hering faithfully rendered Saint-Gaudens's designs. More critically, he would prove to be a stubborn champion for the sculptor when the coin project turned ugly.

Saint-Gaudens went to New York for radiation treatment in June 1906. When he returned to Cornish, he was so weak that he spent most of his time either in bed or consulting with doctors about desperation treatments. His New York physician, a woman in whom Saint-Gaudens invested reverential faith, made frequent trips to Aspet.[43] Saint-Gaudens stopped seeing outsiders in August 1906. On good days, the sculptor was carried to a couch set up on the terrace of his studio, where he watched one of his assistants painting a plaster cast of the Parthenon set into the studio wall. On bad days, he just stayed in a sunny spot on the porch of the main house.

EVEN AS Saint-Gaudens withered in Cornish, his old antagonist, Charles Barber, was blocking the progress of his coin designs in Philadelphia. Saint-Gaudens had known since he accepted Roosevelt's commission that Barber would be trouble. He had even warned the president that at the U.S. Mint, bureaucracy usually trumped art. Back when Roosevelt first proposed a high-relief coin, Saint-Gaudens replied, "The authorities on modern monetary requirements would, I fear, 'throw fits' to speak emphatically. . . . Perhaps an inquiry from you would not receive the antagonistic reply from those who have the say in such matters that would certainly be made to me." Roosevelt conferred with the secretary of the treasury and wrote back to the sculptor: "He said with great kindness that there was always a certain number of gold coins that had to be stored up in the vaults, and there was no earthly objection to having those coins as artistic as the Greeks could desire." Then the president quipped, "I think it will seriously increase mortality among the employees of the mint at seeing such a desecration, but they will perish in a good cause!"

"All right, I shall proceed on the lines we have agreed on," Saint-Gaudens responded to Roosevelt on January 9, 1906. "Whatever I produce cannot be worse than the inanities now displayed on our coins and we will at least have made an attempt in the right direction, and serve the country, by increasing mortality at the mint." But he closed his letter with a prophetic comment about Barber: "There is one gentleman there, who, when he sees what is coming, may have the 'nervous prostitution' as termed by a native here, but killed, no. He has been in that institution since the foundation of the government and will be found standing in its ruins."

Saint-Gaudens didn't tell Roosevelt in 1906 that his cancer had returned. (Homer Saint-Gaudens, in fact, told the president that his father was merely suffering from sciatica.) The sculptor did, however, inform Roosevelt after his cancer surgery in March that he would not be able personally to take the plaster casts of his coin designs to Philadelphia to be converted into dies from which coins could be struck. He was sending Hering to take care of all that, Saint-Gaudens said in a May 29, 1906, letter to Roosevelt, but he still doubted that Barber would permit the president's scheme to come off: "If you succeed in getting the best of the polite Mr. Barber down there you will have done a greater work than putting through the Panama Canal," the sculptor wrote. Saint-Gaudens ended the letter with words especially poignant because he had not told the president how sick he really was: "Nevertheless, I shall stick at it, even unto death."[44]

Henry Hering took a nine-inch, high-relief plaster cast of the Saint-Gaudens double eagle to the Philadelphia Mint at the end of May 1906. Charles Barber rejected it almost as soon as Hering walked into the building. Hering had known the high-relief model wouldn't translate into a die capable of producing a coin in one stamp of the Mint's coin press. He explained to Barber that he simply wanted to make a die from his model for experimental purposes, to find out how many stamps it would take to re-create all the details of Saint-Gaudens's design. "After considerable discussion," Hering wrote forty-two years later, still seething at the Mint engraver, "he finally decided to make the die."[45]

Hering returned to Cornish and began work on a second model of the double eagle, much lower in relief. When he was notified that the die from the first model was ready, he traveled again to Philadelphia, this time bearing his second model. Once again, he ran smack into Charles Barber. "When I showed it to Mr. Barber [he said] it was no more practical than the first model and he refused to have anything to do with it," Hering reported.[46]

Roosevelt did what he could. Through the president's intervention, Hering managed to extract a bit of revenge from the obstructionist engraver in the matter of the reducing machine, the device that miniaturized the large plaster models created by sculptors, transforming them into coin-size dies. At the turn of the century, a French man named Victor Janvier had revolutionized the reduction process with a new machine, the Janvier lathe, which Saint-Gaudens favored. The U.S. Mint, however, was still using an outdated, forty-year-old machine to reduce plaster casts. Hering complained about the quality of the dies made at the Mint to Saint-Gaudens, who asked Roosevelt to order the Mint to purchase a new Janvier lathe. Roosevelt said the word, and the new machine was purchased. When Hering next arrived in Philadelphia, Barber showed him a poor reduction of the cast of Saint-Gaudens's design for the $10 piece and informed him triumphantly that it had been made with the new French reducing machine purchased on Hering's recommendation. "Of course I had to tell him that a bad reduction can be made from a good machine, and that probably he was not sufficiently well acquainted with its mechanism," wrote Hering. And Hering had the evidence. He and Saint-Gaudens had secretly sent the plaster cast of the double eagle to France before taking it to Philadelphia. Janvier himself had made three superior reductions, at three different levels of relief.[47]

The Mint produced a small number of double-eagle coins, between sixteen and twenty-two,[48] from Saint-Gaudens's first high-relief model. The coins required nine strikes of the Mint's special hydraulic press—stamping down with 172 tons of pressure on a one-ounce disk of gold—to reproduce all of the detail of the design. These high-relief specimens were magnificent, more beautiful even than the Greek pieces that had inspired them. Liberty is stalwart yet graceful, her hair flowing as she marches forward, the sun rising behind her. She holds a torch in her right hand and brandishes an olive branch in her left. The eagle on the reverse side flies in profile above the sun, every feather and talon detailed, its beak so sharp it seems almost dangerous.

Roosevelt was thrilled with the high-relief pieces—described by America's foremost gold-coin expert as "without question . . . the most beautiful coin ever made"—and handed them out to selected friends. Even Charles Barber recognized Saint-Gaudens's extraordinary achievement. He made sure to keep at least one of the brilliant high-relief pieces for himself.[49]

But nine strikes, and on the high-pressure machine intended for medals, was not feasible for commercial coins. Almost a year after Hering first took plaster casts to Philadelphia, Roosevelt informed Saint-Gaudens that the dies from Hering's second model had failed as well. "I am sorry to say I am having some real difficulties in connection with the striking of those gold coins," he wrote to the sculptor on May 8, 1907. "It has proved hitherto impossible to strike them by one blow, which is necessary under the conditions of making coins at the present day. . . . Of course I can have a few hundreds of these beautiful coins made, but they will be merely souvenirs and medals, and not part of the true coinage of the country." Still not realizing the extent of Saint-Gaudens's illness, Roosevelt asked, "Would it be possible for you to come on to the Mint?"

It would not. Saint-Gaudens had worsened drastically since the winter and was now near death. "[I] grew used to his gaunt face," Henry Hering wrote to another of the sculptor's assistants. "And his look of being hunted by death and knowing it, but turning at bay with sheer will and self-creation. When they could carry him out to the studios and place him in front of his work, the dejection, the grim unhappy will, the constant looking over his shoulder so to speak, as if death were there, would vanish in an illumination of beauty; his eyes would burn again in the moment's victory." On July 28, 1907, Hering sat with Saint-Gaudens on the porch at Aspet, watching the sun set. Hering noted "a great stormy surge of clouds over Ascutney that gave way at their base to a low level of orange light—chaos pacified." Saint-Gaudens, lying on his couch, spoke of leaving Cornish for a place even more isolated. Five days later, he died.[50]

AND STILL Barber would not yield. Saint-Gaudens had vowed to Roosevelt that he would "stick at" getting his coins past the Mint engraver, "even unto death." Now the sculptor was dead, his beautiful coins were not being minted, and Roosevelt was furious. On August 7, 1907, he wrote to the secretary of the treasury. "I do not want to wait about those new coins. I would like the Director of the Mint to go ahead with the dies of the coins as they are now, and then if experience shows that the clear-cut finish must be obtained, make the change in the original after submitting it to me. Mr. Saint-Gaudens is dead. . . . There has been altogether too much delay about this matter and I want it finished immediately."[51]

Henry Hering took a third model of Saint-Gaudens's design for the double eagle to the Mint at the end of September. Barber once again rejected it. The engraver complained about the whole Saint-Gaudens mess in a letter to the Mint superintendent on October 10, 1907. He was trying to alter the relief, he said, but he wished coin design had been left to people who knew how to design coins. "That [the double eagle] will ever be satisfactory I cannot say, though I have very grave doubts."[52] Treasury officials, under pressure from Congress, suggested striking double-eagle coins on the special hydraulic press. Barber refused.

Into the fray stepped Frank Leach, the brand-new director of the U.S. Mint. Before Leach even had a chance to get settled in Washington in the fall of 1907, Roosevelt sent for him to apprise him of the Saint-Gaudens double-eagle situation. "He suggested some details of action of a drastic character for my guidance, which he was positive were necessary to be adopted before success could be had," Leach later recalled. "All this was delivered in his usual vigorous way, emphasizing many points by hammering on the desk with his fist."[53]

Leach, a former newspaperman from San Francisco, proved that his reputation for efficient leadership was deserved. "I had every medal press in the Philadelphia Mint put into operation on these coins with an extra force of workmen, so that the presses were run night and day,"[54] he wrote. Several days before the deadline Roosevelt had imposed, Leach delivered more than 12,000 Saint-Gaudens double eagles—not as sculptural as the dozen or so specimens struck from the first Saint-Gaudens model, but still high enough in relief to show the details of the sculptor's design. Roosevelt was delighted. He called them "the best coin that has been struck for two thousand years. . . . No matter what is its temporary fate, it will serve as a model for future coin makers."[55]

The coins received a lukewarm reception from the public. Roosevelt and Saint-Gaudens were lauded by the country's coin collectors; the upper-crust American Numismatic Society issued a proclamation approving the new coins. The *Philadelphia Press* chided those of its readers who didn't like the coins as Philistines unfamiliar with the traditions of Greek medal design.[56] But the coins also prompted controversy. Mary Cunningham, an Irish-born servant from Cornish, achieved momentary celebrity when word somehow got out that she had been a model for the face of Liberty. Some sniffed that a servant, and an immigrant at that, had no business appearing on America's coins. "Good heavens!" one man told a reporter from *The New York Times*. "Shall a waitress personify the spirit of free America?"[57]

The flying eagle, with his talons extended behind, was also derided by critics who said the bird was not true to life. Mint Director Frank Leach visited President Roosevelt in late 1907 to discuss the eagle. "I spoke of the position of the talons as being incorrect," Leach wrote. "This the President promptly denied, and said that if I would visit the large aviary at Rock Creek Park I would find the eagles flying about just as represented by the Saint-Gaudens design." Unaware that the president was a student of ornithology, Leach did indeed make a field trip to the aviary. "I did not have to wait to be convinced of the correctness of the President's assertion," he reported, "for the very first flight of an eagle across the aviary showed the talons extended out behind."[58] So much for the eagle controversy. (Leach was similarly convinced of the accuracy of Saint-Gaudens's depiction of a standing eagle on the reverse side of the $10 piece. Though critics complained that the bird, whose legs were thick and heavily feathered, looked as though it were wearing pantaloons, Leach noted that Saint-Gaudens's eagle had been inspired by a John James Audubon drawing.)[59]

Two concerns, however, were more difficult to ignore. First was the question of the motto. Since 1866, coins of the United States had included the motto, *In God We Trust*. Between them, Roosevelt and Saint-Gaudens agreed to omit the motto from both the $10 and the $20 designs. When the new double eagles began circulating, the omission caused a scandal, provoking such a clamor that some ministers actually sermonized about Saint-Gaudens's godless coins. Roosevelt's mail, Mint Director Leach reported, was filled with letters of protest.[60]

Roosevelt, who insisted that using God's name on money was profane, might have withstood the motto outcry had it not been for the final double-eagle problem. Because of their high relief, the coins had a raised rim, almost like a wire running around their edges. Bankers complained that the coins didn't stack properly and were impractical for commercial purposes. Even Roosevelt could not overrule the exigencies of trade. In December 1907, Leach ordered the U.S. Mint to stop producing Saint-Gaudens's high-relief double eagles.

In their stead, the Mint began producing a modified version of the coin. The relief was lower, and the date was changed from Roman to Arabic numerals. Beginning in July 1908, *In God We Trust* appeared above the sun on the eagle side of the coin. Who had reworked Saint-Gaudens's design? None other than Charles Barber. It was the Columbian Exposition medal controversy all over again.

Even Barber's meddling, though, couldn't quell the power of Saint-Gaudens's Liberty and his soaring eagle. As the double eagle went into widespread circulation, it became known as America's most beautiful coin. Collectors rushed to buy the early mintings—the quickly obsolete 1907 high-relief coins with Roman numerals—routinely paying $30 for the coins. Augusta Saint-Gaudens, always more financially savvy than her husband, instructed her lawyer to buy up all the wire-rimmed double eagles he could find. From the very beginning, the Saint-Gaudens double eagles were coins to treasure.

Chapter Two

"All Persons Are Hereby Required to Deliver All Gold Coin Now Owned by Them"

A WISE MAN NAMED William Woodin, in the introduction to a 1913 book cataloguing his many years of numismatic research, observed that coins "are the metallic footprints of nations."[1] The epigram reflected both Woodin's devotion to coins—he was one of the most prominent and discerning collectors of his day—and his economic insight. Woodin was a railroad-car tycoon and financier, a man acutely aware of monetary intricacies. He understood as well as anyone then alive that a country's coinage, in the aggregate, reflected its economic history. Was a nascent economy succeeding? Coin production increased. Had gold been discovered? Higher denominations were authorized. A depression? Mintage numbers dropped. In our day, the money supply is conceptual, an announcement of interest rates by the Federal Reserve. In Woodin's time, it was material, expressed in gold, silver, and copper.

So it is appropriate, even inevitable, that this country's worst economic crisis, the Great Depression, was marked by its most drastic change in coinage: the end, after 138 years, of gold coins. The Double Eagles of 1933 were the last gold coins minted in America, the final footprints in the trail of American gold coinage. They were produced in the depths of the Depression and banned as part of its resolution before ever leaving the Mint. The elimination of gold coins would have been sad under any circumstances—no more shining Liberty to travel the world shouting America's might—but the particulars of the ban in 1933 were especially poignant. Franklin Roosevelt's secretary of the treasury, the man who quietly eliminated gold coins as a means of exchange in the United States, was none other than William Woodin. Theodore Roosevelt and Augustus Saint-Gaudens lent passion and pathos to the saga of the double eagle. William Woodin introduced irony to the story. The same man who in his day amassed one of the greatest collections of American numismatic rarities was responsible for the unique scarcity of the 1933 Double Eagle.

ON THE night of March 3, 1933, there was no more consequential man in Washington than the tiny, sprightly William Woodin of New York. Franklin Roosevelt was to assume the presidency from Herbert Hoover the next day, and Woodin was ensconced with the president-elect in his suite at the Mayflower Hotel, answering the phone as it rang with incessant updates from Hoover, Hoover's treasury secretary, and governors from Federal Reserve Banks all over the country. The nation's gold supply was perilously low. Unless Woodin and the rest of FDR's brain trust did something, the entire United States economy might collapse before Roosevelt took the oath of office the next morning.

The economy had seemed to be in an irreversible death spiral for months, after the burst of optimism that followed Roosevelt's election in November sputtered out. In the cities, unemployed families picked through garbage and slept in shanties. In the heartland, farmers burned corn and wheat to stay warm; grain prices were too low to justify selling their crops. A dangerous spirit of rebellion was taking hold, with armed farmers showing up at foreclosure sales to scare off bidders. The inaugural address Roosevelt planned to give the next day captured the state of the nation on March 3 with mournful eloquence: "The means of exchange are frozen in the currents of trade, the withered leaves of industrial enterprise lie on every side, farmers find no market for their produce, and the savings of many years in thousands of families are gone," Roosevelt wrote. "Only a foolish optimist can deny the dark realities of the moment."

The immediate crisis was bank failure. By March 3, a panic that began in Michigan had spread across the country like an influenza outbreak. In state after state, people were lining up outside their banks, demanding gold and cash. Banks couldn't come up with the money and were failing at such an unsustainable rate that the governors of twenty-one states declared bank holidays, shutting the doors to desperate depositors. Gold was streaming to Europe, bought up by speculators who knew Roosevelt was considering a departure from the gold standard that had long backed U.S. currency with federal gold stores. Federal Reserve Banks in the money centers of New York and Chicago simply didn't have enough gold to keep up with demand from banks struggling to satisfy depositors.

Roosevelt had seemed maddeningly unconcerned as the bank panic worsened. On February 18, 1933—two weeks before Roosevelt was to take office—President Hoover had dispatched a Secret Service agent from Washington to New York City to deliver a handwritten letter of appeal directly into the president-elect's hands. The messenger found Roosevelt at the Astor Hotel, laughing at the hijinks of New York City's political reporters at their annual jamboree.[2] The president-elect received Hoover's grim letter, a plea for Roosevelt to end speculation and deflation with an announcement of his intended economic policies. Roosevelt read it and, without interrupting the festivities, passed it to his chief New Deal economic adviser, a former Columbia University political science professor named Raymond Moley. Hoover was so distraught that he had misspelled Roosevelt's name on the letter's envelope, yet Roosevelt, Moley noticed, showed no sign of distress—not at the dinner and not even later that night at the Roosevelt mansion on 65th Street.

"The letter from Hoover was passed around and then discussed. Capital was fleeing the country. Hoarding was reaching unbearably high levels. The dollar was wobbling on the foreign exchanges as gold poured out. The bony hand of death was stretched out over the banks and insurance companies," Moley later wrote. "And Roosevelt was, to all appearances, unmoved."[3] It was left to Moley and William Woodin—Roosevelt's designated treasury secretary—to worry over reports of the worsening crisis in the next two weeks, and to sit up night after night debating remedies.

Woodin had not been Roosevelt's first choice to serve as secretary of the treasury. The president-elect had initially offered the position, perhaps the most critical in his inaugural cabinet, to Carter Glass, the white-haired Virginia senator who'd been treasury secretary under Woodrow Wilson. Glass was the Democratic savant on banking and finance, and Roosevelt agreed with party elders that Glass's appointment would send a message of reassurance to Congress and the nation. Glass, however, declined Roosevelt's invitation—publicly citing his wife's health, privately dubious about Roosevelt's unorthodox New Deal plans. Roosevelt's advisers, who had worried that the old Virginian might not cotton to their economic theories, were secretly relieved.[4] Moley then suggested to the Roosevelt brain trust that Woodin would be an even better man for treasury secretary than Glass. Moley and Louis Howe cabled in code to the president-elect, who was aboard his yacht: "Prefer a wooden roof to a glass roof over swimming pool." Once Roosevelt figured out his advisers' cryptic cable, he endorsed Woodin's appointment. The choice made good sense. Not only was Woodin entrenched in the banking and industrial establishments, he was also an old friend of the president-elect—a lifelong Republican who had nonetheless lent his credibility, and considerable cash, to FDR, beginning when Roosevelt first campaigned to become governor of New York. (Woodin always referred to FDR as "Governor," even after Roosevelt was elected president.)

That rogue streak was typical of Woodin, a man with a restless and flexible mind. He was born in Berwick, Pennsylvania, in 1868, into an already prosperous family. His grandfather had started a pig-iron foundry in Berwick in 1835; Woodin's father, Clemuel, had expanded the foundry successfully enough that by the time William was a young boy, Jackson & Woodin, as the company was known, was one of the chief suppliers of railroad equipment in the United States.

William, an only child, was devoted to his mother, Mary Louise Woodin, who was descended from one of the first families of Pennsylvania. She spent her winters in New York, so for several months a year William lived with her and attended the New York Latin School. His relationship with his father was more complicated. Woodin's young adulthood was a serial of attempted escapes from Clemuel's dominion. At sixteen, Woodin later told reporters, Clemuel gave him $10,000, instructing him to spend it wisely[5] but almost surely realizing that William wouldn't. Six months later, the money was gone, and Woodin, who said he had intended to become a physician, was instead, as his father had wanted, headed for the School of Mines at Columbia University, where he would learn to run the family business. When Woodin left school, Clemuel ordered him to start work at the foundry, beginning with a job cleaning casings at a salary of ninety cents a day. "The work was hard, dirty, and unpleasant," Woodin said years later. "There were times I revolted at it. But I kept on. As my father had wisely foreseen, not only did I learn the business from the ground up, but I also received many valuable lessons in self-control, and the men I worked with were my teachers."[6]

Whatever the moral lessons he claimed to have absorbed, it's almost impossible to imagine Woodin—a tiny man with an impish, triangular face; an aesthetic sensibility; and a penchant for bon mots—sweating on the foundry floor with the Pennsylvania ironworkers in his father's employ. Little wonder that he fled to Europe in the mid-1890s to study music in Vienna and work as a journalist in London. Woodin wrote for *The New York Herald* and *The Times of London*, covering an Armenian massacre and winning an assignment to accompany England's Lord Horatio Kitchener on his expedition to Khartoum.[7] He was proud of his writing and excited about going to Africa, but once again

Clemuel intervened, summoning William home to Berwick before he could leave with Kitchener.

Woodin resigned himself to the railroad equipment business, for which, once he got off the factory floor, he turned out to be surprisingly well suited. He was president of Jackson & Woodin by 1899, when he escaped Clemuel's control for good by resigning the family firm to join the newly established American Car & Foundry. He eventually rose to the presidency of both American Car & Foundry—which took over Jackson & Woodin—and the American Locomotive Company. Under Woodin's leadership, American Car & Foundry became the biggest railway equipment manufacturer in the world, and he became known as one of the sharpest businessmen of his time. When, for instance, New York was thrown into chilly chaos by the months-long strike of anthracite coal miners in 1922, Governor Nathan Miller named Woodin to serve as fuel administrator, with responsibility for equitably distributing the state's limited fuel. "You have taken a load off my mind," a grateful Governor Miller told Woodin at the press conference announcing his appointment.[8] Dozens of companies invited Woodin to join their boards of directors, and the New York Federal Reserve Board appointed him a director. As a businessman, Woodin lived in the charmed circle of financiers on the "preferred list" of J. P. Morgan & Co., from which he bought stock at reduced prices in the late 1920s.

Woodin and his wife, Annie, a Pennsylvanian whom he married in 1889, seemed to enjoy thoroughly the prerogatives of their position. Their promenades through New York City parties and charity galas, their comings and goings from Europe, the weddings of their children—all were duly chronicled in newspaper society pages. Woodin belonged to the most exclusive clubs: the Union League, the India House, the Metropolitan, the Century, and the Devon Yacht Club, among others. In East Hampton, where the Woodins summered, they were among the founding members of the Maidstone Club, of which William served as the first president. When the Woodins bought a penthouse apartment on Upper Fifth Avenue, it was regarded as a signal that penthouses were now "worthy to rank among the mansions that formerly constituted that world-famous row of homes." And why not? The Woodin triplex, with terraces on all three levels, featured a living room with "a heavily gilded Renaissance ceiling," a music room festooned with damask curtains, and a wondrous third-floor playroom with wraparound windows overlooking the city.[9]

Yet Woodin continued to chafe—no longer at Clemuel, but at the life Clemuel had imposed on him. "I never wanted to be a business-man," he told a Boston financial writer later in his career. "I do not want to be one now, and would give most anything to get out of it, but one gets tied into things in such a way that it is impossible to shake loose."[10] Woodin's heart belonged to the arts, not business. He was a collector of the etchings of George Cruikshank, the nineteenth-century British artist and caricaturist whose work amused and scan-dalized the high society he satirized. Woodin was also a lifelong musician, proficient at both piano and guitar. In middle age, he began to compose his own pieces. His most popular success was a songbook called *Raggedy Ann's Sunny Songs*, which accompanied a story by *Raggedy Ann* author Johnny Gruelle. In appreciation, Gruelle named a character in the story for Woodin: Little Wooden Willie.

Of course, Woodin wouldn't have been able to indulge his passions in quite the same way had he not been a wealthy man. When he was ready for his public debut as a composer, he hired a thirty-piece orchestra to play eight of his works for an audience of his friends. The performance took place at Schubert Hall, donated for the occasion by Woodin's pal Lee Schubert, and was covered by *The New York Times*.[11] Not many first-time composers could expect the same.

MOST OF the men who shared Woodin's love for coin collecting in the early 1900s were, like him, rich. Numismatics demanded the cap-ital to purchase rare coins and the leisure to study and plan acquisi-tions. Only the wealthy—men like William Woodin—had the money and time for the hobby.

For as long as there have been coins, there have been coin aficiona-dos. The Greeks treasured their carefully wrought pieces so devotedly that pilgrims left coins as offerings at such temple shrines as Delos and Delphi; numismatic scholar Elvira Clain-Stefanelli posited that the display of coins at these temples was, in effect, the first public museum exhibit.[12] The Romans treated coins as artifacts to be saved and catalogued. In 107 AD, when Emperor Trajan ordered the re-issuance of 300-year-old coins from the Roman Republic, it was because "Trajan not only recognized, as did his predecessors, the political and religious importance of coins," wrote Clain-Stefanelli, "but also their historical significance."[13]

Coin collecting went into hibernation in the Middle Ages, when gold and ancient coins rarely circulated in Western Europe. It was reborn in the Italian Renaissance, as artists looked back to ancient Greece and Rome for inspiration and rediscovered the mastery of ancient coinage. Petrarch, the fourteenth-century poet, was a devoted coin collector, as were any number of Renaissance kings, popes, and lesser nobles, who spread numismatics across Europe in subsequent centuries. Coin collecting became known, at least according to coin dealers, as "the hobby of kings." Universities built collections and made numismatics an area of academic pursuit.

In the United States, the first coin dealer of note was an illustrator and medal designer named John Allan, who, according to numismatic historian and writer Q. David Bowers, began buying and selling medals and coins in New York City in around 1820.[14] At first ancient coins, foreign coins, and commemorative medals predominated in American collections; John Adams and his son Charles Francis Adams, for instance, collected coins from the nations they visited as diplomats. By the 1830s, however, a small number of people had begun to collect United States coins as well. Matthew Stickney, a wealthy grocer in Salem, Massachusetts, assembled the first significant collection of American coins. Stickney began collecting when he was quite young, starting with coppers acquired at his grocery store. As he prospered—he evolved into a trader of goods imported from the West Indies—Stickney worked with a New York bullion dealer to find rare gold and silver coins. He became famous in American coin circles for his close relationship with William E. Du Bois, the curator of the U.S. Mint's coin collection, who traded Stickney an 1804 silver dollar that once reigned as the most valuable coin in the world.[15]

One of Stickney's few rivals in the mid-1800s was an eccentric

Philadelphian named Joseph Mickley, who made a living as a piano- and violinmaker. A warm and generous man, Mickley lived in a succession of big, messy houses on Market Street—pianos in every corner, musical instruments and oil paintings crowding the walls, workbenches here and there—where he would entertain the curious, even small boys, with displays of his coins. When part of his collection was stolen in 1867, Mickley was so heartbroken that he sold what was left for $12,000 and vowed he was through with coins. He wasn't. Soon thereafter, Mickley embarked on a three-year coin-buying spree through Europe.[16]

Coin collecting remained an arcane pursuit in the United States in the latter decades of the nineteenth century, when the Victorians pursued all manner of collecting. Coin shops opened, particularly in New York and Philadelphia. Dealers began publishing auction lists and numismatic journals. Inevitably, several used their publications to snipe at one another. Edward Cogan, the Philadelphian, went at it with New Yorker E. L. Mason in their respective magazines. Lyman Low, a true numismatic scholar who was known for his snow-white goatee and ubiquitous cigars, feuded with the thin-skinned Edouard Frossard, a literature professor–cum–coin dealer who published a delightfully gossipy and influential magazine.[17] Everyone griped about the Chapman Brothers of Philadelphia, probably because they were so successful. The Chapmans put out glossy auction catalogues with gold-lettered covers, lavish photographs, and puffy descriptions of the coins for sale.[18]

WILLIAM WOODIN began collecting coins around 1888, at the age of only twenty. He was determined to be smart about it. "An important and scientific collection of anything," he wrote many years later, "cannot be formed unless the collector is intensely interested in the subject and willing to devote much time to the study of all matters close to the line he has selected."[19] Woodin did, indeed, devote himself to his coin collection. He researched undervalued coins and decided to focus his buying on $3 and $5 gold pieces. At the 1890 sale of a renowned collection, Woodin acquired two notable rarities, a unique eagle and half-

eagle produced at the New Orleans Mint in 1844, when only Philadelphia was supposed to be minting gold. Woodin also owned—he didn't
say exactly how he acquired it—a unique $3 piece minted in 1870 in
San Francisco. According to numismatic legend, the Mint superintendent in San Francisco had the "S" on the coin engraved by hand on
the $3 die he received from Philadelphia. The superintendent was said
to have minted only two of the $3 gold coins in 1870, burying one in
the cornerstone of the new Mint building under construction at the
time.[20] Woodin ended up with the other. He owned a 1792 half-disme,
one of the coins said to have been produced from Washington's own
silver; and a silver dollar struck from the first set of dies ever used for
the denomination. His collection ultimately included the finest rarities
of every denomination, with examples struck in gold, silver, copper,
and aluminum. It was the assemblage of a man with plenty of money
and considerable discernment.

His greatest triumph as a coin collector was very nearly a disaster.
In 1909, Woodin purchased from two Philadelphia dealers, John W.
Haseltine and Stephen K. Nagy, a unique pair of coins: two $50 gold
pieces minted as an experiment in 1877. William Barber designed the
coins, which Mint officials ultimately rejected as a solution to the
overabundance of gold emerging from California. The coins had been
part of the Philadelphia Mint's own collection, but they somehow
found their way into the hands of Haseltine, who had an uncanny
knack for such sub-rosa acquisitions. Woodin bought them for
$10,000 each—a price that broke the previous record of $6,200 dollars and shocked the coin world. The deal made headlines in the June
1909 issue of *The Numismatist*: "The World's Highest-Priced Coins,"
the magazine trumpeted. "The Two Unique U.S. Pattern Quintuple
Eagles Sold for $10,000 Each—Specialists Consider Them Cheap at
This Price."

Unfortunately for Woodin, the U.S. Government took note of the
purchase and demanded the return of the coins to the Mint.
Woodin—who had, after all, spent $20,000 on the pair—pulled
strings. He obtained a letter of introduction from the president of the
New York Central Lines to the postmaster general, and another to
Theodore Roosevelt himself. The controversy ended up on the desk of

Secretary of the Treasury Franklin MacVeagh, who met with Woodin in Washington in April 1910. The Treasury Department, MacVeagh said, could not permit unauthorized pattern coins to slip out of the Mint. No one wanted to cause a financial loss to Woodin—who, as the New York Central Lines president had noted in his letters of introduction, was then a major Republican contributor and fund-raiser—but the government assumed he could recover his $20,000 payment from the dealers who'd sold him the coins. Haseltine, however, refused to refund Woodin's money. Several months of negotiations ensued, involving Woodin, his lawyer, and government representatives from the Treasury Department, the Mint, and the Department of Justice. In the end, Woodin surrendered the $50 coins to former Mint Superintendent A. Loudon Snowden. Snowden returned them to the Mint.[21] The details of the transaction are still unknown, but somehow Woodin walked away with a treasure chest of pattern coins.[22]

Woodin acquired some of the great coins of American numismatics in the deal, enhancing even his unparalleled collection of patterns (experimental coins produced as test pieces). Along with his numismatic adviser, New York coin dealer, writer, and photographer Edgar Adams, Woodin began compiling the reference book *United States Pattern, Trial, and Experimental Pieces*, which he and Adams published in 1913. When he sold most of his pattern coins at auction in March 1911, it was one of the signal events in the coin world.

THAT SALE was a distant memory on March 1, 1933, as Woodin awaited Franklin Roosevelt's arrival in New York City, where the president-elect would spend the night before traveling to Washington for the inauguration. Crowds had gathered in every village along the Hudson to cheer the eight-car entourage from Hyde Park. The Roosevelt parade picked up twenty motorcycle-riding police officers at the city line and proceeded along Riverside Drive to the family residence on 65th Street, where a throng roared its greeting. Roosevelt appeared as jaunty as ever, posing for photographs on his doorstep. Newspapermen knew Woodin was inside, waiting to brief the president-elect on the escalating bank panic, but Roosevelt was determined to avoid the subject. "We were just talking about a place for him to stay in Washington," he quipped to reporters.[23]

Woodin did all the worrying. The next afternoon, March 2, he accompanied the Roosevelt family on the president-elect's special train to Washington from Jersey City, too preoccupied with the latest news to enjoy the historic trip. On Hoover's orders, the Federal Reserve Board in Washington was in the midst of urgent meetings to decide whether a nationwide bank holiday should be declared—and whether the president had the authority to do so. After the Roosevelt party arrived in Washington that evening, Hoover's Treasury Secretary, Ogden Mills, called Woodin at his hotel to tell him of the Federal Reserve Board's conclusion: Hoover could order the closure of banks for the days immediately before and after FDR's inauguration, provided that Congress be called into special session to figure out what to do thereafter.[24] Mills believed a nationwide bank holiday might be the only way to save the country from running out of gold.

That night, in Roosevelt's suite of rooms at the Mayflower Hotel in Washington, Woodin advised Roosevelt and Raymond Moley of Mills's dire prediction. The Federal Reserve wanted a nationwide bank holiday and Hoover's Treasury Department wanted a bank holiday but Hoover, hog-tied by Congress throughout his presidency, wanted to avoid a bank holiday and instead proclaim presidential power under the wartime Trading with the Enemy Act to halt withdrawals of gold from the nation's banks. Everyone wanted Roosevelt's endorsement. Moley and Woodin called key congressional Democrats to join the conference at the Mayflower. The men debated long into the night. Did the president have the power to close the banks? Could he act without Congress? And if Congress challenged the action, might the president weaken his power to act in a future emergency? Finally, Roosevelt's men reached a consensus: Roosevelt would duck. Hoover was still president and should do as he thought best. There was no need for joint action or Roosevelt's acquiescence.[25]

On the last day of his presidency, as gold and currency withdrawals continued unabated, Hoover ambushed Roosevelt during the president-elect's traditional pre-inaugural visit to the White House. Mills and Federal Reserve Board Governor Eugene Meyer were waiting at the White House when Roosevelt arrived for what was supposed to be a social call. Hoover demanded a meeting to discuss the banking crisis. Roosevelt, who quickly sent a messenger to fetch Moley to the meeting, stood firm: Hoover must act on his own. Roosevelt wasn't going to compromise his own presidency by tying the lame-duck Hoover around his neck. As he left the White House late in the afternoon of March 3, Roosevelt told Hoover, "I shall be waiting at my hotel, Mr. President, to learn what you decide."[26]

Woodin was in the Roosevelt suite back at the Mayflower, along with Senator Carter Glass and congressional Democrats, when Roosevelt and Moley returned from the meeting with Hoover. For the next eight hours, the phone didn't stop ringing. At the Federal Reserve Board, where Meyer went after the disastrous White House meeting, the governors decided that Hoover had to do something that night. Unless the nation's banks were closed the next day, the United States faced insolvency. In the Chicago district alone, the Federal Reserve was expecting demands for $100 million in gold—just about everything the Fed in Chicago had. The New York Federal Reserve reported that it was also dangerously close to exhausting its gold supply. The Roosevelt suite received continuous reports from bankers and politicians in Washington, Chicago, and New York. Hoover kept calling his successor—terrified about doing nothing, terrified about taking an action that might be repudiated by Congress. At one in the morning, with no resolution of the crisis, Roosevelt told Hoover they should both get some rest.

Moley slipped out of Roosevelt's Mayflower suite to return to his own room. When he stepped out of the elevator in the lobby of the Mayflower, William Woodin was waiting for him, fully dressed and ready to go. In precarious health from an ulcerated wound in his throat, Woodin had previously been ordered to bed by Roosevelt. "Don't say it," he told Moley. "I really tried very hard. But I couldn't even get to the stage of undressing. This thing is bad. Will you come over to the Treasury with me? We'll see if we can give those fellows there a hand."[27]

Ogden Mills and a ragged Hoover team were still encamped at the Treasury Department, working frantically in their last few hours in office. They'd hit on an ingenious solution to the banking crisis. The governors of twenty-one states had already declared bank holidays. If the rest of the state governors would follow suit, there would be no need for a presidential proclamation or a showdown with Congress. By the time Moley and Woodin arrived at the Treasury Department, only Illinois and New York, the two major banking centers, had not yet agreed. Illinois wasn't expected to be a problem; Mills and his people simply hadn't been able to reach the governor yet. But New York was balking. The issue was the commercial and investment banks. New York Governor Herbert Lehman had said he wouldn't declare a statewide bank holiday without a formal request from New York's commercial banks—and the banks wouldn't do it. Banking leaders told Lehman that much as they would like to avert additional bank failures, the potential damage to their prestige prevented them from requesting a shutdown of New York's banks. Such was the impasse that awaited Moley and Woodin in the early morning hours before Roosevelt's inauguration.[28]

Bankers from J. P. Morgan, Lazard Frères, and National City Bank had been gathered that night at the New York Bank, along with the state banking superintendent and the president of the New York Stock Exchange. At midnight, sixteen of them piled into waiting limousines and rode up Park Avenue to Governor Lehman's house.[29] They were with Lehman when Woodin and Moley joined Mills at the Treasury Department.

Woodin knew all of these men, as colleagues and as friends. He advised the group in Mills's office to call Lehman again, and to be more forceful. Hoover's men did, repeatedly. Together, Mills and Woodin decided to send the governor of the New York Federal Reserve Bank to Lehman's house to convince Lehman how untenable the gold situation was. Finally, at four-twenty in the morning Lehman proclaimed a two-day bank holiday in New York. The banks in every state would be closed the next morning, the day of Roosevelt's inauguration.

Woodin awakened Raymond Moley, who had fallen asleep in Mills's office. "It's all right, Ray," he said. "Let's go now. Lehman's agreed." The crisis was over, at least for the next few days. The gold supply was safe.

AT ROOSEVELT'S inauguration, Woodin enjoyed a brief respite from the bank emergency. Squeezed out of his place of honor by the crowds jamming the presidential platform near the Capitol entrance, the new secretary of the treasury climbed up on a railing of the Capitol veranda. Perched beside a movie cameraman and a newspaper reporter, he watched FDR assure the nation on that bleak gray day that they had nothing to fear but fear itself. "[Woodin] seemed just as happy as if he had got to his regular place," the newspaperman observed.

Journalists loved Woodin. As he dug into the hellish job of drafting the emergency bank legislation that Congress would consider in its special session later that week, Woodin seemed to the Washington press corps to be exactly the savior the economy needed. His elfin appearance, his resolute cheeriness, his silly jokes, even his never-askew gray toupee endeared him to reporters, who sketched warm portraits for readers. "When the Press trooped in to see what manner of man this was that President Roosevelt had called . . . to run the Treasury at a moment of greatest national emergency," *Time* magazine reported on March 20, 1933, "they found small William Hartman Woodin, his eyes as blue as his shirt and collar, his cupid mouth pursed in an easy little smile, sitting informally on the edge of his desk, swinging his legs. Piped a pert newshawk: 'Mr. Secretary, you're in a pretty hot spot, aren't you?' The brand-new Secretary reached down to his big black leather chair, rubbed his hand slowly over its seat and softly replied: "No, it isn't hot, really.'"[30] The "hot seat" became something of a running joke between Woodin and reporters; much ado was made over a pair of asbestos breeches that outgoing Treasury Secretary Ogden Mills was said to have had made for Woodin.

In that first week of the Roosevelt presidency, Woodin worked day and night. He had promised Roosevelt that he'd have an emergency banking bill ready to present to the special session of Congress on March 9. On March 5, the day after the inauguration, the planning sessions began. Bankers from all over the country, Federal Reserve governors, and Hoover treasury officials arrived at Woodin's offices to help him figure out how to get the banks reopened without reigniting the panic. The government had to convince depositors to leave their money in their banks, instead of demanding to withdraw it in gold. Speed was essential, Woodin believed, if public faith was to be restored; his motto that week was "swift and staccato action."[31]

His first decision was whether to permit the issuance of scrip. With no one able to obtain U.S. coins or paper money during the bank holiday, banks and businesses were pressing to issue their own emergency private currency to customers. Woodin was reluctant to introduce scrip, which might undermine confidence in the country's official paper currency. On the night of March 6, Woodin sat up late, playing his guitar and pondering scrip. The next morning he told Raymond Moley that he'd had a revelation. "We don't have to issue scrip," he said, banging his fist on the breakfast table. "We don't need it. These bankers have hypnotized themselves and us. We can issue [paper] currency against the sound assets of the banks. The Reserve Act lets us print all we'll need. And it won't frighten people. It won't look like stage money. It'll be money that looks like money."[32]

Woodin's revelation—that the government had the power simply to print enough paper money to withstand the bank panic, regardless of the precarious state of the Fed's gold reserves—was the guiding principle of the emergency banking bill, in Moley's assessment. Beginning almost immediately after Woodin reported his breakthrough to Moley, the drafting of the bill began. With Eugene Meyer and George Harrison of the Federal Reserve, Senator Carter Glass, and Treasury officials from his own and Mills's staffs, Woodin presided over a thirty-six-hour marathon that finally ended at two in the morning on Thursday, March 9, 1933. Later that morning, after Roosevelt had looked it over, Woodin took the bill to Glass's Senate office for a meeting with congressional leaders. On his way out of the conference, he was accosted by a group of reporters. "We are newspaper men, Mr. Secretary," they shouted. "Is the bill finished?"

"Yes, it's finished," he said. Then, as *The New York Times* reported,

"Thinking doubtless of his many sleepless nights, he added, smiling: 'My name is Bill and I'm finished too.'"[33]

CONGRESS PASSED the emergency law—which provided for the reopening of sound banks and the provision of currency sufficient to meet demand—by the end of that day. (Eleanor Roosevelt, distressed at her husband's disheveled appearance at the historic bill signing, called to Woodin to smooth FDR's hair. Woodin "gave the President's head a few playful pats.")[34] Woodin's people began the mind-numbing chore of checking thousands of bank reports. Within the week, banks began reopening. Roosevelt made a fifteen-minute radio address to the nation, urging people to "unite in banishing fear," dismiss any rumors of panic, and permit the restoration of the banking system. His plea, and Woodin's bill, saved the day. There was no resumption of the panic as banks reopened. "We're on the bottom now," Woodin announced. "We are not going any lower."

Raymond Moley believed the nation had William Woodin, whom he affectionately described as "half businessman, half artist," to thank for the end of the crisis. "Capitalism was saved in eight days, and no other single factor in its salvation was half so important as the imagination and sturdiness and common sense of Will Woodin,"[35] he wrote. Woodin's hard work continued through March and April, as the Roosevelt administration introduced permanent banking bills to supplant the emergency legislation.

His heroic image, however, faded quickly. By April, Woodin was denying reports that he and Roosevelt disagreed on the bank bill under consideration in Congress, and that he intended to resign. In May, after a Senate subcommittee forced J. P. Morgan to testify about his "preferred list," opportunistic congressmen began calling for the treasury secretary to resign. With his health failing, Woodin left Washington in June 1933. At first Roosevelt insisted that he merely take a medical leave from his cabinet post, but when it became obvious that Woodin wasn't going to recover from the throat infection that had plagued him for months, the president regretfully accepted his resignation on December 20, 1933. Woodin died on May 3, 1934, only fourteen months after FDR took office.

WOODIN'S LEGACY was the survival of the American banking system, albeit a system changed in a fundamental way: America was off the gold standard. The currency of the land was no longer backed by gold. Woodin had known how frightening that idea was—not only for the people but also for foreign governments expecting the United States to meet its obligations in gold. Right after Roosevelt took office, Woodin had assured reporters that the nation was still on the gold standard, despite the president's March 4, 1933, injunction against payments in gold from banks. "Gold merely cannot be obtained for several days," Woodin had insisted. "In other words, gold payments have been suspended for that period."

But Roosevelt's proclamation of March 6, 1933, and the emergency banking legislation passed three days later, put the lie to Woodin's avowals. Banks were not permitted to pay out or export gold, only paper currency. Government offices were prohibited from paying out gold except under license from the Treasury Department. Ordinary people were supposed to turn in to the Federal Reserve Banks whatever gold they held, exchanging it for paper money. There was at first no formal order for people to return their gold, but Roosevelt knew and used the power of mass pressure. "It is my belief," he said in his radio address of March 12, 1933, "that hoarding has become a very unfashionable pastime." For those unwilling to rise to their patriotic duty, there were also intimations, even in the early days of the Roosevelt administration, that Americans who did not return their gold to Federal Reserve Banks in exchange for paper currency would soon suffer unspecified penalties. To track hoarders, Woodin ordered the Federal Reserve to begin compiling lists of people who had made large withdrawals of gold before the bank holiday began and hadn't brought it back.

Gold strictures continued in those first months of Roosevelt's presidency. On April 5, 1933, Roosevelt issued an executive order codifying his call for Americans to surrender their gold: "All persons are

hereby required to deliver on or before May 1, 1933, to a Federal
Reserve Bank or a branch or agency thereof or to any member bank of
the Federal Reserve System all gold coin, gold bullion, and gold cer-
tificates now owned by them or coming into their ownership on or
before April 28, 1933." On April 19, Woodin essentially banned all
gold exports. Woodin's friend J. P. Morgan, not yet disgraced by his
Senate testimony, wired Roosevelt his approval. "The way out of the
Depression is to combat and overcome the deflationary forces," he
telegraphed. "I regard the action now taken as being the best possible
course."[36] After April 1933, gold was no longer available as a means of
exchange in the United States.

Even in the midst of this quiet revolution, William Woodin had
been careful to protect his old friends in the coin world. Everyone else
was expected to line up at Federal Reserve Banks to relinquish their
gold, but the rare gold coins of numismatic dealers and collectors
were safe from recall. Woodin mailed assurances to his favorite coin
dealer, Thomas Elder, who reprinted a portion of the letter in an auction catalogue. "You are advised," Woodin had written, "that there is
no present intention to require the delivery to the Treasurer of the
United States of gold coins having a recognized special value to collectors of rare and unusual coins."

Roosevelt's April 5 executive order included the same language in
its specific exemption of gold collectibles from the general recall, and
coin collectors continued to receive protection in every iteration of
the subsequent series of antihoarding orders and laws. When there
might have been some confusion—such as in Roosevelt's executive
order of August 28, 1933—Woodin's successor, Henry Morgenthau,
Jr., corrected it. In January 1934, soon after Morgenthau formally
assumed the office of secretary of the treasury, his staff, apparently
responding to requests from coin dealers, asked the attorney general
to approve an amendment to the August 28 executive order—an
amendment that echoed the language Woodin had used in his letter to
Elder. The attorney general quickly forwarded the proposed amendment to the president. "It is understood that the issuance of the proposed order is urgent for the reason that a sale of gold coins of the
kinds covered by the order is to be held in New York City tomorrow,"

he wrote. Roosevelt approved the amendment, permitting coin collectors to trade and hold "rare and unusual coin" without a special license, and to permit the export, with a license, of "gold coin having a recognized special value to collectors of rare and unusual coin."[37]

When Congress formalized Roosevelt's executive orders in the Gold Reserve Act of 1934, the legislation included an official exemption from prohibitions against gold trade for coin dealers and collectors. Once again, the key phrase echoed Woodin's letter to his old friend and dealer Thomas Elder: Under the Gold Reserve Act of 1934, to be legally held or exported, gold coins had to be of "recognized special value to collectors of rare and unusual coin." Almost seventy years later, the fate of Stephen Fenton's 1933 Double Eagle would turn on those words.

BUT THE collectors' exemption from the Gold Reserve Act doesn't answer the question of why any 1933 Double Eagles ever existed to be exempted. No 1933 Double Eagles had been officially delivered to the Mint cashier on March 5, the day on which William Woodin decreed that the Mint could not pay out gold without a special license; nor on March 12, when Roosevelt's radio address encouraged Americans to return their gold coins to Federal Reserve Banks. There was never any need, in other words, for $20 gold coins to be minted in 1933; the coins were obsolete before they ever officially existed. So why on earth did the Philadelphia Mint, in March and April 1933, turn out almost 500,000 new Double Eagles? An anonymous Mint official explained the situation to *The Philadelphia Inquirer* on Tuesday, March 7, 1933. Despite the tumult resulting from the bank holiday, everything was business as usual at the Mint, he said. The Mint had not received instructions from the Treasury Department or anyone else to halt production, so workers just kept turning out the coins scheduled to be minted. After all, the unnamed official shrugged, "This is just a factory."[38]

Chapter Three

The Mysterious Man at the Money Factory

INSIDE THE U.S. MINT, then and even now, coins are factory output, considerably smaller but otherwise not much different from cars rolling off an assembly line. Philadelphia Mint workers of the 1930s hardly remembered that the raw materials they processed every day were gold and silver, and that their end product was money. They strapped on their thick canvas aprons and took their stations alongside the bulky Mint machinery, feeling lucky to have held onto good jobs in the midst of the Great Depression.

One of the luckiest in March 1933 was George McCann, who had worked at the Mint for more than a decade, and not just as a line worker. McCann, who was thirty-seven years old in 1933, had begun his Mint career in the transfer weigh room, but he'd managed to work his way up to the plum job of assistant cashier, which meant that he was in line someday to take over as cashier, one of the Mint's most prestigious posts. The Philadelphia Mint had always been a clubby place to work, prone to power struggles and fiefdom-building in the top ranks. McCann had played politics wisely, ensconcing himself as the junior member of the Mint's ruling oligarchy, a clique known to resentful underlings as "the Four Horsemen."

The institution that the Four Horsemen ruled was actually the third United States Mint to be built in Philadelphia. It was an imposing structure, a three-story steel-and-granite behemoth squatting just beyond the city's main business district and looming over its neighbors—a public library, a junior high, and a hospital. McCann's office was down the hall from the grand, gilt-ceilinged entrance on Spring Garden Street, close to the offices of two of his mentors, Assistant Mint Superintendent Fred Chaffin and Chief Clerk Ralph Roland. As assistant cashier, McCann had heavy responsibilities. Money constantly moved into and out of his hands. He and his boss were in charge of officially receiving the coins produced by the Mint, memorializing them in the Mint's account books, and seeing to their storage in the basement vaults. When coins were shipped out of the building, the cashier recorded their transfer in his daily log; if the Federal Reserve or the United States treasurer returned coins to the Mint, the cashier logged them in. McCann and the rest of the cashier's staff also dealt with customers who came to the Mint to exchange gold and silver bullion and scrap metal for gold and silver coins. Their transactions were conducted at the cashier's office, which had a special window and counter for such exchanges.

At the beginning of March 1933, the Mint's coin production rooms were humming, operating as if there had been no bank panic, no frenzied meetings to save the economy, no late-night telephone and bill-drafting heroics from Treasury Secretary William Woodin. The coining of 1933 Double Eagles was already underway when Franklin Roosevelt took office. Beginning on February 18, Mint workers in the rolling and cutting room fed gold bars through machines that flattened them into strips, then into the furnace where they were heated red-hot, cooled, and rolled again. The strips proceeded into the cutting presses, which spit out blank disks of the right size to make double eagles. The blanks were weighed, cleaned, and sorted—by women hunched over huge trays—before the end of February. The first 1933 Double Eagles were stamped in the two-story-high coining room on Thursday, March 2,[1] as Franklin Roosevelt and William Woodin traveled to Washington on Roosevelt's special train. The next day, while Roosevelt was being ambushed by a frantic Herbert Hoover at the White House, Mint workers in Philadelphia continued coining 1933 $20 pieces. On Monday, March 6, the day that President Roosevelt proclaimed an extension of the bank holiday and prohibited banks from paying out gold, oblivious Philadelphia Mint workers began weighing the first of the freshly minted 1933 Double Eagles to be sure they contained the proper amount of gold, just shy of an ounce. On March 15, the first 25,000 of the 1933 "Saints" were delivered to George McCann's boss, Mint Cashier Harry Powell. Following Mint custom, Powell reserved 250 1933 Double Eagles for testing by the federal Assay Commission and another two for the Bureau of the Mint laboratory in Washington.

But what was to be done with the rest of the 1933 Double Eagles—brand-new gold coins entered in the Mint's books at a time when the president and his treasury secretary had ordered Americans to return their gold to the government? All over Philadelphia, even as those first 1933 Double Eagles went through the final stages of production, gold was flowing back to Federal Reserve vaults. On March 10 alone, *The Philadelphia Inquirer* reported, almost $1 million in gold was returned to the city's Federal Reserve Bank, coincident with an order to all members of the Philadelphia Stock Exchange to prepare a record of their firms' previous gold withdrawals. By March 15, more than $5.5 million in gold had been turned in. The city's newspapers were full of stories of patriotic Philadelphians scurrying to comply with the anti-hoarding exhortations of FDR and William Woodin. One man went to his bank with a cheap suitcase filled with gold coins worth $25,000, declaring he was "through with hoarding." A woman emptied $1,000 worth of double eagles from the pockets of her fur coat, after receiving a promise that she wouldn't be fined.[2] Another Philadelphian insisted upon returning a pair of cuff links made of quarter-eagles, even though bank officials assured him that they weren't illegal. From under the mattresses, from inside the drawers, from the toes of long underwear and the fingers of pigskin gloves, the gold of Philadelphia was delivered out of hiding and into government vaults.

The Mint, meanwhile, received instructions to hold onto its gold.

The last shipment of gold coins from the Mint had taken place, at William Woodin's direction, on Sunday, March 5, 1933, to shore up bank reserves before anyone knew whether panicked withdrawals would resume when the bank holiday ended. The Mint's chief clerk, Fred Chaffin, had supervised the crew that came in that Sunday to transfer nineteen tons of half-eagles, eagles, and double eagles from the basement vaults to the courtyard shipping area, and then onto trucks bound for Federal Reserve Banks. There were no 1933 Double Eagles in the emergency Sunday shipment; though some of the coins had been minted, none had yet been logged into the cashier's books. The next day, March 6, Mint Director Robert J. Grant telegraphed from Washington to all of the mints and assay offices, stipulating that they were not to pay out gold without a special license from the Treasury Department. Gold, he wrote in a private letter the same day, was not supposed to be leaving the mints in any form.[3]

Grant's injunction seemed clear enough, but in the chaotic first days of the Roosevelt administration, contradictory advice also arrived in Philadelphia from Washington. An assistant treasury secretary telegraphed to the Mint on March 7 that it was, in fact, "authorized to issue gold coin or bars in exchange for gold bullion received." If a customer came to the cashier's window with gold bullion, this telegram suggested, McCann or another of the cashier's assistants could pay out the bullion's value in gold coins. The confusion didn't end definitively until a week after Roosevelt's April 5, 1933, executive order officially forbidding private citizens to own gold. On April 12, a telegram from the Treasury Department specifically advised the U.S. Mint that Roosevelt's executive order banned exchanges of gold coins for gold bullion. If any gold coins had left the Philadelphia Mint between March 6 and April 12, none were supposed to leave thereafter.

And yet Mint workers in the coin production rooms in Philadelphia continued stamping out 1933 Double Eagles, coins that were unquestionably obsolete before they even left the Mint presses. By the end of March, the Philadelphia Mint had produced 100,000 1933 Double Eagles. Another 200,000 were minted in April. The final 145,500 1933 Double Eagles—the last run of the $20 gold pieces Augustus Saint-Gaudens had designed under Theodore Roosevelt's aegis—were produced in May. In all, 445,500 of the 1933 Double Eagles were received by George McCann and the Mint cashier in the spring of 1933.

On June 27, 1933, McCann was one of the four men who stood outside Cage 1 of Vault F on the east side of the Mint basement as a heavy steel door closed on all but 500 of the coins. The vault, constructed of ten-foot, steel-reinforced walls, was filled with bags and bags of gold—not just the 1933 $20 coins, but half-eagles, eagles, and double eagles from 1928, 1929, 1931, and 1932—all to be removed from circulation forever. In compliance with Mint regulations, a three-man settlement committee placed a seal on the vault door, confirming the number and type of bags of coins locked within. McCann, the fourth man, had been designated to serve as the Mint superintendent's representative at the official closing of the vault. He affixed his signature to the seal. McCann was earning less than $2,000 a year in 1933. The vault he had just sealed contained more than $50 million worth of gold coins.

EVERY ONCE in a while in the history of the United States Mint, men like George McCann have succumbed to the temptation inherent in routinely handling amounts of money far in excess of what they took home in a week, a month, a year, or a lifetime. Mint chicanery is part of the long, dark tradition of minor-league American corruption. Not every worker in Mint history, it turns out, subscribed to the view that coins are mere factory output.

Security at the Mint, particularly in the 150 years of operation before World War II, always focused on threats from the outside rather than thievery from within. As far back as 1793, there was a Mint police force, complete with a patrol dog, to surveil the grounds, but inside the Mint, the only control over the precious metal and coins was careful recordkeeping.[4] The system assumed that the adversarial relationship among various Mint departments—coiners, cashiers, weigh-room clerks, and vault custodians, all checking the work of the others so they wouldn't be blamed for losses themselves—would keep everyone honest.

Of course, it didn't. There are Mint legends of men smuggling coins in hollowed-out wooden legs and other unlikely hiding places ranging from coffee urns to the gas tanks of heavy machinery. One Mint worker in the late 1800s was said to have brought a dead rat in his lunchbox every few days. He would surreptitiously stuff gold coins down the rat's throat, then toss it out a window. When he left work, the rat would still be lying on the sidewalk—who would pick up a big, dead rat?—and he'd scoop it up and take it and the gold coins home. The scheme was exposed only because one day the fellow became greedy and overstuffed the rat. When he tossed it out the window, it burst, spilling its guts as well as the gold coins stuffed inside it. A passerby called the police, who staked out the splattered rat. When the unsuspecting thief went to claim his rat and his gold, he was arrested.[5]

More serious thefts were perpetrated by men who controlled the records, such as the ingenious George Edward Adams, a turn-of-the-twentieth-century cashier in the Seattle assay office. Prospectors would bring their raw gold to Adams's office to be tested for purity and then refined, since gold mined in the Northwest was usually mixed with black sand. That sand was the key to Adams's ruse. When prospectors brought in their impure samples, Adams would weigh the raw deposits. Then he would siphon off pure gold as the samples were refined, making up the weight of the stolen gold with black sand that he secretly bought in bulk. Adams transported his stolen gold dust to small smelting companies on the West Coast, where he had it assayed under a series of assumed names. On his honeymoon, he even made a deposit at the Mint's own New York assay office, his most brazen escapade. Adams was eventually unmasked by the always-enterprising Frank Leach, the San Francisco Mint superintendent who later became Theodore Roosevelt's Mint director, but before Adams was caught, he stole about $150,000.[6]

And even Adams's theft looks clumsy compared to the most sophisticated Mint intrigues, which depended on the willingness of coin collectors to pay huge sums to indulge their passion. A single rare coin might not be worth as much as a stolen gold bar, but no Mint official would go to jail for selling or trading it. So, for almost as long as the U.S. Mint has existed, insiders have used their positions to appropriate, or even create, unregulated rarities. The most valuable coins in

American numismatics—the 1933 Double Eagle among them—have all left the Mint under suspicious circumstances.

Consider the 1804 silver dollar, which until 2002 was the highest-priced American rarity. In the early 1830s, a diplomatic envoy named Edmund Roberts traveled to the Far East and managed to secure valuable trade treaties with the prime minister of Siam and the imam of Muscat. On his return, Roberts complained of the poor quality of the diplomatic gifts the State Department had furnished for presentation to the foreign heads of state. He suggested instead a fancily displayed set of U.S. coins, which he would carry back to the Far East on his next trip. The State Department approved Roberts's suggestion and ordered the Mint to assemble special sets of the gold, silver, and copper coinage of the United States, to be housed in velvet-lined presentation boxes.

The U.S. Mint had a problem, however, in complying with the order: The United States was no longer coining silver dollars. A disparity between the silver content of U.S. dollars and lower-weight Spanish coins had led to such widespread export of U.S. dollars that Congress suspended their minting in 1804. Mint records indicated that silver dollars had last been coined that year, so Mint officials decided they should include an 1804 dollar in the diplomatic presentation sets the State Department had requested. But no one at the Mint could locate an 1804 silver dollar.[7] Unsure how to proceed, Mint officials found a set of old silver-dollar dies, engraved the 1804 date, minted two coins, and included them in the velvet-lined boxes. Roberts, the diplomatic envoy, delivered one set of coins to the sultan of Muscat in 1835 and the other to the king of Siam in 1836.

In 1835, the U.S. Mint coined two additional 1804 silver dollars, intended for presentation sets for the emperors of Cochin-China and Japan, with whom Roberts expected to sign treaties. When Roberts died on the island of Macao in 1836, after contracting dysentery during the celebration of the Siam treaty, the two newly minted 1804 silver dollars stayed in Philadelphia. Another four 1804 silver dollars, all with lettering on their edges, were struck at the Mint in the 1830s or 1840s.

Those silver dollars, dated 1804 but minted more than thirty years later, became the most desirable of American coins. (The complete King of Siam Presentation Set, which is said to have been given by the king to the Englishwoman Anna Leonowens, who was memorialized in *The King and I*, was on the market for $10 million in 2004.) For as it turned out, no 1804 silver dollars were coined before 1834. The silver dollars actually coined in 1804 bore the date 1803. The only existing 1804 silver dollars were the ones created at the Mint thirty years later.

Coin collectors became rabid to own 1804 silver dollars, and a Mint insider named William Du Bois was willing to oblige them. Du Bois, by both birth and marriage, was part of a web of families that dominated Mint affairs through the 1800s. He was the first man at the Mint who truly understood the infant rare-coin market and the first to take advantage of that knowledge. Du Bois began his Mint career in 1833 as a twenty-three-year-old clerk for Director Samuel Moore. Five years later, he and Jacob Eckfeldt, a member of the Mint's reigning family and Du Bois's future brother-in-law, formally established the Mint Collection, the nation's official coin collection. Du Bois championed the Mint Collection tirelessly for almost forty years. He was a delightful, soft-spoken man, a trained attorney who became the Mint's chief chronicler and spokesman. Every time a new outcry arose over rare coins that had mysteriously appeared on the market, Du Bois could be counted upon to calm the outrage. His charm, and his family's influence, hid a multitude of Mint sins.

Du Bois's first 1804 silver-dollar deal was a trade with Matthew Stickney, the pioneer collector of American coins. Stickney wanted the 1804 silver dollar described in Du Bois and Eckfeldt's 1842 manual of American coins; Du Bois swapped it for some of Stickney's rarities that he wanted for the Mint Collection. After the success of the Stickney trade, Du Bois and other Mint insiders "commenced restriking rarities to service the market,"[8] usually not for their own profit but for the benefit of the Mint's coin collection. The Mint director during the 1850s, James Ross Snowden, was part of the conspiracy. Snowden's particular interest was the Mint's collection of medals depicting George Washington, and he admitted to Philadelphia coin dealer Edward Cogan that he ordered the striking of pattern pieces to trade

for Washington medals when opportunities arose.[9] Collectors of the
time worked with Snowden to fill holes in their collections, thus
enabling him, in turn, to fill vacancies in the Mint's collection.

In 1858 or 1859, outright greed surfaced as a motive for the covert
restriking of rarities. A young Eckfeldt relative working in the
engraver's office created additional specimens of the by-then-famous
1804 silver dollar and began peddling them up and down the eastern
seaboard. A Boston collector wrote to the Mint director to ask
whether the 1804 coin he'd just been offered for $75 was genuine.[10]
Reports also surfaced of 1804 silver dollars for sale in New York and
Philadelphia, prompting a storm of angry letters to Snowden. Careful
examination of the newly circulating 1804 silver dollars revealed a
fatal flaw in young Eckfeldt's enterprise: His coins, unlike the 1804
dollars produced earlier, didn't have lettered edges. Snowden quietly
confiscated four of the fakes,[11] dismissed the wayward Eckfeldt, and
drove private Mint enterprise underground.

Secret coining didn't end, however. Philadelphia had become a hub
of the coin trade, with at least a half-dozen full-time coin dealers.
Mint officials simply began making clandestine sales and trades
through dealers. Don Taxay, a groundbreaking Mint historian, has
speculated that private Mint deals in 1859 and 1860 generated
$50,000.[12] Even 1804 silver dollars, so recently the cause of a scandal,
were fair game. This time, the anonymous yet enterprising Mint official who caused the restriking of the famous coins was careful to letter the edges and conceal the coins until years later, when they began
to be offered for sale through a Philadelphia dealer.[13]

Mint corruption was so blatant under the leadership of Mint Director Henry Linderman in the late 1860s that a congressional subcommittee commenced an investigation in 1878. Linderman, the nephew
of a U.S. senator from Pennsylvania who wrangled the job for Linderman, was an active coin collector who, along with a coterie of Mint
cronies, supposedly engaged in the routine restriking of desirable
coins. They would then distribute the restruck rarities and one-of-a-
kind pattern coins through a small group of favored dealers.[14] Linderman's own collection contained such a concentration of suspect

rarities—including a restruck 1804 silver dollar—that when his coins were catalogued for auction after his death, Treasury Department agents conducted a raid and stopped the sale.

The most notorious Mint caper took place long after the proclaimed end of the Mint's unofficial manufacture of rarities. In February 1913, as part of Theodore Roosevelt's remaking of American coinage, the Mint adopted a new design for the nickel. James Earle Fraser—a protégé of Augustus Saint-Gaudens who had spent his childhood in the American West—sculpted the distinctive five-cent piece, with a noble Indian profile on its face and an almost frighteningly realistic bison on its reverse, to replace the pedestrian Liberty Head design of Charles Barber. All nickels dated 1913 were supposed to have been of the Fraser design, but in 1919, the country's premier coin-collecting journal, *The Numismatist*, ran an advertisement offering to buy theretofore-unknown coins: 1913 nickels of the Liberty Head design. Samuel Brown, a resident of North Tonawanda, New York, had placed the advertisement, in which he said he would pay $500 for any 1913 Liberty Head nickel.[15] Brown ran another ad the next month, upping the offer price to $600. Several months later, he turned up at a convention of the American Numismatic Association with five 1913 Liberty Head nickels.

Those five were the only 1913 Liberty Head nickels ever to emerge. Samuel Brown never disclosed how he obtained the coins, but he was the assistant curator at the Philadelphia Mint from 1904 to 1907, so he surely understood numismatic rarity. He was also the clerk of the Mint in 1913, the year his rare nickels were struck.[16] It is widely supposed that someone at the Mint, likely Brown or a confederate (perhaps engraver George Morgan), illicitly struck the five coins, knowing full well that they'd become treasures of coin collecting. And so they did. From Samuel Brown, all five coins passed through the hands of three dealers and into the possession of Colonel E. H. R. Green (the wastrel heir of Wall Street miser Hetty Green) who collected boats, railroad equipment, stamps, and pornography as well as coins. After Colonel Green's death, the five nickels were split up and for many years reigned as the most famous of American coins. One appeared on an episode of *Hawaii Five-0*, the object of a coin-theft story line. Another of the coins was carried in pocket change by a disabled war veteran named James McDermott, a coin dealer who liked to shock bartenders by taking his Liberty Head nickel out of his pocket and explaining its worth. A third was thought to have disappeared in the 1960s after its owner died in a car accident. In 2004, when that coin turned out to have been in the owner's family all along, but simply misidentified as a forgery, the coin made national headlines. In the most recent sale of a 1913 Liberty Head nickel, a private deal in May 2004, the coin brought a reported $3 million.[17]

GEORGE McCANN, the assistant Mint cashier who stood before Vault F in June 1933 as the newly minted Double Eagles were locked inside, was versed in numismatic rarity. He was a coin collector, apparently tutored by a man named Ira Reed, a Philadelphia coin dealer who used to turn up at the cashier's window to buy special coins before they were publicly issued. McCann was no coin scholar—none of his colleagues at the Mint remembered what his specialty was—but he had so palpable a desire for money, so tactile a connection to coins, that it was evident to some of the people with whom he worked. Two Mint workers noticed that McCann seemed to spend an unwarranted amount of time in the counting and weigh room, where boxes of worn and mutilated coins would arrive for accounting before being melted. One remembered McCann fiddling with coins piled on the scales in the weigh room, though he had no reason to do so. Another worker, Charles Rumpp, said that McCann used to ask him to phone the cashier's office when coins were ready to be counted. McCann would then show up to offer his help in moving and stacking boxes. "The employees in the mint are so used to handling coin that they do not play with it in their hands," Rumpp said. "But I now recall that Mr. McCann, while standing at the boxes filled with uncurrent coin on the trucks, would be handling the coin."

Rumpp was not the most reliable of witnesses, since he later admitted to having stolen coins from the same counting and weigh room. But he wasn't the only one of George McCann's colleagues who thought there was something suspicious about the man. A bookkeeper named John Carey swore that McCann was a thief who had stolen 500 ounces of fine gold from the weigh room back in the 1920s and had only gotten away with it through the intervention of his powerful friends. A few other Mint workers later said that they'd also registered complaints about McCann, though he was never disciplined. George McCann was an influential man at the Mint. Hibberd Ott, who'd been appointed cashier in the spring of 1933, was out sick most of the time. McCann was, for all intents and purposes, the Mint cashier.

He and Chester "Doc" Ziegler, the chief assayer and another of the Four Horsemen, were in charge of the 500 1933 Double Eagles that had not been locked into Vault F, the coins that had been reserved for testing. Twenty were sent to the Treasury Department's Bureau of Standards in Washington, where they were destroyed during laboratory examination in early 1934. At around the same time, thirty-four of the 1933 Double Eagles reserved for the Assay Commission were added to the stash already sealed in Vault F. That left 446 coins, selected from the March 15 and April 26 mintings of 1933 Double Eagles, for the Assay Commission to examine.

The Assay Commission was an appointed group that had convened every February since 1792 to ensure the weight and purity of the country's gold and silver coins. The 1934 commission, composed mostly of dignitaries whom the Treasury Department wanted to honor, was charged with evaluating the coins of 1933. Until it met, the 1933 Double Eagles that the commission would examine were held in a sealed chest at the Philadelphia Mint called the "pyx box." The pyx box was stored in the Mint cashier's office, George McCann's province.

On February 14, 1934, McCann and assayer Doc Ziegler removed the 446 1933 Double Eagles from the pyx box for the Assay Commission, an assemblage that included a U.S. senator, a federal judge, and the comptroller of the currency. B. G. Shields of the Mint's New York assay office oversaw the commission's testing. He took randomly selected specimens from the cashier's office on the first floor of the Mint upstairs to Doc Ziegler's assay office on the third floor. Two of Ziegler's assistants conducted the actual tests. The assistants later said that they paid no attention to the dates on the nine coins they assayed. They simply took the coins, hammered down their edges, and placed them in the roller to be turned into strips of gold.

The nine coins they tested were, obviously, destroyed, but the other 437 1933 Double Eagles that had been reserved for the Assay Commission were still in perfect condition. On February 20, 1934, those coins were returned to the pyx box in the cashier's office. A month later, George McCann officially succeeded Hibberd Ott as cashier. For the next three years, the remaining 1933 Double Eagles were in his care. When, for instance, the Mint director requested that two 1933 Double Eagles, along with two examples of other 1933 coins, be sent to the Smithsonian Institution (then known as the United States National Museum) for inclusion in the National Numismatic Collection, it was McCann who carried out the order.

Around the time McCann was promoted to Mint cashier, he began playing the stock market. His salary as cashier was less than $2,500, and he had a wife and a teenage son to support, but in 1934 he opened a brokerage account and deposited more than $1,100, putting at risk a large percentage of his net worth. (His home in Camden, New Jersey, was worth $7,500.) McCann did well in the market in 1934 and 1935. By 1936, he was worth more than $20,000. That year, he managed to deposit almost $10,000 in his brokerage account— cash that was untraceable to his salary or his other investments.

Things were changing at the Mint, though. No more would men like William Du Bois, Henry Linderman, and the Four Horsemen operate with unbridled power. The new director of the Mint was the dynamic Nellie Tayloe Ross, who had been the first woman governor in the United States. (Ross served out the last two years, 1925 and 1926, of her husband's term as governor of Wyoming after he died in office.) She was a staunch Democrat, a vice-chairman of the Democratic National Committee, and a women's-rights activist. In 1933, Franklin Roosevelt rewarded her hard work for his campaign with the Mint directorship, which Ross held for the next twenty years.

Ross worried more about Mint security than her predecessors had, particularly as the Depression ebbed and the demand for silver and copper coins outstripped the Mint's normal capacity. "The demand," the Treasury Department announced in a 1934 press release, "is far out of proportion to any that has ever occurred before at this time of the year in the whole history of the mints." The Philadelphia Mint began operating on three shifts, hiring dozens of new workers to keep coin production rolling twenty-four hours a day.[18]

To make sure the coins stayed within the Mint, Ross asked the chief of the Secret Service to survey the building, "in order to determine how it is guarded against possible attack or theft."[19] Agent William Houghton of the Secret Service's Philadelphia field office received the assignment, and on April 14, 1934, made a surprise visit to the Mint. He was not at all satisfied with what he saw. The guard at the main entrance on Spring Garden Street was wholly occupied with herding a bunch of noisy high-school students through the Mint gallery. A second entranceway guard, who was supposed to be locked into a steel-reinforced secure room with a direct telephone line to the police station, was wandering around the lobby, absent from his post. Another set of guards, stationed at the truck entrance on 16th Street, was well trained and well equipped but had no means of communicating with the guards at the main entrance if anything happened. Finally, Houghton noted, the guard at McCann's office was entirely too lax. The gate to the cashier's office was supposed to be locked. It wasn't, and the cashier's-office guard stood talking to a cluster of scrap-gold dealers sitting on a bench holding their deposits. "His revolver," Houghton reported, "which I am sure he could not shoot, was so dirty it was not serviceable."[20]

Houghton continued to monitor Mint security, albeit sporadically. On October 26, 1934, after insisting that the Mint guards take pistol practice, he called Assistant Superintendent Fred Chaffin, one of George McCann's buddies, to report the results: Not only had several of the guards failed to qualify at target shooting, but some of them hadn't even hit the target at all. Houghton was equally concerned about threats from within. "It is my understanding," he commented, "that over one-hundred men have recently been employed at the mint, and no investigation has been made as to their character or past history."[21]

Houghton asked a special operative named William Valentin to follow up. Valentin was adept at sniffing out opportunities for criminal-minded Mint workers. In the rolling room, for instance, employees on the night shift might be able to throw parts of silver bars out the window to be picked up, Valentin warned, "by fellow conspirators." The night workers were all questioned, and, not surprisingly, said they'd never attempted any such plot. "Too many Secret Service around," one said. The Mint's practice of issuing passes to carry parcels out of the building also troubled Valentin. "An employee intending to carry a bundle out at quitting time goes to his or her foreman sometime during his tour of duty and asks for a pass, and as far as I can determine, gets it without the foreman making any effort to learn the contents of the bundle that is to be carried out," Valentin noted in a prescient June 1935 report. "How easy it would be for a dishonest person to secrete about his person coins or ingots during working hours, and then in the locker rooms slip the purloined articles into a bundle and successfully carry them off."

ON FEBRUARY 3, 1937, almost four years after Franklin Roosevelt effectively banned gold coins from circulation, the Treasury Department finally ordered the Philadelphia Mint to destroy all of its remaining gold coins. That day, George McCann broke the seal on Vault F, Cage 1, where hundreds of thousands of gold coins had been locked away since June 27, 1933. When the vault's contents were audited, a $5,000 bag of 1928 double eagles was discovered to be missing. The Secret Service opened an investigation, quickly focusing suspicion on Edward McKernan, the vault custodian who had retired in October 1936. George McCann reported that McKernan might have stolen the coins in the frenzy of the last shipment of gold from the Mint on March 5, 1933; McKernan, McCann told agents, had been there that day, and he was also known to show off gold coins outside of work. McKernan was arrested and questioned, but he was never convicted of stealing the missing bag of $20 pieces.

During the investigation of the missing double eagles, no agents seem to have suspected George McCann of the theft. That was a rare bit of luck for McCann in 1937, which was otherwise not a good year for him. Fred Chaffin's sudden death in 1936 had weakened the sovereignty of the Four Horsemen. Moreover, McCann was getting killed in the stock market, losing more than $7,000—a third of his net worth. After depositing almost $10,000 in his brokerage account in 1936, he made no deposits in 1937.

He carried on at work as always, though. Beginning on February 6, 1937, McCann supervised the transfer of bags of 1933 Double Eagles from Vault F in the basement to the melting room on the west side of the first floor. There the coins were weighed, sorted into lots of 7,000 ounces, and heated to almost 2,000 degrees, the melting point of gold. Molten gold was poured into molds and converted to bars, which were then reweighed to account for all of the gold content of the melted coins. On March 18, 1937, the Mint was able to report that all of its 1933 Double Eagles had been melted down into gold bars.

But they hadn't. On February 15, nine days after the meltdown commenced, a Philadelphia jeweler named Israel Switt sold a 1933 Double Eagle to Philadelphia coin dealer James Macallister for $500.

Chapter Four

The "Gold Coin Bootlegger" and the Coin Dealers

ISRAEL SWITT WAS A SQUAT, balding redhead who wore thick-rimmed glasses, cheap suits, and a perpetual sneer. He was a thoroughly nasty piece of work. He'd fawn over desirable clients and scorn everyone else—be they competitors, colleagues, or customers he didn't consider worthy of his attention. He was so cocky that he used to keep the door to his shop locked and the CLOSED sign posted in the junk-shop disarray of his front window to dissuade uninformed shoppers. Switt permitted only the wealthy and connected to penetrate his defenses. When he died in 1990, he left a million-dollar legacy, a trove of the finest estate jewelry and objets d'art of Philadelphia's Main Line—all crammed into his four-story shop on Jewelers' Row.

His success was a testament to hard work and ruthlessness. Switt came from nothing. Philadelphia-born and -raised, he started working at the age of seven, running errands for a local pawnbroker. He graduated to scrap-gold dealing, and by the time he was twenty-five, after serving in the Navy during World War I, Switt had his own scrap-gold business.[1] Over the years, he transformed it into one of the landmarks of Jewelers' Row. Switt was married and had a daughter, but he was almost always at the store.

He did occasionally go out on buying trips. In the late 1930s and 1940s, Switt was the only dealer in Philadelphia who seemed to have cash to buy jewelry, and nothing made him happier than snatching treasures at fire-sale prices.[2] Widows, families ruined in the Great Depression, fellow jewelers—Switt gave no one a break when he was buying. (He could occasionally be generous when he was selling, if you were one of his rare favorites and you didn't try to bargain with him or otherwise annoy him. Then he might give you a good price and take you to the tavern next door for a roast beef sandwich.) One Philadelphia antiques dealer recalled accompanying Switt on a visit to an elderly widow who needed to sell her beloved collection of Art Deco jewelry. Switt arrived at the widow's house and began rifling through her jewelry, handling it roughly and describing it dismissively. The antiques dealer had valued the collection at $30,000, but he didn't have the money to buy it. Only Switt had that kind of cash, and Switt didn't get it by treating sellers kindly. "I wouldn't give you eighteen thousand for the whole lot," Switt informed the widow.[3]

The mystery was how Switt acquired his reserves of cash in the late 1930s—a particularly perplexing question given the events of August 22, 1934. On that day, several months after the Gold Reserve Act made the ownership of gold coins illegal, policemen at Philadelphia's Thirtieth Street Station spotted Israel Switt lugging a suspiciously heavy suitcase. The officers stopped him, opened the suitcase, and found it filled with $2,000 in old gold coins, apparently purchased from gold hoarders. Switt was arrested for illegal possession of gold. He forfeited the old gold coins, and his gold-trading license was revoked.[4] For a scrap-gold dealer, this should have been a disaster.

Yet Switt's business not only survived his arrest, it flourished. Many years later, when Secret Service investigators were asking questions about Switt, the Philadelphia coin dealer to whom Switt sold the first 1933 Double Eagle explained the paradox. Israel Switt, James Macallister said, was "a gold coin bootlegger," continuing a back-room trade in illicitly hoarded gold. The gold coins for which

Switt would be remembered—gold coins that forever tied this dumpy Philadelphia jeweler to the likes of Augustus Saint-Gaudens and William Woodin—were the 1933 Double Eagles.

SWITT SOLD two 1933 Double Eagles to James Macallister in February 1937—the first on February 15 and the second on February 20. Five months later, Macallister bought two more 1933 Double Eagles from Switt, and in December a fifth coin. He paid either $500 or $550 for each of the five. Macallister later said that when he asked Switt how he had obtained the 1933 Double Eagles, Switt offered vague and inconsistent explanations. He'd bought them from an old woman who was related to a Treasury Department official, he once told Macallister. Another time, Switt said that a fellow named Norris, somehow connected to the Philadelphia Federal Reserve Bank, had sold the 1933 Double Eagles to him. Macallister didn't much care about the coins' dubious provenance, nor about Switt's arrest record. He stopped buying the $20 pieces from Switt only when Switt's ready supply made him begin to doubt that the coins were rare enough to justify their price.[5]

But Macallister wasn't the only coin dealer Switt knew. In New York, the jeweler sometimes visited a dealer named Abe Kosoff. He would appear unannounced at Kosoff's office, bearing rare American coins and, according to Kosoff, less-than-credible accounts of acquiring them from some banker or another. Kosoff seldom bought from Switt, but in 1937, when the Philadelphian showed up with a 1933 Double Eagle, Kosoff bought it.[6] About two years later, in 1939, Switt sold three more 1933 Double Eagles to Ira Reed—a Philadelphia coin dealer who knew George McCann—for $500 apiece. Sometime thereafter, Switt sold a tenth coin, the last 1933 Double Eagle he is known to have sold, to Ira Reed.[7]

Israel Swift was never part of the fraternity of coin dealers; his business was scrap gold and jewelry, and though he kept a box of gold coins in his store, he was no numismatic expert. When he sold those 1933 Double Eagles to Macallister, Kosoff, and Reed, prominent coin dealers all, Switt launched the coins into a new world, a peculiar fellowship of buyers and sellers who all knew one another, traveled together, and bought and sold each other's coins. For the next several years, the ten 1933 Double Eagles sold by Israel Switt whirled about in this little universe, which was so close-knit that word of the rare $20 coins spread fast within it, and so isolated that no one outside seemed to know or care about the coins' existence.

COIN DEALERS were the keystones of the coin world of the 1930s and 1940s. Successful dealers not only acted as judges of a coin's quality, they held the community together: Dealers inevitably knew more than their clients about the whereabouts and provenance of rare coins. That was all they necessarily had in common, though. There was no particular training required to become a coin dealer—no courses to take, no degree to earn, not even a minimum age. Anyone could buy and sell coins, though not everyone could do it profitably.

The three dealers who first handled 1933 Double Eagles all thrived in the business despite their quite different styles. Macallister was the high-toned Philadelphian, with a clientele of rich Wall Streeters. Every Wednesday, wearing a tailored suit and a homburg, he'd ride the train to Manhattan and then travel downtown with coins to sell.[8] After meeting with his clients—and before settling down for the night at the Waldorf-Astoria, where he always stayed—Macallister would usually visit with a few New York dealers, particularly Wayte Raymond, with whom Macallister occasionally conducted auctions on West 47th Street under the name of Morgenthau Galleries. Raymond, who kept offices on Park Avenue, was a luminary of the coin fraternity in that era. An accomplished numismatist as well as a good businessman, he was famous for having bought one of the finest collections of the day, in its entirety, for $100,000. When Wayte Raymond and James Macallister teamed up for a Morgenthau sale, it was an event.

Ira Reed was less of a swell. Reed was an old Pennsylvanian who never stopped using the Quaker "thee" and "thou," a country auctioneer whose girlfriend called him "The General" for his habit of ordering people around.[9] Though Reed would not scruple to buy almost anything, from Native American artifacts to fine antiques, if he thought he could sell it for a profit, he specialized in coins, and he used his proximity to the Philadelphia Mint to gain an advantage over other dealers. Reed was known to cozy up to men at the cashier's window—including George McCann—to obtain desirable coins before they were publicly available.[10] By 1939, when he first bought 1933 Double Eagles from Israel Switt, Reed had begun holding regular coin auctions in Philadelphia, a successor to the famous Chapman Brothers of that city. Abe Kosoff called Reed, "the greatest auctioneer of them all."[11]

Kosoff ended up better known and better remembered in the coin world than either of the Philadelphians who bought Switt's 1933 Double Eagles. He epitomized the midcentury coin dealer, his style an amalgam of scholarship and salesmanship. The son of a Brooklyn butcher, Kosoff fell into the business by accident. In 1929, he had finished high school and needed a job to work his way through college. A high-school friend set him up with an antiques dealer who had a sideline in coins, to which Kosoff found himself drawn.[12] With coins, you either feel the romance or you don't. Kosoff did. He also reveled in the camaraderie of dealers and collectors. He and some friends founded a coin club in Brooklyn, and Kosoff enthusiastically attended its meetings, even when they ended in a tavern. When his friends ordered beer, Kosoff, a straight arrow, always ordered milk.[13]

Business was slow at first—he started working six weeks before the stock-market crash in October 1929—but Kosoff was a charmer, a handsome, confident man with a way of winning over clients. He had a narrow face with full lips and brown eyes that crinkled at the corners; he wore his hair long enough to show its wave. Even when Kosoff wasn't smiling, the lines on his face proved him to be accustomed to humor. People wanted to like him and to help him. Kosoff married in 1933 and was devoted to his wife, Molly, who traveled the world with him buying and selling coins. But within the business, one of his nicknames was "The Widow's Best Friend," an acknowledgment of his success at persuading wives to sell their husbands' collections through him.[14]

Kosoff finished his accounting degree at New York University and enrolled at Columbia University for graduate work, but by the mid-1930s he was so successful as a part-time coin dealer that he decided to make it a career. He broke off from the antiques dealer who'd given him a start and struck out on his own in 1937, the year he bought a 1933 Double Eagle from Israel Switt. In 1939, Kosoff opened a shop on 57th Street in Manhattan.[15]

His timing was good. The locus of the coin business was shifting from Philadelphia (where Reed and Macallister were) to New York, with its concentration of serious collectors. Of the ten 1933 Double Eagles that Israel Switt sold between 1937 and 1941, six passed through New York.

Wayte Raymond, who sponsored auctions with Macallister and became a mentor to Kosoff, was the king of New York dealers in the 1930s, but there were plenty of others of good reputation. The Guttag brothers and I. Klein had successful shops downtown. Thomas Elder, William Woodin's favorite dealer, was still running auctions. The Stack brothers, Morton and Joseph, founded their shop in 1933 and by 1935 were holding important auctions. Hans Schulman, the son of an old Dutch numismatic family, came to New York to escape the war in Europe in the late 1930s, found he liked the city, and stayed, establishing a New York pipeline to world coins and foreign collectors. Max Berenstein had a fancy antiques and jewelry shop on 57th Street, where he also dealt in coins. Berenstein, in fact, bought the first of James Macallister's 1933 Double Eagles only days after Macallister had obtained the coin from Israel Switt. Berenstein paid extravagantly for it, too—$1,600, according to Macallister's records.[16]

Macallister's second 1933 Double Eagle went to another New Yorker, a famous collector named Frederick C. C. Boyd. F. C. C. Boyd, as he was known, was a onetime printer's apprentice and traveling salesman who'd become a very wealthy man, one of the few businessmen who prospered in the Great Depression. By the end of the 1930s, Boyd was a high-ranking executive of the Union News Company, which operated a network of newsstands and soda fountains in railroad stations around the country. Boyd dabbled in coin dealing—he ran advertisements in *The Numismatist* and was hired to appraise the million-dollar collection of Colonel E. H. R. Green in

1937—but he had the heart of a collector, not a dealer. He ended up, for instance, buying most of Green's coins for himself. He also bought and held the choicest items from William Woodin's collection of pattern coins. Rumor in the coin world had it that Boyd, who lived in New Jersey, maintained a Manhattan apartment just to house his coin collection. He was so wealthy that when he received a $50,000 check from Abe Kosoff for his collection of gold coins from California's territorial days, Boyd let it sit in a desk drawer, undeposited, for months. When Kosoff finally called Boyd's secretary to inquire why the check—which he and his partner had scrambled mightily to fund—hadn't been cashed, he found out that it was wedged, forgotten, behind Boyd's desk drawer.[17]

Boyd dealt regularly with Kosoff, but he acquired his 1933 Double Eagle from Macallister, with whom he had had good luck; in his 1937 address to the American Numismatic Association, Boyd spoke of a pair of rare 1933 $10 pieces he had obtained from the Philadelphia dealer. (Several dozen $10 eagles, unlike their $20 counterparts, were legitimately acquired by coin dealers and collectors in 1933 before Roosevelt took office.) In his speech, Boyd said that when he learned that the National Numismatic Collection at the Smithsonian lacked a 1933 eagle, he decided to donate one of the pair he owned to the museum in honor of Macallister. He described the 1933 eagles—not their even-rarer $20 Double Eagle cousins—as "the last gold pieces issued by the United States Mints."[18]

Boyd, in other words, must have known that the 1933 Double Eagle he owned had not been officially issued by the Mint. But neither he nor any other of the more than fifteen dealers and collectors who handled 1933 Double Eagles in the years between 1937 and 1944 seemed to consider the $20 pieces illegal in any fashion. There was, after all, plenty of history in the coin world of private citizens owning coins that had left the Mint under suspicious circumstances. The misdated silver dollars of 1804 were then the most coveted of American coins, with their dubious provenance adding to, rather than detracting from, their value. Boyd himself owned a fine collection of experimental pattern coins, many of which had been sold on the sly by Mint officials. And he had catalogued the Green collection, which included all five of the famous 1913 Liberty Head nickels, unofficial coins at best. For a collector like F. C. C. Boyd, obtaining a coin as rare as the 1933 Double Eagle was an achievement to be celebrated. And Boyd did. He exhibited his 1933 Double Eagle at a spring meeting of the New York Numismatic Club in 1937[19] and took it to the convention of the American Numismatic Association in 1939. There he and his wife, Helen, displayed their 1933 Double Eagle alongside five varieties of Saint-Gaudens double eagles minted in 1907. The 1933 Double Eagle was intriguing enough to the coin world that *The Numismatist* reported on the Boyds' display, noting that their 1933 Double Eagle was "one of just four known."[20]

IN THE early 1940s, the hobby of coin collecting—and the business of coin dealing—was changing. Finally people had money to spend, and more of them than ever were spending it on coins. "Coins were difficult to obtain. All of the ads were 'WANTED' ads, [and] very little was being offered for sale," Abe Kosoff wrote years later. "Dealers and collectors had their tongues hanging out. A choice coin could start some excitement."[21] The high end of the hobby, where dealers such as James Macallister and Abe Kosoff dwelt, was as exclusive as ever, with men such as Fred Boyd, Lammot du Pont, and Baltimore banker Louis Eliasberg competing for the great rarities. Pressure on prices, however, was coming from below, as the lower ranks of collectors expanded. The hobby's growth was due, in the main, to two influences: the introduction, in 1938, of twenty-five-cent, preprinted coin albums that encouraged young collectors; and the advertising and publicity generated by a Fort Worth, Texas, coin dealer named B. Max Mehl. More than any other dealer, Mehl inspired thousands of people to check their pockets for treasures, singlehandedly producing a generation of coin collectors.

Benjamin Max Mehl—who brokered three 1933 Double Eagles as they changed hands between 1937 and 1944—was a phenomenon without precedent in the coin world. Mehl was an immigrant, born in Lodz (then Russia, now Poland) in 1884; he came to America in the early 1890s. By the end of the decade, he was clerking in a Texas shoe store owned by his brother and spending all of his extra money on his coin collection. "I must have started during my cradle days," Mehl later wrote, "as I do not recall of [sic] my ever not being interested in coins."[22] He started out just trading coins with other collectors, but in 1900, while still working at the shoe store, he established a part-time coin business.[23] "I heard of and read about the great rarities, which I did not even hope to ever see, much less own," he wrote. "I thought that by dealing in coins it may be possible for me, if not to add to my earnings, to at least add to my numismatic joy."[24]

As a novice dealer, Mehl concentrated on making his name known, beginning with an ad in the most prominent coin collector's magazine, *The Numismatist*, in 1903. One of the responses to the ad came from C. W. Cowell, a Denver collector who wanted to sell his $50 gold pieces as well as other items from his collection. Mehl later told a reporter from *The Saturday Evening Post* that Cowell's letter was the real start of his career. He didn't have the money to buy the coins outright, so he wrote to the collector requesting permission to sell them on a commission. Cowell agreed to let the young dealer try. Mehl's first circular advertising the coins brought $350 in orders and persuaded the Denver collector to permit Mehl to sell his entire set.[25] In the July 1906 issue of *The Numismatist*, Mehl announced that he was now a full-time coin dealer. "I am in a position to serve you most satisfactory," the ad said, in Mehl's imperfect English. "Kindly let me hear from you whether buyer or seller. Give me a chance to show you how nice I can take care of your favors."[26]

Mehl was an elfin man, five feet one or two at the outside, with slicked-back hair, old-fashioned wire-rimmed glasses, and ears that stuck out so far that they seemed almost perpendicular to his head. He lived in a town better known for cows than coins, yet he became the most famous coin dealer of his time, perhaps of any time. Mehl was no scholar, though he fancied himself one and would talk endlessly, to anyone who would listen, about coins and their connections to world history. Nor was he a sophisticate like Abe Kosoff. Mehl fit right in at the Fort Worth Rotary Club and the local Shriners Temple, both of which he eventually headed. The one time Mehl considered moving his business out of Fort Worth, in an aborted 1912 partnership with New Yorker Wayte Raymond, he retreated to Texas before he'd been gone a month. He didn't need to be anywhere but Fort Worth, Mehl said. "FROM NEW YORK CITY TO TEXAS," was the headline on one of his 1948 advertisements, which gloated about several of the New York collections he had sold. "You and I know that these truly great collections from New York City were not acquired by me on the strength of my good looks. Somehow I feel that my forty-eight years of proven success, unquestionable past and present financial responsibility and reliability had something to do with it."[27]

Mehl's genius was his understanding that the best way to expand his business was to expand the market. "I noticed that no effort was being made by anyone to popularize coin collecting and to create new collectors," he recalled long after he was well established. "The idea occurred to me to try advertising in general publications. My first 'large' advertisement appeared in *Collier's* [in 1906]—a five-liner at the huge cost, at least to me then, of $12.50."[28] That ad, and the others that followed, accomplished what Mehl intended. Two years later, in *Mehl's Numismatic Monthly*, the magazine he began publishing in 1908, Mehl boasted, "Within less than two years I have succeeded in obtaining a good share of the confidence and patronage of numismatists of the country. My sales in 1907 aggregate $25,000."[29] By the 1930s, Mehl was spending $50,000 a year—a shocking amount—on magazine and newspaper advertisements, which frequently pictured him standing in front of Fort Worth's Mehl Building (which he erected in 1916) or his Victorian mansion. He sponsored a fifteen-minute radio show on more than fifty radio stations, and he sold tens of thousands of copies a year of his one-dollar *Star Rare Coin Encyclopedia*. Even President Franklin Roosevelt had in his personal correspondence files an order form for the *Star Rare Coin Encyclopedia*. Mehl's most famous ad campaign, which ran for years and was said to have cost him millions of dollars, was his offer to pay $50 (and later $75) for the famous 1913 Liberty Head nickel. Mehl knew perfectly well that no one was going to find a 1913 Liberty Head nickel in his pocket change; for most of the duration of the ad campaign, all five of the rare nickels were held by Colonel Green, a client to whom Mehl sold about a half-million dollars' worth of coins over the years. But the advertising persuaded people to pay attention to coins, attracting thousands of new collectors to the hobby. (According to legend, it also caused delays on trolley routes as conductors examined the nickel fares for stray 1913 Liberty Heads.) Moreover, despite the grating folksiness of his technique—the corny advertising, the overblown catalogues, the soap-operatic radio show—Mehl managed to attract some of the very best coin collections of the first half of the century to his building in the coin hinterland of Fort Worth.

Mehl operated only by mail-bid auction. He would persuade a collector to sell his coins through Mehl's dealership, publish a lavish and hyperbole-ridden catalogue, set an auction closing date, and await the flood of bids sent to the Mehl Building in Fort Worth. Mehl's own office in the front of the building was decorated in high British-men's-club style, with a fireplace, oiled wood paneling, and a glassed-in library of rare coin books. Hidden from view was the back-room operation: the dozens of women, coming and going through a back door, whom Mehl employed to handle his mail. The mail, which included bids for auction items, orders for catalogues and *Star Rare Coin* books, and inquiries about the worth of particular coins, ran to hundreds of thousands of pieces a year.[30] Mehl rarely did business in person, never even accepting visitors who showed up in Fort Worth without appointments. A noted coin writer, J. Hewitt Judd, once tried to visit Mehl unannounced. Despite his famous name and long acquaintance with Mehl, he was turned away.[31]

Mehl so disliked conducting business face-to-face that he once refused to sell an 1804 silver dollar to Louis Eliasberg, the Baltimore banker who was intent on assembling a collection that included an example of every American coin ever minted. Eliasberg, pre-equipped with an appointment, flew to Fort Worth specifically to talk Mehl into selling him the 1804 silver dollar that was part of the collection of William Cutler Atwater, a New Yorker whose holdings Mehl was selling in a mail-bid auction. (Mehl, never one to shy away from superlatives, modestly described his catalogue for the Atwater sale as "the most beautiful specimen of Numismatic Literature ever published.") Mehl told *The Saturday Evening Post* that he entertained Eliasberg in grand style, lunching at the Exchange Club, golfing at the country club, and touring the sights of central Texas by car. They talked coins for hours, but every time Eliasberg reminded Mehl that he wanted to take the 1804 silver dollar home with him, Mehl politely refused, advising Eliasberg to send him a bid by mail after he had returned to Baltimore. Eliasberg did, and he won the coin. "You can't do business with people when they come to see you," Mehl told the *Post*. "I wasn't sure he really wanted to buy it. . . . When they buy coins from me I want to be sure they do so without any feelings of obligation."

The mail-bid-only auctions also provided latitude for side deals that Mehl couldn't have pulled off in live auctions. Mehl beat out other dealers for the right to sell the famous collection of William Forrester Dunham, which included not only a first-class example of an 1804 silver dollar but also an 1822 half-eagle, one of only three known to exist and a coin hotly pursued by J. P. Morgan. Mehl published a catalogue for the sale, which, of course, attracted enormous interest. But he had actually sold most of the collection, before circulating the catalogue, to a Cincinnati insurance executive named Charles Williams. The dealers and collectors who bid on Dunham rarities all came away from the sale disappointed—just another reason for many of them to resent the Texan. Mehl was not particularly popular with his coin-dealing brethren. "Many did not like him," admitted Abe Kosoff in a 1978 column in *Coin World*. "Many disagreed with his advertising policy. I agree that today he might have himself a peck of trouble. But we are talking about the days of P. T. Barnum, of the huckster, of the patent medicine man."

Competition among dealers in those days was intense, particularly for notable collections. In 1943, for instance, a Columbus, Ohio, dealer named Michael Higgy decided to dispose of his private coin collection. Higgy wanted to sell the collection outright, rather than wait for the proceeds of an auction. Abe Kosoff, James Macallister, and an Ohio dealer named James Kelley were all invited to submit bids. Kelley offered the most money, but because he held a high draft number, his bank wouldn't lend him the funds to complete the deal. Kosoff ended up with the Higgy collection when he persuaded a wealthy friend to advance him the money to buy it.[32] The Higgy auction was a raging success for Kosoff, but it was the rare blockbuster of the era that wasn't Mehl's. "It was almost as though Mehl had a stranglehold on the important consignments as they came on the market," wrote numismatic historian Q. David Bowers, "with the leavings, such as they were, going to competitors."[33] Abe Kosoff was a friend and defender of Mehl, but even *he* never quite forgave the Texan for beating him out for the right to sell the collection of composer Jerome Kern. "Mehl crowed about the Kern collection because he walked away with it from right under my nose after all kinds of assurances that I was to get it," Kosoff noted after Mehl's death in 1957.[34]

B. Max Mehl handled three 1933 Double Eagles. One of them, purchased by Mehl from James Macallister in December 1937, wound up in the collection of Charles Williams, the same Cincinnati insurance-company president to whom Mehl had sold the rarities of the Dunham collection.[35]

The other two had more consequential trips through history—at least the history of the 1933 Double Eagle. One would kick off the investigation that led to the destruction of all the 1933 Double Eagles known to have originated with Israel Switt. The other would be the storied survivor of that destruction.

On February 23, 1944, Mehl bought a 1933 Double Eagle from Jake Shapiro, a Chicagoan who traded coins under the name J. F. Bell. This coin had the longest ownership history of Switt's 1933 Double Eagles. Originally purchased from Switt by James Macallister, it had passed through the hands of a New York collector named B. L. Taylor to Max Berenstein, the New York jeweler and sometime coin dealer. Berenstein sold the coin to another collector, who in turn sold it to Ira Reed, the Philadelphia dealer and auctioneer who'd already turned a profit on the four 1933 Double Eagles he'd bought directly from Israel Switt. Reed sold this coin, as well as another 1933 Double Eagle he'd been able to acquire, to Jake Shapiro. Shapiro sold the coin to B. Max Mehl, who had a client waiting anxiously for a 1933 Double Eagle.

Mehl's client—one of the best clients of all the major American coin dealers of the 1930s and 1940s—was King Farouk, the ruler of Egypt and an ardent coin collector. Mehl made the sale to Farouk on February 23, 1944, the same day he bought the 1933 Double Eagle from Jake Shapiro.[36] Two days later, an official from the Egyptian

Royal Legation in Washington, DC, took the coin to the director of the U.S. Mint and requested an export license. Gold ownership and export was still illegal under the Gold Reserve Act of 1934, except in the case of gold considered to be of "recognized special value to collectors of rare and unusual coin"—the exemption insisted upon by Treasury Secretary William Woodin.

King Farouk's 1933 Double Eagle received royal treatment from Mint officials. Mint Director Nellie Tayloe Ross asked her own personal assistant, Mrs. W. D. Fales, to take the coin to the curator of history at the Smithsonian to find out whether it qualified for the collectors' exception. The curator, Theodore Belote, typed a quick answer to Ross at the bottom of her letter to him: The 1933 Double Eagle was of recognized value to coin collectors, and had been before and since Roosevelt's executive order of April 5, 1933.[37] Farouk, in Belote's evaluation, was eligible for an export license for the 1933 Double Eagle. On February 29, the Treasury Department issued the Egyptian Legation an export license for the coin.

For ten days, Mint officials stored Farouk's 1933 Double Eagle in the cashier's safe at the Philadelphia Mint. Then on March 11, 1944, a Mr. Fahim of the Royal Legation retrieved the coin and sent it, along with Farouk's export license, to the king's Abdine Palace in Cairo via diplomatic pouch.

The third 1933 Double Eagle brokered by B. Max Mehl, a coin Mehl purchased from James Macallister in July 1937, was sold to a collector named James Flanagan. Flanagan, an honorary colonel and a resident of Palm Beach, Florida, held onto his 1933 Double Eagle until 1944, when he decided to sell his entire collection. The colonel consigned his coins to Morton and Joseph Stack, the New York brothers who were beginning to be known as New York's premier coin auctioneers.

If Mehl's trademark was folksiness, the Stack brothers' was elegance. Their shop on West 46th Street was like a fine jewelry store, with coins resting on velvet in long glass cases. No junk-shop dust was evident at Stack's; the brothers intended to do business with "dignity," in a "decorous, museum-like ambience."[38] In private, Joseph and Morton had a tumultuous relationship, according to John Ford, a protégé who later became a renowned dealer in his own right. "They were so busy arguing with each other all the time," Ford said. "They were volatile, particularly J. B. When he screamed and yelled, steam would come out of his ears."[39] But in front of clients, the shouting ceased. Stack's worked with most of the major collectors of the day: Colonel E. H. R. Green, J. P. Morgan, Lammot du Pont. It was Stack's that sold Louis Eliasberg the Clapp collection, which launched Eliasberg on his quest to acquire an example of every U.S. coin ever minted. Josiah Lilly, the pharmaceutical heir, entrusted Stack's to build for him one of the greatest collections of U.S. coins in history, without ever disclosing that the collection existed. Stack's became a landmark for coin collectors in New York at exactly the same time that New York became the coin-collecting capital of the United States. "It was a shop people wanted to walk into," said Harvey Stack, Morton's son and Joseph's nephew. "On Saturdays, people worked a half-day [at their jobs]. After work they'd come to Stack's. It was like a clubhouse where collectors would gather for lunch on Saturdays. That's what it was called, The Clubhouse."

Stack's catalogues, which treated coins as important artifacts worthy of serious scholarship, were a hallmark of the brothers' auctions. The March 1944 Flanagan sale was no exception. Morton and Joseph saved the last page of the catalogue for the pièce de résistance of what they billed as a "celebrated collection": Flanagan's 1933 Double Eagle, which would be sold as the final lot of the auction. The catalogue described the coin as "excessively rare," noting that Flanagan's was the first 1933 Double Eagle to come up for sale at a public auction. The Stacks had big ambitions for the Flanagan sale. They took out an advertisement in *The Numismatist*, announcing their intention to "realize the world's record in total amount of dollars!"[40]

Ernest Kehr, the stamp and coin columnist for *The New York Herald Tribune*, noticed the advertising for the Colonel Flanagan sale. Kehr was more of a stamp man than a numismatist, but he knew a news story when he saw one. The last page of the Stack's catalogue for the Flanagan sale, with its "excessively rare" 1933 Double Eagle, was a story. Kehr contacted the U.S. Mint to ask a question: How many 1933 Double Eagles had been released to the public?

Kehr's inquiry was the snowball that started an avalanche. The 1933 Double Eagle, unknown for eleven years outside of the coin world, was about to be discovered by the United States Secret Service.

Chapter Five

The First Investigation

ERNEST KEHR'S QUESTION—How many 1933 Double Eagles had been released to the public?—landed on the desk of Associate Mint Director Leland Howard in Washington. On Monday, March 20, 1944, Howard telegraphed the Mint superintendent in Philadelphia: "Does your record show that double eagles minted in 1933 were ever paid out. Your institution only one to manufacture double eagles 1933. Reported sale of same in New York schedule [*sic*] for next week. Please get information Tuesday if possible."[1]

Howard, an imperious fellow, received his answer in a memo the next day. The records of the Philadelphia Mint indicated that no 1933 Double Eagles had circulated publicly. Of the 445,500 $20 pieces minted in March, April, and May 1933, 445,000 had been classified as "uncurrent" and locked in Vault F in June 1933. Thirty-four additional coins were soon thereafter added to the stockpile in the vault. The other 466 coins were reserved for the Bureau of the Mint and the Assay Commission. Twenty-nine of those were destroyed in testing. Two were sent to the Smithsonian's National Numismatic Collection.

The rest of the coins reserved for testing, stored for a while in the cashier's pyx box, were supposed to have joined the 1933 Double Eagles already locked in Vault F. On this point, the records kept by vault custodian Edward McKernan were sketchy, but they did show that the coins left over from the Assay Commission's testing were at some point added to the Mint's total gold holdings.[2] And all of the Mint's gold coins were supposed to have been melted down and converted to bullion in 1937.

Yet the Stack's catalogue for the sale of Colonel James Flanagan's coin collection, as Leland Howard knew from Ernest Kehr's inquiry, claimed that eight or ten 1933 Double Eagles were known to exist. Howard believed there could be no innocent explanation. The associate mint director called Frank J. Wilson, the longtime chief of the U.S. Secret Service, to request an investigation. Wilson referred the case to his New York office and sent along a high-ranking Washington agent, James Haley, to watch over the investigation. On March 24, 1944, a young and well-scrubbed New York agent named Harry W. Strang was assigned to the case of the 1933 Double Eagle. He began the investigation at the Herald Tribune building, where he and Haley went to interview Kehr, the newspaper coin columnist. Kehr showed Strang and Haley the catalogue for the Colonel Flanagan sale, which was already underway at Stack's. The 1933 Double Eagle, Kehr noted, was due to be sold the next day, as the final lot of the auction.

The agents hurried over to Stack's, on 46th Street just off Fifth Avenue, to speak to Morton and Joseph Stack. The brothers reluctantly showed Strang and Haley Flanagan's 1933 Double Eagle, as well as a letter from B. Max Mehl noting that he'd sold Colonel Flanagan the coin in 1937 for $1,250. (Mehl was correcting an error on the sale price listed in the auction catalogue.) Morton and Joseph were distressed to see a pair of Secret Service agents at the auction, and not just because they hated to lose bragging rights to the first public sale of a 1933 Double Eagle. Buying and selling gold in 1944 required a government-issued license. When two agents walked through the doors of their shop with badges and guns, the Stacks—like most of the coin dealers Agent Strang would confront in his investigation—believed they had no choice but to cooperate.[3]

Morton and Joseph told Strang and Haley that other 1933 Double Eagles were, in fact, circulating among coin collectors. They directed the agents to a man whom they knew to have one of the coins, Max Berenstein, the New York jeweler and antiques dealer who'd bought the first 1933 Double Eagle to appear on the market. Strang and Haley left Stack's, taking Colonel Flanagan's 1933 Double Eagle with them, and went around the corner to Berenstein's shop on Madison Avenue. There they found Berenstein, who was eager to help. The jeweler told the agents about a half-dozen 1933 Double Eagles and their owners: Philadelphia dealers James Macallister and Ira Reed; and collectors F. C. C. Boyd, Jake Shapiro, and James Clarke. Strang and Haley asked Berenstein to surrender his 1933 Double Eagle. The obliging antiques dealer did.

After leaving Berenstein, the agents took the two $20 pieces they'd seized to the Mint's New York assay office, where the coins would be stored in a vault. Strang made plans to return to Stack's the next day; several of the collectors named by Berenstein were going to be in attendance at the auction house on 46th Street for the last day of the Flanagan sale. Then he and Haley began drafting an initial report for Chief Wilson in Washington. The 1933 Double Eagle investigation was officially under way.

To UNDERSTAND why, for the next several months, the Secret Service would devote so much time and so many agents to finding and seizing a handful of ordinary gold coins, one has to understand the history of the agency. The Secret Service was established in 1865 not to protect the president—the service's best known responsibility in modern times—but to prevent counterfeiting. At the time, that was a mission of the most profound importance to the United States. The federal government was just beginning to issue U.S. paper currency, which before the Civil War had been the exclusive province of state-chartered banks. Counterfeiting of state banknotes was rampant. Nearly eighty percent of the banknotes in circulation in 1862, according to David R. Johnson's definitive history of the early years of the Secret Service, were fakes.[4]

When the Civil War began, the federal government reclaimed from the states the power to control paper currency. A pair of laws—the Legal Tender Act of 1862 and the National Banking Act of 1863—banned state banknotes and created a nationwide standard for paper money that could be issued only by the government of the United States. Congress realized, however, that for the federal paper to be accepted, people had to believe in its integrity. Some kind of national anticounterfeiting police force would have to be established. As Johnson noted, "Having asserted its constitutional rights, the federal government had to defend itself or jeopardize its role in national economic development."[5] Nothing less than the economic credibility of the United States, in other words, was at stake.

Looking back, it seems something of a miracle that everything worked out. Congress assigned the job of policing the federal paper money supply to the Treasury Department, though at first it authorized no funding for the enforcement agency. A swashbuckling Civil War hero, Colonel Lafayette Baker, was the first anticounterfeiting operative; he staged a few flamboyant raids on counterfeiting operations in the Midwest in 1864 before returning to his regular detective job at the War Department. Baker was succeeded by William P. Wood, formerly the supervisor of the Old Capitol Prison in Washington, DC.

Wood was a man of conveniently flexible scruples, educated by the spies and fraudsters in his charge at the prison. Counterfeiting was an urban crime that was particularly unrestrained in New York, the printing capital of the country and the home of a large and hungry underclass. Saloons tended to be the centers of counterfeiting networks, which employed skilled manufacturers to produce fake notes—printing operations required the outlay of thousands of dollars—and unskilled "shovers" to push the bogus currency into circulation. Shovers, almost always young people, might be peddlers, laborers, porters, even housewives.[6] This was a milieu Wood's Capitol Prison inmates knew well. From them, he learned to use bribes, make deals, and induce low-level informants to squeal on ringleaders.

His exploits received enough attention that in 1865, after Congress appropriated $100,000 to fight counterfeiting, Wood was appointed the first chief of the newly created United States Secret Service. He set up a headquarters for himself in New York, hired agents with experience in the underworld of New York and Philadelphia—nearly half of Wood's operatives had criminal records—and achieved quite remarkable success. In the Secret Service's first official year of operation, agents arrested more than 200 counterfeiters.[7]

When Wood was knocked out of office by a change in presidential administrations, the Secret Service's freewheeling ways ended. Subsequent chiefs tightened standards for recruiting and hired more men from the middle classes, usually ones with some background in law enforcement. The service also reformed its investigative techniques, though apparently without sacrificing results. The agency was small, with no more than forty-seven operatives before 1910, but its reputation for effective and honest federal policing was outsize. It was the Secret Service, for instance, that investigated the New York Customs House and Whiskey Ring scandals during the administration of Ulysses Grant, the growth of the Ku Klux Klan in the 1870s, and Spanish spy rings in the years leading up to the Spanish–American War.

The service's primary mission, however, remained the integrity of the money supply. And Secret Service agents continued to make counterfeiting an unattractive criminal enterprise. One celebrated operative, Andrew Drummond, joined up in 1871 after a stint as a ship's purser acquainted him, involuntarily, with a widespread smuggling operation of cigars and bay rum. Drummond—notably moral and devoted even among the generally moral and devoted agents of the Secret Service—roamed the country, cultivating informants and busting up counterfeiting rings. Drummond typified the agency's doggedness. He was once outfoxed by a Philadelphia counterfeiter named Harry Cole, who agreed to inform on one of his cronies in exchange for Drummond's testimony on his behalf. After Drummond helped win his acquittal, Cole returned to his corrupt ways and managed to evade the seriously irritated agent for three years. Finally, though, Drummond found Cole in upstate New York, planted two informants within his operation, and succeeded in arresting not only Cole but also the stationers and printing suppliers who abetted him. Cole died in prison.[8]

As notable as Drummond's persistence was his humorlessness in matters involving the nation's money. Secret Service historian Johnson recounted the story of Drummond's crusade against play money in the 1880s. "Having obtained the names of toy-money manufacturers from a Manhattan toy dealer, [Drummond] personally visited each company and confiscated all their supplies and equipment," Johnson wrote. "Drummond also had the district attorney write to other manufacturers, who promptly surrendered all their supplies. In November 1881 this campaign climaxed when R. H. Macy surrendered one hundred and sixty boxes of toy money to Drummond for destruction." Nor was Drummond an exception when it came to this sort of priggishness. Other agents were known to have advised a candy-store owner not to sell gold-foil–covered chocolate dollars, and to have confiscated a painting of a dollar bill hanging in a saloon. "From the Service's perspective, these were not trivial cases," wrote Johnson. "Rather, they demonstrated how dedicated the operatives had become to the proposition that, in Drummond's words, 'the Securities and Coins of all countries should be held sacred.'"[9]

By THE turn of the twentieth century, the Secret Service had essentially eliminated the counterfeiting of paper money. Federal banknotes were universally accepted, and the credibility of the government was assured. It was then that the service's mission expanded. In 1902, after President William McKinley was assassinated, Congress assigned the agency the responsibility of guarding the president and his family. The investigative skills of its agents, meanwhile, continued to be put to use in the highest-profile scandals of the day: the Louisiana Lottery debacle in the 1890s; a spy case that exposed a high-ranking undercover agent of Kaiser Wilhelm just before World War I; and the Teapot Dome scandal in the 1920s.[10]

Counterfeiting remained under control through the 1920s, with seizures of bogus money never exceeding $533,000 in a year. But in the 1930s, probably because of the Great Depression, that situation began to change. In 1933, Secret Service agents confiscated almost $1 million in counterfeit money. In 1935, the total was almost $1.5

million. Counterfeiting was becoming a crisis again, and to resolve it, Treasury Secretary Henry Morgenthau, who had succeeded William Woodin, called upon the most respected detective in the country. Frank J. Wilson was a big, slow-moving man whose ordinary looks—he was bald and could hardly see without his round, black-rimmed glasses—hid his quite extraordinary talent.

Frank Wilson had wanted to be a detective ever since, as a boy, he had watched his father, a farmer-turned-cop in Buffalo, New York, help guard President McKinley on a tour through the city. His severe nearsightedness kept him out of World War I, so he took the civil-service examination and got a job as an investigator, first for the wartime Food Service Administration and then for the Internal Revenue Service (IRS). Wilson aquired an abiding disgust for what he called "boss justice" at the IRS, when a case he'd built against corruption in the issuance of federal alcohol licenses was dismissed by a judge whom Wilson considered to be part of the same political machine that sponsored the corruption. "It gave me a sober insight into the workings of crooked politics," he wrote in his autobiography, "which was later to stand me in good stead when I fought other cases of 'boss justice' versus American justice."[11]

For the next twenty years, Wilson enjoyed one celebrated adventure after another. He helped snare Bruno Hauptmann, the kidnapper of Charles Lindbergh's baby, and was an unwavering witness at the Hauptmann trial. An admiring Adela Rogers St. John, who covered the trial, described him as a "relentless glacier." Wilson brought down "The Kingfish," Huey Long of Louisiana. He was also, in the view of Al Capone biographer John Kobler, far more responsible for the capture and conviction of the notorious gangster than the "untouchable" Eliot Ness. It was Wilson who recruited a breakthrough witness from inside the Capone organization—a St. Louis dog-track owner whose silent partner was Capone—and who installed one of his men undercover in gangland Chicago. Wilson tracked down a pair of Capone accountants who proved to be key, if extremely reluctant, witnesses against the boss. In his day, the detective was so famous that in 1949 he and his wife were the subjects, albeit unnamed, of a film called *The Undercover Agent*. Wilson was played by Glenn Ford.[12]

In 1936, Treasury Secretary Morgenthau appointed Wilson to head the Secret Service. His orders, Wilson later wrote, were clear: "See that counterfeiting is reduced—promptly!"[13] Wilson was impressed by the pomp of his new office—leather chairs, massive mahogany desk, giant windows overlooking the White House, and a life-size portrait of former Treasury Secretary Salmon Chase—but distressed at the archaic state of the Secret Service's investigative resources. He immediately ordered all the agency's offices to be equipped with teletype machines, and most with still and movie cameras to document evidence. The most important field offices received newfangled lie-detector machines, and agents were sent to school in Chicago to learn to use them. Wilson required all Secret Service agents to attend Treasury Department courses in "modern and improved techniques in criminal investigation," the first such instruction many of them ever received.[14]

Inspired by their new boss, agents worked as never before. The annals of the Secret Service from the 1930s and 1940s are filled with accounts of captures of significant counterfeiters. There were also, however, any number of aborted—even ridiculous—investigations. In the Wilson era, no case was too petty, no investigation too thorough. A Syracuse teenager who drew a pen-and-ink picture of a $1 bill for his own amusement, a New York City toy store selling novelty dollar bills, a man with an ashtray made of gold coins: All received undoubtedly terrifying visits from Frank Wilson's unsmiling agents. Money, to the Secret Service of the 1930s and 1940s, mattered.

And that included coins. After the Gold Reserve Act of 1934 banned gold ownership, violations of the gold laws also fell under the jurisdiction of the Secret Service. Here again, the records show an agency determined to fulfill its mandate, no matter how preposterous a case seemed. Consider the prosecution of John Mayer, a jewelry-store owner who made the mistake of displaying nine foreign gold coins in his shop window on Lexington Avenue in Manhattan. Some alert New Yorker contacted the Secret Service, which dispatched agent John Fitzgerald to Mayer's store. "He stated that he is not a numismatist, and not a member of any numismatic society but knows a little about numismatic coins. He said he purchased the nine coins on display, about three years ago, believing them to be rare coins," wrote Fitzgerald. The hapless Mayer surrendered his nine gold coins and promised never to buy more.[15] In another case, Memphis Secret Service Agent Austin Sutterfield spent days tracking down a moonshiner named Hanson Sutton, who was said to have claimed to have $8,000 worth of eagles and double eagles buried in a metal box in Marked Tree, Arkansas. When Sutterfield cornered Sutton at his farm for questioning, "He told me that he had no gold coins, had not at anytime had any, but that he sure would like to find some," the agent reported. Sutton confessed that he'd made up the story about the coins and told people about it just in case he happened to find any. "Sutton may not be mentally deficient but he certainly has a wonderful imagination and is an accomplished prevaricator," concluded Agent Sutterfield, in the deadpan language of the Secret Service. "I am returning the complete file."[16]

Harry Strang, the young agent in charge of the 1933 Double Eagle investigation, had been involved in his share of inconsequential cases,[17] but he nonetheless managed to impress Chief Wilson. In 1942, when an acquaintance of the chief named Edgar Olivere needed help establishing the place and date of his birth, Strang received the assignment—routine, but of personal interest to the boss. Olivere praised Strang in a letter to Wilson: "A very fine fellow—and certainly knowledgeable."[18] For Strang, the 1933 Double Eagle case was a chance to show what he could do with a real mystery, one with very valuable coins at its center—not bogus stamps or play money. Harry Strang was determined to find out how these gold coins had gotten out of the U.S. Mint, how many were circulating, and who had them.

STRANG RECEIVED some answers on his second day on the case, March 25, 1944, when he and James Haley returned to Stack's to conduct interviews with collectors and dealers at the Colonel Flanagan sale. Fred Boyd, the renowned New York collector, admitted to the agents that he owned a 1933 Double Eagle. He'd bought it from James Macallister, he said, and he wasn't going to turn it over to the Secret Service until the agents could prove to him that the coin had been stolen from the Mint. Jake Shapiro (the Chicago dealer and collector who also used the name Bell) was unlucky enough to have his 1933 Double Eagle with him at Stack's that morning. A volatile man, Shapiro did some shouting when Strang and Haley demanded that he surrender his coin, but he finally turned it over to the agents. Ira Reed, the Philadelphia dealer, was cagey when Strang and Haley questioned him at Stack's. He had owned two 1933 Double Eagles, he confessed, but he'd sold them both. One had gone to Shapiro, Reed said, but he couldn't remember to whom he'd sold the other.

In his initial report, filed on March 27, 1944, Strang detailed everything he'd learned from Kehr, the Stack brothers, Berenstein, and the others. The head of the New York Secret Service briefed Chief Wilson and the assistant chief on Strang's report. They then ordered Strang to go to Philadelphia and continue the investigation there. Fred Boyd had told Strang that all of the 1933 Double Eagles in circulation among coin collectors had originated from one source, supposedly a son of the president of the Philadelphia Federal Reserve Bank. He was said to have had a bag of the coins when the gold recall order was issued and to have extracted ten before returning the bag to the Fed. Boyd's tip needed to be checked out.

In Philadelphia, young Strang was assigned a new partner: George Drescher, a squint-eyed, stone-faced agent—a decorated World War I veteran who'd first joined the Secret Service in 1919.[19] On Strang's first day in Philadelphia, he and Drescher called on Ira Reed, whom Strang had already interviewed once in New York. Reed was only slightly more cooperative this time, revealing little Strang didn't already know. He had sold three 1933 Double Eagles, Reed now admitted—the Shapiro coin that Strang had already seized, a coin that he sold to B. Max Mehl, and a coin that still belonged to James Clarke, a collector whose name Strang had received from Max Berenstein. Reed refused to produce any of his records, at least not unless the agents would promise that owners of 1933 Double Eagles seized by the Secret Service would ultimately get them back. "We, of course, could make no promises to that effect," Strang noted.

The agents finally obtained solid information later that day when they went to see James Macallister at his shop. Macallister took out all of his records, offering up dates, buyers, and purchase prices for the five 1933 Double Eagles he'd handled. He told the agents that he had always been suspicious about the coins and, in fact, had asked questions about their history. Once he'd been told that an old woman related to someone at the Treasury Department had first owned the 1933 Double Eagles; another time, he heard that the coins originated with a man who was somehow connected to the Federal Reserve Bank in Philadelphia. Macallister couldn't be sure either story was true, but he did know where he'd obtained the coins. His source, he told Strang and Drescher, was a Philadelphia jeweler, a hustler with an arrest record. The man's name, Macallister said, was Israel Switt.[20]

This was the first Strang had heard of Israel Switt, and his first tangible lead for the original seller of 1933 Double Eagles. Strang and Drescher returned to the Philadelphia Secret Service office, where they found the records of Israel Switt's 1934 arrest and 1937 conviction for violations of the Gold Reserve Act. They also visited the Mint to ask some questions. By the end of the day, they were fairly certain that the stories they'd heard from Fred Boyd and James Macallister about a mystery source at the Federal Reserve weren't true. No bag of 1933 Double Eagles ever went to the Fed. This was an inside job. Someone at the Mint had stolen the coins, and Israel Switt probably knew who had done it.

The next day, the two agents went to Switt's store on 18th Street. He was expecting them: Ira Reed had already warned him of the Secret Service's investigation. For the next four hours, Strang and Drescher grilled Switt—first at his store, then back at the Philadelphia Secret Service offices. They also accompanied him to his safe-deposit box, which he opened in their presence. Israel Switt was as tough as an undercooked brisket. In those four hours of questioning, he was willing to admit only that beginning in 1937 he had sold nine 1933 Double Eagles to three dealers—James Macallister, Ira Reed, and Abe Kosoff. The agents wanted to know where he had obtained the coins. Conveniently, he had no records. "I do not remember when, where, or from whom I purchased them," Switt asserted in a signed statement, "as they were received by me in collections with other coins at different times." Did he know people at the Mint who could have slipped him the 1933 Double Eagles? He knew a couple of Mint employees, Switt conceded, but no one important. He only talked to people at the Mint about scrap gold, not coins. "I never had any conversation about or obtained any gold coins from or through any employees of the U.S. mint," he said in his statement.

Strang and Drescher pressed Switt about one Mint employee in particular. They'd already pinpointed the weak spot in the Mint's records of the 1933 Double Eagles: those 400 or so coins that had come back to the Mint after Assay Commission testing. Two, the records indicated, had been sent to the Smithsonian. But the other 435 1933 Double Eagles, entrusted to the Mint cashier, still had to be accounted for. "The whereabouts . . . of these double eagles during the time they were apparently in the cashier's hands is rather vague," Strang and Drescher noted in the April 1, 1944, report that discussed their interview with Switt. "There is no record of them having been placed in the sealed vault." The cashier at the time, the agents reported, was nominally Hibberd Ott, but he'd been out sick beginning in March 1934. Acting as cashier during Ott's illness, under the supervision of Chief Clerk Ralph Roland, was Ott's assistant, George McCann. And George McCann, Strang and Drescher had learned, made a very convenient suspect in the 1933 Double Eagle case. Like Israel Switt, he had a criminal record: On May 29, 1940, McCann had been arrested for stealing silver coins from the Mint.

In no small way, the U.S. government had George McCann to thank for the tight security in place at the Philadelphia Mint when America's entry into World War II forced the Mint quickly to escalate coin production. By then, the Secret Service, working with the Federal Bureau of Investigation and local police departments, was already running background checks on every man and woman hired by the Mint. These were the result of the service's investigation of the once-mighty George McCann.

Back in the spring of 1940, the Philadelphia Secret Service bureau had been summoned to the Mint to investigate reports of theft from the weigh room. Agents discovered that McCann, then cashier, and Charles Rumpp, the foreman of the cashier's counting and weigh

room, had independently been stealing "uncurrent" silver coins—
coins returned to the Mint because they were too worn or mutilated
to stay in circulation. McCann's seemed the pettiest of crimes; he was
arrested with a total of $339.90 in stolen money, mostly obsolete half-
dollars and quarters. But as they investigated, the agents also heard
numerous "reports of previous irregularities," as a June 12, 1940,
report delicately phrased the matter. Mint employees said that on several occasions, McCann had been questioned by higher-ups but never
disciplined. Unfortunately, the Secret Service found Mint personnel
records pitifully inadequate, with nothing in the files to confirm these
accounts of McCann's other alleged offenses.

On the recommendation of the Philadelphia Secret Service office,
and with the endorsement of Chief Wilson, the Mint set up not only
files on current employees but also a system for checking future hires.
McCann, meanwhile, was fired from the Mint and prosecuted for
stealing the money that agents found on him at the time of his arrest.
In March 1941, he pled guilty to embezzling government property,
admitting in open court to having stolen a total of about $1,200 over
two years. McCann was sentenced to pay a fine of $500 and to serve a
federal prison term of a year and a day.

DID ISRAEL Switt know George McCann? That was the critical
question Harry Strang sought to answer in the 1933 Double Eagle
investigation. Switt told Strang that he did not, and claimed not to
know Ralph Roland, the former chief clerk, either. But the agent suspected Switt of lying. So in April 1944, he and Drescher began a
series of interviews with former Mint workers.

The only man who seemed to know both McCann and Switt well
was Robert Graham, a since-retired deposit and weigh room clerk.
Graham admitted he was a friend of the two men (though he owned
up only to being "more or less friendly" with the notoriously irascible
Switt). He said he didn't know of any coin transactions between them
but did tell the agents that McCann was a coin collector, information
that would explain how the Mint cashier knew that 1933 Double
Eagles would be valuable to collectors.

More clues about McCann's experience with rare coins came from Willard Boyce, McCann's successor as cashier. Boyce told Strang and Drescher that after he was named cashier, Ira Reed approached him with a request to buy some of the Mint's special wartime zinc-coated pennies before they were released publicly. Reed promised to pay Boyce for his trouble, and for future service in securing rare coins. He also intimated, Boyce told Strang and Drescher, that he'd had a similar arrangement with George McCann. "Another employee of the mint," Boyce reported Reed saying, "made himself quite a piece of money dealing with me." Boyce told the agents that he'd once seen McCann, when McCann was cashier, come into the deposit and weigh room to weigh a handful of gold coins. Strang speculated that McCann might have been checking the weight of common-date Saints that he planned to substitute for stolen 1933 Double Eagles.[21]

But connecting McCann to Switt—or even linking Switt to anything illegal—remained a problem. (Strang and Drescher resisted simply interviewing McCann—whom they knew to be out of prison and living in Westmont, New Jersey—until they'd determined how good a case they had against him.) On April 14, Strang and Drescher met with Chief Wilson in Washington to brief him on the 1933 Double Eagle case and to solicit his advice on how to proceed.

Wilson had taken a personal interest in the case, which was turning out to be exactly the kind of sprawling, document-intensive investigation that he'd run successfully at the Internal Revenue Service. The chief had sent out teletypes to Secret Service bureaus all over the country, ordering agents to fan out and interview coin collectors and dealers with rumored links to the stolen 1933 Double Eagles. At the meeting with Strang and Drescher in his palatial office in Washington, Wilson suggested an old trick from his Capone days: squeezing Israel Switt with his income-tax returns. Switt had claimed that he didn't have records on the 1933 Double Eagles, but two of the dealers to whom he'd sold them did. Macallister had told Strang and Drescher about his five purchases from Switt; and Abe Kosoff had given New York Agent Milton Lipson the same information about the one 1933 Double Eagle he admitted he'd bought from Switt. What did Switt's tax returns say? Wilson sent Strang and Drescher back to Philadelphia to find out.

The chief followed his order with another suggestion, fired off via teletype: "There are three persons mentioned who might be referred to as suspected of being involved in the handling of these coins, namely, Switt, Reed, and McCann," Wilson wrote. "It is believed that serious consideration should be given to endeavoring to have all these men (or any of the three who will agree to it) submit to the lie detector test."

Switt's lawyer squelched Strang's request that his client submit to a lie-detector test. But the chief's exhortation to follow the money was just the advice Strang and Drescher needed. They demanded Switt's income-tax returns and requested transaction records from everyone known to have bought and sold 1933 Double Eagles. From James Macallister they obtained the canceled checks by which Macallister had paid Switt for his five coins. The checks had been endorsed not only by Switt but also by a man named Edward Silver. The agents went back to Macallister to find out about this new character.

Edward Silver, they learned, was Switt's brother-in-law and business partner. In fact, Macallister now said, Switt had told him that it was Silver who could acquire more 1933 Double Eagles.[22] "My partner Ed," Macallister quoted Switt as saying, "can get all he wants of these as we had twenty-five and only sold fourteen." Was Edward Silver the link between Switt and McCann? Strang and Drescher once again dug into Mint records and found that Silver had obtained a license to deal in scrap gold in September 1934, two weeks after Switt lost his gold-trading license. Silver had deposited huge amounts of gold in the years since: almost $82,000 in 1935, $50,000 in 1936, $68,000 in 1937, and more than $100,000 in 1938, 1939, and 1940. Surely Silver had met George McCann when he was making these deposits.

Strang and Drescher checked with Willard Boyce, McCann's successor. Boyce reported seeing Silver and McCann in conversation any number of times. He'd also overheard McCann talking to Silver on the phone. Jake Pepper, the foreman of the deposit and weigh room, supported Boyce's account. He told the Secret Service agents that he'd seen Silver walk into McCann's office several times after transacting business in the weigh room.[23]

But when the agents finally interviewed Silver in May, he insisted that he didn't know George McCann. He admitted that he conducted business at the Mint four or five times a week, but he said he only knew deposit and weigh room employees, not the cashier himself.

Strang and Drescher were only permitted to interview Silver in the presence of the lawyer he and Switt had hired to represent them, a Philadelphian named Emanuel Friedman. Friedman was proving an immovable obstruction to the agents' investigation. "His attitude was anything but cooperative," Strang reported on May 12, 1944. "He stated that he had conferred with his clients but declined to state what they had told him, except that they had not obtained the coins directly from a mint employee, and that there were others involved whom Friedman declined to name. Friedman also intimated that his clients had handled a considerable quantity of these coins but refused [to divulge] the details." With Chief Wilson pestering them for progress on the case, Strang and Drescher repeatedly returned to Friedman's office to push him to allow Switt and Silver to talk. Friedman was always polite, always obliging, and always intransigent. He told the agents he was willing to help and would consult with his clients, but after Silver's interview on May 16, he never permitted Strang and Drescher to question Switt or Silver again.

So Strang and Drescher were forced to develop evidence against the brothers-in-law from other sources. First on their list was a pair of felons, Bernard Kushner and Jack Rubin, with whom both Switt and Silver admitted doing business. Kushner and Rubin were well known to the Secret Service. Jack Rubin had been convicted of receiving jewelry stolen from the Waldorf-Astoria Hotel in 1939; he was serving a seven-year sentence at Sing Sing Prison. Kushner had been arrested for smuggling gold bullion from Canada; he was serving four years at the federal prison in Lewisburg, Pennsylvania. Strang and Drescher traveled there to see Kushner on May 26, 1944. Anxious for the agents' help at his upcoming parole hearing, Kushner talked for six hours about Switt and Silver. Kushner claimed that they ran a melting operation in their shop, transforming illegal gold coins into bullion they sold to Kushner. They were clever about it, Kushner said, and always added dental and scrap gold to diminish the purity of the bullion so authorities couldn't figure out that it came from coins.

Jack Rubin was less helpful when Strang and Drescher interviewed him at Sing Sing in June. With no imminent parole hearing to refresh his memory, Rubin refused to back his erstwhile partner's story of buying melted gold coins from Israel Switt and Edward Silver. But he did inadvertently confirm another possible link between Switt and George McCann. In 1936, Rubin said, he bought a number of pristine 1931 and 1932 double eagles from Israel Switt. His account confirmed what Strang and Drescher had already heard: In 1936, before the first sale of a 1933 Double Eagle, Israel Switt had sold dozens of 1931 and 1932 double eagles, which had become extremely valuable after the gold recall in 1933. Rubin's story was more evidence that 1933 Double Eagles weren't the only $20 gold-coin rarities Switt had been peddling.

And George McCann was probably his source for the 1931 and 1932 double eagles as well. Strang and Drescher discovered that McCann, as Mint cashier, had access to these double eagles, as well as their 1933 counterparts, via the stash of coins reserved for the Assay Commission. George McCann had deposited $10,000 in his brokerage account in 1936; at the time of his arrest in 1940, he could not explain its source. Had Switt paid McCann for rare 1931 and 1932 double eagles that year?

ON JUNE 28, 1944, after more than three months of intensive investigation by Strang, Drescher, and a supporting cast of Secret Service agents, Chief Wilson was growing impatient with the case of the 1933 Double Eagles. He teletyped the head of the Philadelphia bureau, Agent Fred Gruber, and instructed him to contact the federal prosecutor in Philadelphia for a meeting. Wilson ordered Gruber, Strang, and Drescher to attend, and said he would send Washington, DC, Agent James Haley as his representative. The chief also instructed Strang and Drescher to prepare a summary report on the evidence against Switt, Silver, and McCann to be presented to U.S. Attorney Gerald Gleeson.

Gleeson wanted to question Switt and Silver himself. Once again, Emanuel Friedman, their lawyer, stood in the way. Through the summer of 1944, as Chief Wilson fretted in Washington, Friedman put off the U.S. attorney. Finally, on September 26, Bureau Chief Gruber and Agents Strang and Drescher met with Gleeson and Friedman in Gleeson's office. It was a fruitless meeting, producing just another in the long string of vague promises from Friedman about consulting with Switt and Silver. On October 10, Friedman at last admitted what had been evident for months: Switt and Silver would not cooperate with the 1933 Double Eagle investigation. They would never reveal how they had obtained 1933 Double Eagles, nor how many they had handled. The Secret Service would not be able to learn anything more about Switt's enigmatic comment to James Macallister of having once had twenty-five 1933 Double Eagles.

Chief Wilson ordered Strang—who had spent much of the summer at his regular posting in New York—to return to Philadelphia and resume the coin case. The agent and his new partner, Charles Rich, headed for Westmont, New Jersey, to question George McCann. If they couldn't catch McCann through Switt and Silver, maybe they could catch Switt and Silver through McCann. Strang and Rich paid an unannounced visit to the former Mint cashier at Muller's Real Estate office, where he'd found a job after his release from prison. McCann wasn't entirely surprised to see them; at Chief Wilson's suggestion, the government had attached his retirement funds, claiming that McCann was responsible for the never-solved theft of a $5,000 bag of double eagles from Vault F at the U.S. Mint. Strang noted that McCann was "apparently very much agitated" by the government's action, particularly since he'd received notice that the government intended to recover the present-day value of the missing coins—about $8,500—from him.

McCann spoke to Strang and Rich for two hours. He denied knowing Switt or Silver and said he had never had custody of the 1933 Double Eagles returned to the Mint by the Assay Commission. He insisted that the box containing the coins was always in the possession of the vault custodian, Edward McKernan, whom McCann named as the likely thief of the 1933 Double Eagles as well as the missing

$5,000 bag of coins. Strang and Rich wanted McCann to agree to another interview, but the former cashier said he wouldn't talk to them without his lawyer. When the agents called McCann's lawyer the next day, they were informed that McCann had epilepsy, and his health would not permit any more questioning.

To check McCann's assertion that McKernan had stolen the coins, Strang and Rich scheduled another interview with the former vault custodian, who was eager to cooperate. They concluded that McKernan had been a sloppy bookkeeper, but not the man who stole the 1933 Double Eagles. His account of the coins returned by the Assay Commission—that they were placed in a special box, to which only the cashier and the assayer held keys—matched what other Mint workers had already told Strang. McKernan suggested that Strang and Rich investigate McCann's cronies—Fred Chaffin, Ralph Roland, and Chester "Doc" Ziegler.

Fred Chaffin had died suddenly in 1936 on a train in Wyoming. He had been a coin collector, but he had turned in his gold coins after the passage of the Gold Reserve Act; his silver, sold after his death, brought only $134. Ziegler was dead as well. He killed himself in 1938, jumping in the middle of the night from the window of a private mental hospital to which he'd been admitted. Ziegler left an estate of more than $27,000. His executor was Ralph Roland, whose biggest concern in handling the estate was said to be that Ziegler's housekeeper and common-law wife, to whom Ziegler left only $300, would challenge the will. When Strang and Rich interviewed Ralph Roland—Strang's third session with the former chief clerk—Roland said that Ziegler's estate included no gold coins. Moreover, Roland turned on McCann, his onetime protégé. "It is Roland's opinion that the 1933 [Double Eagle] could not have become circulated without collusion with McCann," the agents reported.[24]

Strang and Rich twisted the scenarios every imaginable way and always returned to McCann, Silver, and Swiit as the men who had removed some number of 1933 Double Eagles—they weren't sure how many—from the Mint and sold them. There wasn't evidence to support any other conclusion. George McCann was the only Mint employee who had had a clear opportunity to snatch the coins. He was a coin collector; he'd been romanced by Ira Reed; and he knew that 1933 Double Eagles would be highly desirable rarities on the numismatic market. McCann must have passed the coins to Silver, whom the agents were sure he knew. Silver connected McCann to Israel Switt, who had sold all nine of the 1933 Double Eagles the Secret Service was able to track down. Strang and Rich believed that McCann had also supplied an unknown quantity of 1931 and 1932 double eagles to Switt and Silver. On November 24, the two agents submitted to Chief Wilson a final report outlining their conclusions.

As Chief Wilson had instructed, Strang had investigated the income-tax returns of both Switt and Silver and had become convinced that the men were substantially underreporting their income. Among Philadelphia jewelers, Switt was regarded as a wealthy man, yet he paid no income tax, Strang noted, until 1940, when he paid a total of $50.79 on gross income of almost $60,000. Silver's returns showed that his business grossed close to $200,000 annually, yet he paid little or no income tax. Strang delivered a copy of his November 24 report to the agent in charge of the intelligence unit of the IRS in Philadelphia. He also gave the IRS copies of the Switt and Silver tax returns and notified Chief Wilson that he'd done so. But nothing ever came of the tax investigation of Switt and Silver.

Nor did anything come of the criminal case involving the 1933 Double Eagle, despite Strang's months of dogged investigation and the persuasive evidence he assembled. U.S. Attorney Gleeson stalled the decision for several months after Strang and Rich filed their final report. He turned over the case to an assistant, who met a couple of times with the Secret Service agents in January 1945. But in the end, when Gleeson telephoned Philadelphia Secret Service Bureau Chief Fred Gruber, he had bad news: He couldn't prosecute Switt, Silver, or McCann. Any case against them, Gleeson said, would be barred by the statute of limitations. Time had run out on any crimes they might have committed in the late 1930s.

Gruber had the unenviable task of informing Chief Wilson. On February 7, he telegraphed Wilson the news of Gleeson's decision: "No criminal prosecution will be instituted by his office in this matter." There is no record of the chief's reaction.

Chapter Six

Seizure

GERALD GLEESON'S REFUSAL TO prosecute Swist, Silver, and McCann didn't end the 1933 Double Eagle case for the Secret Service. There was still the matter of the coins themselves, and what was to become of them. Frank Wilson had been thinking about the disposition of the coins since May 1944, when Harry Strang was just six weeks into his investigation. Wilson had requested a legal opinion from the Treasury Department's chief lawyer to answer the question of whether or not the Secret Service could demand the return of 1933 Double Eagles from collectors who owned them. The lawyer, Joseph O'Connell, said it could. Interpreting a 1939 case, O'Connell said the government didn't have to prove that collectors knew their 1933 Double Eagles had been stolen when they bought them. Instead, he advised, the Treasury Department simply had to notify the coins' owners that their 1933 Saints had been misappropriated and were the rightful property of the United States. Then none of the owners could claim ignorance when the government demanded the coins' return. Anyone who continued to refuse to surrender his coin would be subject to criminal prosecution.

When O'Connell first reported his opinion, the Secret Service had three 1933 Double Eagles in its possession, all of them seized by Agent Harry Strang in New York City in the first two days of his investigation. Over the next year, the owners of these three coins agitated for their return. Colonel Flanagan, whose 1933 Double Eagle was to have been auctioned at Stack's, hired lawyers to barrage the Secret Service with letters, then enlisted U.S. Senator Claude Pepper to lobby on his behalf. Chicago collector Jake Shapiro wrote his own increasingly inflamed letters to Wilson. Max Berenstein, the New York antiques dealer who'd been so helpful to Agent Strang, sent his lawyer to the Treasury Department in Washington to stand at the main reception desk until someone told him whether the Secret Service planned to return Berenstein's coin or else refund the money he paid for it.

Chief Wilson was as impervious to these entreaties as a rock to the rain. Not only did he refuse to return the 1933 Double Eagles the Secret Service had already seized, he also set out to take possession of those the service didn't have. Even as Gleeson, the Philadelphia prosecutor, was deciding not to file criminal charges against Switt, Silver, and McCann, Wilson requested another memo from Treasury Department attorney O'Connell to justify seizing the coins from their owners. O'Connell reiterated the legal opinion he'd previously offered: Owners of 1933 Double Eagles could be prosecuted on criminal charges if they retained their coins after receiving notification that the coins had been stolen from the United States. So on May 15, 1945, letters went out to all of the 1933 Double Eagle owners the Secret Service had identified, advising them that it was illegal to possess the coins. The next month, Fred Boyd, Charles Williams, James Clarke, and James Stack (not related to the Stack brothers of the auction house) reluctantly surrendered their 1933 Double Eagles to Secret Service agents. "Of course, I do not care to have in my possession anything that has been embezzled or stolen," wrote a rueful Fred Boyd. "However, as a collector, I should like to keep this coin."[1]

One 1933 Double Eagle owner, L. G. Barnard of Memphis, decided to challenge the government head-on. Barnard, president of the Memphis Sash and Door Company, hired a law firm and filed a petition in federal court, seeking a court ruling on who owned his 1933 Double Eagle: he or the government. "Mr. Barnard is a wealthy and influential citizen," warned Memphis Secret Service agent Austin Sutterfield. "He intends to contest the recovery of the coin."[2] The U.S. Attorney in Tennessee turned around and sued Barnard, demanding return of the coin. Barnard's defense—his whole case, really—was his good-faith purchase of the 1933 Double Eagle. He was a prominent man and a well-known coin collector, his lawyers contended in their court filings, and he had bought the coin through an equally reputable Memphis banker. The coin was minted and issued by the United States as legal currency, and so, Barnard argued, he had the right to own it. If Barnard's argument prevailed, all the collectors who had acquired their 1933 Saints under similar circumstances could demand that their coins be returned.

Barnard had reason to be hopeful. In at least two previous cases well known in the coin world, the government's attempts to seize suspicious coins had failed. One involved the coin collection of Henry Linderman, the former Mint director and Treasury Department official who'd been at the heart of the Mint chicanery of his time. When he died, Linderman's own collection was found to be filled with rarities, most notably an 1804 silver dollar and all manner of unique pattern coins. New York coin dealer Lyman Low was selected to auction off the collection, and in 1887 he prepared a lavish catalogue for the sale, which he expected to be a blockbuster. It wasn't. Before the auction came off, treasury agents arrived at Low's door and confiscated Linderman's collection, claiming that it contained coins improperly obtained from the Mint. But in the end, without explanation, the government returned the Linderman collection to Low. He'd been financially devasted by the cost of the original catalogue and forced to give up his own coin firm, but the dealership he joined sold the Linderman collection in 1888.[3]

Equally unsuccessful was the government's 1910 pursuit of Captain John Haseltine, the Philadelphia dealer who was famous for having inherited the outstanding inventory of coins assembled by his father-in-law, William Idler, as well as Idler's unparalleled connections at the Mint. Haseltine was the source of many of the great rarities of coin collecting that surfaced around the turn of the twentieth century, including the unique pair of $50 gold pieces that he sold to William Woodin for a shocking $20,000 in 1909. In 1910, a collector named James Manning requested from Haseltine a selection of twenty-four pattern coins. The coins were not particularly valuable, but Manning was a diligent collector, and he sent a letter to the new Mint director, Abram Piatt Andrew, describing his pattern coins and requesting information on the number struck of each. As it happened, Andrew's bête noire was the Mint's surreptitious trading of restruck rarities and experimental coins. Manning's letter hit a sensitive nerve. Andrew sent Manning a reminder that under an 1873 law it was illegal to own pattern coins, which rightfully belonged to the United States. When Manning promised to return the twenty-four pattern coins to Captain Haseltine, Andrew arranged for treasury agents to accompany the package. Andrew's agents seized the coins, and the government sued Haseltine for title. But in October 1910, the government abruptly dropped the suit against Haseltine and returned the coins that the agents had seized from him. Pattern coins, *The Numismatist* crowed, were safe for collectors. The coin world regarded Haseltine as a hero for standing up to the mighty federal government.

BARNARD AND the rest of the 1933 Double Eagle owners were not to be so lucky. Barnard's case went to trial in Memphis in the summer of 1947. The government, represented by a Memphis federal prosecutor and a Treasury Department lawyer, kept the case simple, never even invoking the names of George McCann or Israel Switt. The government's strategy was to argue that no 1933 Double Eagle, except for the two in the Smithsonian's collection, could have left the Mint lawfully, so Barnard's coin must have been stolen. And if it had been stolen, it rightfully belonged to the United States. Barnard had able lawyers—a coin collector from New York named Harry Stein came down to assist Barnard's Memphis attorney—but Judge Marion Boyd found the government's accounting of the coins compelling. "It is a fair inference," Boyd ruled, "that the Double Eagle here involved was taken out of the Mint in an unlawful manner." Regardless of Barnard's good faith in buying it, the judge concluded, the coin had been stolen or embezzled, so Bernard could not keep it. "Title to the coin in litigation," Judge Boyd ruled, "is in the plaintiff, United States of America."

Barnard, who reportedly had nearly bankrupted himself in the litigation over his 1933 Double Eagle,[4] did not appeal, and agreed to surrender his coin to the Secret Service in 1947. Two other challenges to the government's 1933 Double Eagle seizure were equally futile. James Clarke, also represented by Harry Stein, filed suit in 1945, but his case was dismissed in 1947. Another collector, James Stack, sued the government in 1950 to recover the coin he'd already turned over to the Secret Service. Stack's suit, which named Harry Strang as a defendant, dragged on for years, even after Stack himself died. It finally staggered to an end in 1956, with Stack's 1933 Double Eagle remaining the property of the United States.

The government now had undisputed title to eight 1933 Double Eagles that Agent Harry Strang had traced in the 1944 investigation— and to another 1933 Double Eagle that Strang hadn't even heard about in 1944. On August 12, 1952, a registered mail package arrived at the Philadelphia Mint. It was sent from the Baltimore office of Louis Eliasberg, the coin collector who had assembled the only complete set of every type of coin ever minted by the United States. Inside the envelope was a 1933 Double Eagle.

Old Ira Reed, it seemed, had outfoxed the Secret Service, treating Harry Strang's 1933 Double Eagle investigation as if it were no more serious than a friendly chat with the beat cop. On April 15, 1944, the day after Chief Wilson exhorted Strang and George Drescher to continue pressuring the uncooperative Philadelphia coin dealer, Reed had sold a 1933 Double Eagle to Louis Eliasberg. Reed was so wily that he'd lied about the coin to the agents' faces—and then managed to squeeze $1,000 from Eliasberg for the coin, a high price indeed for a coin sought by Secret Service agents across the country. Eliasberg never explained what prompted him finally to send his 1933 Double Eagle back to the Mint; though the coin world was abuzz with talk of the Secret Service investigation in 1944, Eliasberg implied that he'd only heard about it in 1952. "In so far as I have subsequently heard that there was a cloud to the title," he wrote to Associate Mint Director Leland Howard on September 4, 1952, "I decided to surrender the coin."

Eliasberg's 1933 Double Eagle was locked in a safe in the office of the superintendent of the Philadelphia Mint. The other eight 1933 Double Eagles in the possession of the Secret Service were secured at the Treasury Building in Washington, DC. They had escaped from the United States government once. They wouldn't again.

But there was at least one other 1933 Double Eagle elsewhere in the world. The Secret Service knew about the coin, and had known about it from the early days of its 1944 investigation. Even Chief Wilson couldn't order the return of this 1933 Double Eagle, though. The tenth 1933 Double Eagle known to have slipped out of the Mint was not just a rare ounce of gold. It was a hostage of international politics.

Chapter Seven

Farouk of Egypt

SHEER IMPROBABILITY IS WHAT makes the story of the 1933 Double Eagle so unusual—not just the extraordinary, preposterous power of the coin to link an unimaginable collection of people, but also the swoops of fate the coin embodied. What if William Woodin had not insisted on an exception for coin collectors in FDR's emergency banking legislation? What if George McCann had not been a coin collector and Edward Silver had not taken over his brother-in-law's scrap-gold business? And what if B. Max Mehl had not bought one of Jake Shapiro's 1933 Double Eagles in February 1944, a mere month before the Secret Service launched its Double Eagle investigation?

Mehl's lucky timing removed one 1933 Double Eagle from Chief Frank Wilson's hard-boiled detective drama and whisked it into what must have seemed at the time to be a fairy tale. King Farouk of Egypt, Mehl's client and the owner of the last 1933 Double Eagle identified by the Secret Service in 1944, was the world's most notorious playboy. For sixteen dazzling years in the first half of the twentieth century, anything Farouk wanted was his. Any object that piqued his interest or fired his whimsy he acquired, by purchase or by royal expropriation. Farouk's favorite of his four palaces, the gigantic Koubbeh in suburban Cairo, was stuffed with his possessions. Downstairs was his private casino, with 400 decks of pinup-girl playing cards. Upstairs were miles of corridors and hundreds of rooms for Farouk's acquisitions. In his study were paintings and statues of nudes, a crate of magic tricks, seven inkwells of gold and silver, fourteen diamond-studded letter openers, and four desk drawers filled with golden fountain pens. The music room had every instrument imaginable. The gym was loaded with costly exercise machines. Farouk's royal wardrobe included a hundred suits, a thousand ties, two thousand shirts, thirty sets of slippers, and seventy-five pairs of binoculars. The king's jewels—box after box of precious rubies, emeralds, and diamonds—were stored in a hidden room between the first and second floors. Six vaults in the basement housed Farouk's beloved million-dollar collections of stamps and coins, including his 1933 Double Eagle. It was all overwhelming to the Western journalists finally permitted within the Koubbeh's iron gates in 1952.

By then, though, Farouk's run had ended—so ignominiously that *Time* magazine's man at the Koubbeh detected a whiff of pathos rising from the king's piled-up treasures. "Above all," he noted, "the palace gave the impression that someone had feverishly and indiscriminately crammed possessions into the vast rooms, to ward off loneliness, or perhaps despair."[1]

Farouk's life was filled with both, despite his frantic efforts. He was born on February 20, 1920, to King Fuad of Egypt and his beautiful, French-educated second wife, the teenaged Nazli Sabry. The blond-haired prince, whose name means "one who knows right from wrong," had an absurdly pampered but lonely and isolated childhood. Farouk was raised entirely within the walls of one palace or another, glimpsing the outside world only when the family moved between either the Abdine or the Koubbeh Palace in Cairo to the summertime residences, Ras el-Tin and Montazah in Alexandria. He had every imaginable amusement—acres and acres of land to roam, pools and lakes stocked with boats, tennis and squash courts, horses and camels, rooms full of toys and gadgets[2]—but no one to play with except his four younger sisters. Farouk craved the friendship of boys. A Swedish nanny who cared for the royal children later wrote poignantly of the prince's attachment to a photograph of her nephew back in Sweden. And when a palace electrician named Antonio Pulli went to Farouk's room one day to fix the prince's model-train set, nine-year-old Farouk fastened himself to the Italian servant. Pulli became Farouk's best friend, giving the prince entrée to the backstairs roughhousing of the palace's Italian workmen. Farouk was so grateful that he remained devoted to Pulli throughout his reign.

The prince spent far more time with Pulli and the other servants, as well as his beloved British governess, Mrs. Ina Naylor, than with his parents. Farouk saw his mother—whom King Fuad confined in an all-female harem guarded by eunuchs—only twice a day. She spoiled the boy terribly, petting him and feeding him sweets.[3] The rest of his schedule was dictated by his father, the fearsome Fuad. A master politician, adept at playing the British occupiers of Egypt against Egyptian nationalists, Fuad scared everyone, including his son. Years before Farouk was born, Fuad had been shot in the throat and almost killed by the brother of his first wife. Doctors saved his life but were unable to remove the bullet from his throat, so every few minutes Fuad uttered a terrifying bark, which matched his ruling style. The king, rarely seen by his awestruck son, ordered Farouk to be toughened up with a rigorous course of athletics and studies. His intentions, however, were undermined by servants who lavished undeserved praise on the prince. Farouk's education was so spotty that he failed the entrance exam at Eton and could not even be admitted as a regular student to the Royal Military Academy at Woolwich.

Fuad sent the fifteen-year-old Farouk to England anyway. He was determined to get his son into the Royal Military Academy, so he ensconced Farouk and a retinue of twenty servants in a country house near the academy. Twice a week, Farouk drove up to the school for classes. The rest of the time, two tutors selected by Fuad were expected to cram enough knowledge into Farouk's head that the prince could pass the academy entrance exam. Farouk, however, had different ideas. He spent much of his time in London, going to nightclubs and shopping. The teenaged prince, who until this point had had little opportunity to spend his money, was already showing the predilections of a collector. In London he bought antiques and jewelry, rare books, and rubbishy trinkets that caught his eye. Farouk was a charming young man—slim, sloe-eyed, lush-lipped, and impeccably mannered. London merchants called him "Prince Freddy" and doted on him.[4]

Farouk's English idyll ended after only six months, when Fuad died suddenly. Farouk, riding in Richmond Park when he received the news, was famously unmoved. "I'll just do three more rounds of jumps, then I shall return with you," he was reported to have said. (His tutor, the Oxford-educated desert explorer Ahmed Mohammed Hassanein, defended Farouk, arguing that the prince's response was simply that of a very frightened, very young man.)[5] Farouk traveled to Buckingham Palace to accept the condolences of King Edward VIII and then went to Paris to meet with the president of France. Then the dazed young man, sixteen years old and utterly unprepared to rule his country, sailed home to Alexandria.

He inherited all the political uncertainty and tension of his father's monarchy but brought none of Fuad's education or native cunning to the job. Egypt was a maelstrom in 1936. With its rich Nile-delta farmland, the country had for centuries been a target of foreign imperialism. Farouk's family came to power fighting the Mamelukes and Turks, and clung to it as Western Europeans took over control of Egypt at the end of the nineteenth century. Britain had declared Egypt its protectorate in 1914, and the British had thereafter offered endless affronts to the Egyptian people, excluding even wealthy and educated Egyptians from the best hotels and clubs in their own country. Fuad spent the nineteen years of his rule politicking desperately but skillfully, managing to convince both the British and the swelling ranks of Egyptian nationalists that they needed him on the throne.

His young son's leadership was hardly the balm his agitated country needed. Farouk was a sheltered teenager who'd only had six months of freedom from his father while he was in England. Now he was in charge, with essentially unlimited resources. Farouk had inherited something like $100 million, control of 75,000 acres of farmland, and all the royal trappings of palaces, villas, private trains, cars, and yachts.[6] He proceeded to indulge himself in grand style. He didn't like the royal train station at Montazah Palace, so he ordered it knocked down and rebuilt to his specifications, even though the station was used only twice a year. He had his stable of more than 100 cars painted red, then banned the color for all other cars in Egypt so police would know not to stop him as he sped along the highway between Cairo and Alexandria. (Once when the teenaged Farouk crashed his red MG into a tree outside Cairo, the Cairo police helped him find a replacement before his mother found out.[7]) Farouk never read the newspaper and refused to study with the British tutor whom High Commissioner Miles Lampson had installed in the royal entourage. He spent his days smoking, gossiping, and eating.

And collecting. The tentative young man who had charmed shop-keepers in London quickly turned into a voracious accumulator, one who piled up possessions as maniacally as he slurped down dozens of oysters for breakfast. On a trip to Switzerland in 1937, he bought medals, watches, and cuckoo clocks. He brought home boxes full of foreign coins. He amassed beer-bottle tops, razor blades, matchboxes, and playing cards, which his friend Pulli, the onetime palace electrician, stored in his own rooms. Farouk indulged his every fancy. If he coveted something in a friend's home, he demanded that it be given to him. Friends took to hiding their finest possessions before Farouk arrived for a visit.

Even Farouk's 1938 wedding to Queen Farida, one of the most beautiful and cultured girls in Egypt, didn't slow his drive to accumulate. Farouk had become obsessed with collecting old weaponry used in Egypt's battles for independence. He ordered Army General Mohammed Neguib to bring him a selection of arms from the Egyptian Museum, and to search the country to find a Krups cannon that had belonged to his family patriarch, Mohammed Ali. In November 1938, Farouk and Antonio Pulli went to the beach in Alexandria to dig up an old cannon from Napoleon's invasion of Egypt in 1798. They were on the beach digging when Farouk's first child, a daughter, was born.[8]

ALL SERIOUS collectors are at least a little bit crazy, as the more self-aware among them cheerfully admit. Most manage to check their obsessiveness more successfully than Farouk, whose appetite was so unquenchable and undiscriminating that he seemed almost cartoonish. But Farouk was far from the only collector to sacrifice work, family, and even morality for the sake of acquisition. Newspaper baron William Randolph Hearst, another famously voracious accumulator, filled a warehouse in the Bronx to overflowing with his unending purchases of art and antiques, employing a staff of thirty men to juggle crates to make room for new arrivals. Many of the crates were never even opened before Hearst exhausted even his fantastic fortune. He died owing millions to creditors.[9]

Or consider the sad story of Sir Thomas Phillipps, a nineteenth-century collector of books and manuscripts. Phillipps was so determined "to have one copy of every book in the world"[10] that he ignored the death of his first wife and alienated his children, who were forced to live amid the teetering piles and boxes of books that filled not just the rooms but also the hallways and staircases of his mansion. Phillipps reduced the pension he supplied to his aging mother in order to buy more books, and even then he left booksellers waiting years for payment. His second wife had to beg him to divert enough money from his book purchases to pay for groceries. She wrote to him from a seaside boardinghouse to which her doctors sent her when the tribulations of marriage to Phillipps destroyed her health: "Oh, if you would not set your heart so much on your books, making them an Idol, how thankful I should be."

In 1994, a retired professor of psychiatry named Werner Muensterberger published *Collecting: an Unruly Passion*, a treatise on the psychology of collecting. Muensterberger's description of the puzzling condition that prompted his research fits Farouk like one of the king's thirty pairs of slippers:

> Collectors themselves—dedicated, serious, infatuated, beset—cannot explain or understand this often all-consuming drive, nor can they call a halt to their habit. Many are aware of a chronic restiveness that can be curbed only by more finds or yet another acquisition. A recent discovery or another purchase may assuage the hunger, but it never fully satisfies it. Is it an obsession? An addiction? Is it a passion or urge, or perhaps a need to hold, to possess, to accumulate? . . . This ongoing search is a core element of their personality.[11]

Muensterberger concluded that the drive to acquire is rooted in infancy, when some children learn to substitute objects—a stuffed animal, say, or a blanket—for attention and affection from their parents. These children are comforted by their toys, and they come to attribute an almost magical power to them. Yet their very reliance on their possessions reinforces their sense that, in Muensterberger's words, "loving care is not always immediately at hand." Only their objects, which *are* always at hand, relieve their sense of anxiety and uncertainty. When these needy, insecure children grow into adult collectors, Muensterberger theorized, they substitute art or coins or stamps or porcelain, or whatever objects captivate them, for the magic toys of infancy.

Muensterberger also explained why one talismanic object doesn't suffice for collectors like Farouk, who are driven to continue acquiring, forever expanding and refining their collections. First, he said, they need to repeat, over and over, the experience of allaying anxiety by obtaining a new object. Every new object they pursue and acquire "bears the stamp of promise and magical compensation," at least until anxiety besets them again. And second, Muensterberger wrote, collectors come to define themselves through their collections, relying on their objects to make them feel notable and important. These are people, in Muensterberger's assessment, who didn't receive adequate attention as infants and feel a compulsion to continue proving their worth with new objects. They crave the approval of experts in their chosen areas, who almost become substitute parents. Wrote Muensterberger: "The need for authentication and approval by experts is a reflection of two forces existing within the collector—the desire for self-assertion through ownership and a sense of guilt over narcissistic urges and pride." A collector derives his entire sense of well-being, in other words, from his possessions. Individually, his objects offer him security. Collectively, they imbue his life with significance.

MUENSTERBERGER DID not study Farouk, but the Egyptian king might have served to illustrate every aspect of the analyst's psychological portrait. Farouk had the inattentive parents, the lonely childhood, the dependence on his toys. He was desperately insecure about his father's love. After Fuad died, Farouk must have been terrified by his responsibilities, though he was never introspective enough to keep a journal or even write letters admitting his fear. If, as Muensterberger theorized, collectors continue acquiring to ease anxiety, Farouk's ravenous drive makes perfect sense.

His prickly relationship with British High Commissioner Miles Lampson undermined the young king's confidence more irreparably than anything else. Lampson was an enormous man, six feet five inches and 250 pounds of John Bull condescension. He treated Egypt as if it were his private country club, and Farouk as the pesky club manager's son. Lampson referred to Farouk as "the boy." Farouk called him "the headmaster." And as World War II approached, the two scrapped continuously.

Under the 1936 Anglo-Egyptian Treaty of Friendship and Cooperation, Britain pledged to grant Egyptian independence as long as Egypt agreed to side with England in the event of war and to permit the British to establish a substantial military presence in the Suez Canal Zone. The treaty conferred upon the Egyptian king the power to name prime ministers, but from the beginning of Farouk's reign, Lampson habitually disregarded the king's judgment. The high commissioner directed the appointment of prime ministers he favored and the dismissal of those he didn't. In 1940, after Italy had declared war on Britain and the Italian Embassy in Cairo was closed down, Lampson instructed Farouk to replace the prime minister and the head of the Egyptian Army. Farouk refused. Cairo burned with rumors that the young king was planning to flee into exile. Lampson then spread word that Farouk would not be permitted to leave Egypt, forcing the king to accede to Lampson, just as his ancestors had been forced to give in to the British.

Cairo filled with British troops who marched through the streets singing obscene songs about Farouk. In response, Farouk became more compulsive than ever about amassing possessions. He sent servants to loot sequestered German houses. When the British Embassy collected weapons for the British home guard, Farouk skimmed off the best guns for his weaponry collection. He established a relationship with Victor and Armand Hammer in the United States, granting the brothers permission to reproduce his coat of arms on their stationery, along with the phrase, "By Appointment to His Majesty the King." Farouk paid the Hammers millions of dollars to supply him with everything from cheap magic tricks to priceless Fabergé eggs. Armand even sold Farouk a fifty-foot mobile palace in which the king planned to escape Cairo if it fell to the Germans. Like so many of Farouk's purchases, the mobile palace was more junk than treasure. On Egypt's hot desert highways, the tires blew out and the electrical system short-circuited.[12]

In the first years of the 1940s, Farouk also began to collect mistresses. The king's strangely passive sexuality was an open secret in Cairo, where high society whispered about his visits to a medical specialist to stimulate his sex drive. But just as one might expect of a native collector, he cultivated a playboy image, combing Cairo nightclubs for beautiful women to add to his troupe. In 1940, he met Irene Guinle, a young divorcee from a family of Venetian Jews, at a fundraising dance for the Alexandria Red Cross. Guinle later told Farouk biographer William Stadiem that she had wanted nothing to do with the king, whom she considered a German sympathizer, but Lampson persuaded her that she could help the Allied cause as Farouk's mistress. Guinle offered a vivid description of Farouk the collector:

> We played Ali Baba games in the palaces, walking down these rococo corridors in the middle of the night completely nude, opening secret doors into rooms containing the most fabulous jewels. . . .
> He loved having these treasures but he didn't really know what they were. He would open one drawer with millions worth of diamonds, another with emeralds, another with rubies, but he'd close them right away because he thought I might take something. Then we would go down to the royal garage and he would press buttons and doors would open and he would show me all of his cars. . . . We'd drive out to the pyramids in the middle of the night to look at 'his' pyramids and 'his' sphinx, but he had no real interest in history or antiquities. They were just more toys.[13]

•   •   •

COIN COLLECTING was the one arena in which Farouk exercised true connoisseurship. The playboy king was devoted to his coin collection. As he bought up American and world coins in the 1940s—an era in which it was said that the key to success as a coin dealer was having Farouk as a client—he learned to be a numismatist. His coin curator was on duty at night. At eleven, before Farouk went out to indulge himself at Cairo's clubs and casinos, or else at four in the morning when he came back, Farouk would spend a couple of hours lingering over his coin cabinet.

Hans Schulman, a Dutch émigré who'd settled in New York after fleeing the Nazis, was the king's favorite dealer, probably because the high-living Schulman treated the king as if he were more than a mere check-writer. Schulman would buy U.S. and British coins on Farouk's behalf and ship them to Egypt with long descriptions of their condition and history. "When he had studied the coins and selected the ones he liked to keep, he would carefully read the descriptions," Schulman recalled years later. "If I had made a mistake in the date, he would put it in his own handwriting with a red pencil: 'Hans, date error,' or 'Hans, condition overgraded,' or 'price too high' or 'not James I, but James II.' He loved to find an error, and he enjoyed these two hours with his coins more than anything in the world."[14]

Farouk also bought coins from Abe Kosoff, who, though he disapproved of Farouk's carousing, was happy to do business with the king. It's easy to see why. From Fred Boyd and his wife Kosoff once bought a unique 1907 pattern double eagle, with Augustus Saint-Gaudens's flying eagle on the back but the Indian head that Saint-Gaudens had sculpted for the $10 piece on the front. Kosoff paid the Boyds $1,500 for the coin. He then sold it to Farouk, who had developed a particular interest in U.S. pattern coins, for $9,900. The Egyptian king was a coin dealer's dream. Kosoff regularly sent Farouk catalogues of the coins appearing in his auctions. The king would look over the catalogues and then send Kosoff a cable listing the lot numbers of the coins he wanted. Price was not a concern. Farouk expected Kosoff to bid on his behalf until he won the desired pieces, whatever the cost. "When he said buy," Kosoff later wrote, "he meant buy."[15]

And, of course, Farouk bought from B. Max Mehl. Kosoff and

Mehl were both involved in one of the most celebrated incidents of Farouk's coin-collecting career—his inadvertent and nearly simultaneous purchase of two of the famous 1913 Liberty Head nickels. After years of advertising to buy one of the five coveted nickels, Mehl finally got the chance to auction a specimen in 1944, when he sold Fred Olsen's collection. Farouk sent Mehl a bid on Olsen's nickel. But before Mehl's mail-bid auction concluded, Abe Kosoff sold Farouk another 1913 Liberty Head nickel, this one from Fred Boyd's collection. When Mehl's auction ended, Farouk turned out to be the top bidder on Olsen's coin as well. The king tried to decline the purchase, explaining to Mehl that he'd since bought another of the rare nickels, but Mehl was unyielding. "You had to know B. Max Mehl to realize that he would have the 'guts' to tell King Farouk that he had bid on the item and was obliged to accept it," Kosoff later wrote. "I don't think I would have handled it that way, but Max did!"[16]

It was Mehl who located and purchased for Farouk one of the 1933 Double Eagles circulating quietly in the early 1940s. This took some doing. Most of the 1933 Double Eagles had short ownership histories: Israel Switt to James Macallister, Ira Reed, or Abe Kosoff; then from the dealer to a collector who held tight to his rare coin. Farouk's coin was the exception. His 1933 Double Eagle had knocked around, having been briefly in the possession of both James Macallister and Ira Reed as well as New York jeweler Max Berenstein and two other collectors. Mehl acquired the coin from Jake Shapiro, the short-tempered Chicagoan, on February 23, 1944, and sold it that same day to Farouk.

As a longtime collector of American rarities, Farouk knew the regulations governing the export of gold coins from the United States and made sure to follow them. The Egyptian Royal Legation delivered Farouk's 1933 Double Eagle to Mint Director Nellie Tayloe Ross and requested an export license. Ross, in turn, sent the coin to Theodore Belote, the curator of history at the Smithsonian. He authorized the Treasury Department to grant Farouk an export license. The license itself, number TGL-11–1709, was issued on February 29, 1944—less than a month before the Secret Service opened its investigation of the 1933 Double Eagle. Farouk's coin then sat in a vault in the Mint cashier's office until a member of the Royal Legation retrieved it and sent it on to Egypt on March 11, a mere two weeks before Harry Strang opened the 1933 Double Eagle case.

Within the first week of Strang's investigation, the agency found out that Farouk had just been permitted to export one of the illicit coins. Agent James Haley asked Acting Mint Director Leland Howard—the man who had, after all, demanded the Secret Service investigation—for an explanation. Howard sent Secret Service Chief Frank Wilson a rather sheepish reply on March 30, 1944. Yes, the Mint had had possession of Farouk's 1933 Double Eagle. And yes, Theodore Belote had approved its export. "As far as I know," Howard wrote to Wilson, "Mr. Belote did not have information in his possession which would indicate whether or not these coins had ever been paid out from the Treasury. In fact, Mr. Belote may have had the impression that they had been paid out because the mint forwarded two of the above-mentioned coins to Mr. Belote for the Smithsonian Collection."

Once the Secret Service confirmed that the coin had been exported legitimately, the question was what to do about it. In May 1944, Treasury Department lawyer Joseph O'Connell advised, "It would be proper to attempt by diplomatic representatives to have the coin returned to the United States." There is no record, however, that anyone in the U.S. government tried to recover Farouk's 1933 Double Eagle in 1944 when the Secret Service was building its case against Israel Switt and George McCann.

Nor was any attempt made in 1945, when the Treasury Department sent out letters to American collectors demanding the surrender of their 1933 Double Eagles. Treasury lawyer O'Connell had apparently changed his mind about the Farouk coin. In the same opinion in which he justified seizing the other collectors' 1933 Double Eagles, O'Connell wrote, "The coin held by King Farouk does not in my opinion present a problem which this Department should consider at this time." As government lawyers litigated with L. G. Barnard and James Stack to establish title to the 1933 Double Eagles, Farouk's coin remained in Cairo, secure in a palace vault.

More secure, in fact, than Farouk. The war years were a watershed for the Egyptian king. By 1945, the slim young prince who had returned from England to the embrace of all Egypt was a bloated, dissolute monarch in danger of losing the crown. Miles Lampson was to blame. In 1942, provoked by yet another crisis over the prime ministership, the high commissioner had issued Farouk an ultimatum: Appoint Lampson's man or else leave the throne. Lampson assumed Farouk would abdicate. He ordered British troops to establish a presence outside the Abdine Palace in Cairo and made plans to transport Farouk to exile in the Seychelles aboard a British warship. Farouk, supported by all of Egypt's politicians—including Lampson's choice for prime minister—refused the ultimatum. Lampson then proceeded to the palace, accompanied by tanks, armored cars, and 600 British troops. He and seven soldiers shot the locks off the palace gates and shoved their way into Farouk's office, where Lampson waved the ultimatum in the king's face. A humiliated Farouk held onto his crown only by acceding to Lampson's choice for prime minister.

The immediate aftermath of the incident was sympathy for Farouk, but the king was beginning to lose the faith of his people. In the strictest secrecy, some of the most prominent leaders in the Egyptian Army formed a group called the Free Officers and became consumed with Egyptian independence. Farouk's own former tutor, Aziz el Masri, mentored two of the Free Officers, Gamal Abdel Nasser and Anwar Sadat. El Masri and Sadat so despised Britain that both colluded with the Nazis during the war.

Farouk's behavior, meanwhile, appeared increasingly outlandish after the Lampson episode. "He gave in to himself completely," wrote his biographer, William Stadiem. "He became an epicure, a hedonist with an attitude of 'self-indulgence today, because tomorrow we're deposed.'"[17] Wartime Cairo, a crossroads of spies and soldiers, had an end-of-the-world glamour that perfectly suited Farouk's mood. Dressed in a Royal Air Force field marshal's uniform, he gambled at the Royal Automobile Club and watched the dancers at the Kit Kat, the Fleurent, Madame Badia's, and the Auberge des Pyramides. His acquisitiveness outraged even his friends, as he appropriated their gemstones, watches, stamp albums. When the emir of Yemen dined with Farouk, the king asked him to remove his jeweled dagger during the meal. The emir never saw it again.[18] Farouk's devastating car accident at the end of 1943—speeding to inspect his new royal yacht, he crashed his red Cadillac into a British army truck—seemed almost ordained. Farouk was a man driving himself to disaster.

Yet Farouk was also someone the United States did not want to alienate. Egypt had never been more important to America than it was after World War II. The United States needed an ally in the Middle East to protect its access to oil. It needed entrée to the Suez Canal, and it needed a bulwark against Asian communism. U.S. diplomats hoped to keep Farouk in power for their own purposes, though they knew his monarchy was precarious. His greatest threat after the war ended was no longer Miles Lampson, who'd been recalled when the Labour Party took control of Parliament in postwar England, but his own people. Egyptian nationalism, fed now by anti-Zionist as well as anti-British fervor, was spreading dangerously. Egypt was ripe for revolt. Its peasantry was vast, uneducated, and hideously poor. Its ruling class was sybaritic and its government corrupt. The Free Officers and a nationalist movement known as the Muslim Brotherhood grew bolder. Political assassinations and terrorist bombings became commonplace. Desperate to prove his Arab loyalty, Farouk in 1948 ordered the Egyptian Army to join with those of the other Arab nations in a war against the Jewish settlers in Palestine. Egypt's ignominious defeat was a disaster for Farouk. "From the way things are going from bad to worse in Egypt," a British Foreign Officer remarked to a member of the U.S. diplomatic mission in London in January 1949, "it seems to me that a revolution there is inevitable."[19]

The arrival of a new American ambassador in Egypt in 1949 was proof of how perilous the State Department considered Farouk's position to be. Jefferson Caffery was an archaeology-loving Louisianan who had served more than thirty years in the Foreign Service. He had a history of looking out for American interests in foreign crises. He'd been the chargé d'affaires in Greece during the Greek revolution after World War I. He'd been the ambassador in Cuba in the 1930s when the Batista government came to power. After World War II, he was named ambassador to France, where he had the delicate job of squelching incipient communism and acknowledging

French pride while reminding the French that their postwar demands had to be moderate.

In October 1949, Caffery had a long, strange meeting with Farouk. The king denounced America's support of Israel, which he said had encouraged pro-Arab and anti-Western unrest in Egypt. "You have refused everything we have asked for," he told Caffery. Then the King seemed to veer suddenly into minutiae. "Coming down to earth," he complained to the ambassador, "the matter that interests me most, and it interests me a lot, is that of your refusal to accept our military students." Caffery assured him he'd look into it. But the king had another non sequitur to deliver. "As I left," Caffery reported to the State Department, "with reference to nothing in particular, he said, 'Don't think I know nothing of business matters. Don't forget that the founder of my dynasty was a tobacco merchant.'"[20]

So it's little wonder that later in 1949, when the Treasury Department sent a letter to the State Department asking diplomats to seek the return of Farouk's 1933 Double Eagle, the State Department refused. Raising the matter with the king was "politically inadvisable," the State Department informed the Treasury on December 30, 1949. The last thing Ambassador Jefferson Caffery needed was an international incident over a coin.

In 1950, Farouk earned worldwide disgust with an obscenely extravagant, weeks-long bachelor trip through Europe. The king had divorced Farida, his elegant queen, and was engaged to marry a chubby sixteen-year-old commoner named Narriman Sadek. Before the wedding, he intended to enjoy himself. With an entourage of thirty, Farouk sailed one of the royal yachts to France, where he rented out entire floors of the best hotels, gambled all night, and ate enough for three men. The king's party traveled through France, Spain, and Italy in a fleet of brand-new Cadillacs, picking up young women as they went. The press of several nations covered every stop, sending around the world photos of a dumpy man with an unbecoming little mustache. The beautiful boy Farouk had once been was hardly recognizable in the man he had become. His neck and jawline were buried under flesh. His eyebrows had thinned, and balding bared his forehead to the middle of his skull. His face was so fat that his eyes had become slits. Even on his bachelor jaunt, Farouk seemed to wear a look of permanent sadness.

His 1951 wedding to Narriman was his last attempt to recover the affection of ordinary Egyptians. He courted them with donations of food and clothing to hospitals and orphanages, and he gave away land to peasants. But the wedding and subsequent honeymoon showed the people how little such gestures cost Farouk. Narriman was married in a gown studded with 20,000 diamonds. She and Farouk traveled through Europe on a private train outfitted with fourteen telephones and an ostrich-skin interior. In one night of gambling in Cannes, Farouk lost $150,000. The world was outraged. Ambassador Caffery wondered if Farouk would even bother to return from the honeymoon. "There are many who feel that the King would be well advised to return at an early date if he expects to find very much left," he observed.[21]

When Farouk finally did return, Caffery met with him. The king was "fed up," he told the ambassador, with attacks on him by the American press. "I am wholeheartedly on the side of the West, and in case of war you can count on me," Farouk said. "Having that in mind, do not do anything to weaken my position. If I am strong enough I can help you, but if I am weak I won't be able to help you at all." Farouk knew he was in danger. He went out less often, and when he did, he wore a bulletproof shirt, carried a gun, and was surrounded by body-guards. Sometimes he vowed he'd fight for the throne, but sometimes he talked of renouncing everything and decamping to Europe.

Hans Schulman, the New York coin dealer, was worried enough about the king that he took out an insurance policy with Lloyd's of London. Farouk usually paid Schulman twice a year. If the king was killed, Schulman didn't want to be out the hundreds of thousands of dollars owed to him. Schulman suggested to Farouk that he remake his image through his coin collection. The coin dealer hired a public-relations man and composed articles about Farouk the numismatist, the king who lusted for coins, not women.[22] Farouk was interested in Schulman's scheme, but ran out of time to act on it.

The United States, according to Farouk biographer Stadiem, had a different sort of insurance policy in Egypt. Kermit Roosevelt, Theodore's grandson, was a Central Intelligence Agency operative in Cairo. Roosevelt had befriended Farouk on a previous tour of duty in Egypt, but now he began meeting secretly with the Egyptian Army's Free Officers, particularly Anwar Sadat and Gamal Abdel Nasser. The Free Officers were in open defiance of Farouk. They had posted their own candidate for the presidency of Cairo's Officers' Club in early 1952 and had attempted to assassinate Farouk's man. Farouk was shuffling prime ministers on what seemed like a weekly basis, hoping to find someone who could establish a stable government. If Farouk failed, Roosevelt believed the United States could control the Free Officers and keep Egypt, in Caffery's colorful language, from "fall[ing] into the lap of my Russian colleagues like an overripe plum."[23] The CIA agent promised Sadat and Nasser that if they staged a coup, the United States would not intervene to save Farouk.

On July 22, 1952, Farouk issued a challenge to the Free Officers by appointing his brother-in-law minister of war. Sadat and Nasser had to act, or face arrest. With the tacit support of the British and the Americans, they launched their coup on the night of July 23. Within hours, Nasser and the Free Officers had stormed through Cairo, capturing and imprisoning army officers loyal to Farouk. Sadat broadcast a message of revolution on Cairo Radio.

The next morning, the Free Officers dispatched a list of demands to Farouk, who was summering at Montazah Palace in Alexandria with Narriman and their infant son. The Free Officers called for Farouk to disband his cabinet, surrender much of his personal power, and appoint General Neguib (the same general whom Farouk had once sent to fetch weapons for the king's collection) as commander of the Egyptian Army. Farouk, who had been frantically telephoning the British and American Embassies for help, had no choice but to accede. Nasser and Sadat sent hundreds of soldiers to surround Montazah.

Farouk wasn't quite finished, though. He loaded his family and Antonio Pulli into two red Mercedes sedans and fled to Ras el-Tin, the official summer residence, which was guarded by 800 faithful troops. The Free Officers followed. Farouk's soldiers killed several of the Free Officers' troops. The Free Officers then retaliated with a clear message to Farouk: They killed Princess Ferial's white pony and three little dogs belonging to his daughters.[24] Farouk alternated between standing at a palace window with his rifle and pleading for his life in telephone calls to Ambassador Caffery. Caffery finally intervened, persuading the Free Officers to agree to a cease-fire in order to negotiate Farouk's departure from Egypt. "Let us spare Farouk and send him into exile," Nasser said. "History will sentence him to death."

Farouk asked for only a few things in exchange for his abdication. He wanted permission from the Free Officers to take the ever-faithful Pulli with him into exile. He wanted to sail away on the newest royal yacht, the *Mahroussa*. He wanted to retain his family's land in Egypt. And he wanted to keep his stamp and coin collections, which were back in Cairo, in the vaults at Abdine.[25]

Nasser agreed only to guarantee Farouk safe passage to the yacht and a twenty-one-gun salute as he left Egypt. Farouk was in no position to bargain. He accepted Nasser's terms and began packing the dozens of trunks and suitcases, some loaded with jewels and gold, that he and his family would take out of Egypt.

That evening, July 26, 1952, Ambassador Caffery and General Neguib went to Ras el-Tin to accompany Farouk to the royal quay. The general saluted Farouk, who wore a naval uniform. An honor guard stood on the dock, and a military band played the Egyptian national anthem. The king shook hands with Caffery and the Egyptian politicians in attendance. He boarded the launch that would take him to the *Mahroussa*, along with his family, General Neguib, and two other army officers. Once Farouk was aboard the yacht, he shook hands with Neguib, who saluted him again before returning to shore. When the *Mahroussa*'s gangway was raised, all the navy vessels in Alexandria's harbor hoisted their flags in salute, and twenty-one guns fired a farewell to King Farouk.

All of the possessions he left behind—all of the junk and all of the treasures he'd bought and found and stolen and stuffed into his palaces in the sixteen years of his reign—now belonged to the Egyptian people. Including the 1933 Double Eagle.

Chapter Eight

Disappearing

HANS SCHULMAN, THE COIN dealer who had supplied Farouk with so many of his American coins, was owed more than $300,000 at the time Farouk sailed into exile on the *Mahroussa*. After the deposed king and his entourage arrived safely in Italy, Schulman telephoned to remind Farouk of his debt. Farouk was polite but discouraging. "Hans, your coins are in Cairo," he told Schulman. "You have to get paid by the Egyptian government. I don't have the coins so I cannot pay you."[1]

Farouk would never again see any of the possessions he had so frantically accumulated. Whatever passion and direction his collections had provided him was missing from his exile in Italy, which Farouk endured in a haze of dissolution, smoking, gambling, and eating as insatiably as ever, and running through a string of young mistresses after Narriman left him in 1953. From time to time in the first two years of exile, Farouk threatened to sue to recover his treasures, even hiring lawyers to advise him, but his fulminations were in vain, particularly after the revolutionary government passed legislation dispossessing the ex-king and his family.

Farouk's dealers, as dealers always do, adjusted quickly to the new situation in Egypt. Farouk was forgotten, except by the softhearted Schulman, who even years later visited the ex-king at his apartment in Rome.[2] Now there were deals to be made with the revolutionary government. "We reasoned that something had to be done with [the coin] collection," Abe Kosoff calculated. "Would it be housed in a museum? Would additions be required? Would it be sold? I intended to find out."[3] Kosoff sent a letter to the custodian of Farouk's coins on February 4, 1953, hoping to be hired to complete the Royal Collection—or, if not, to liquidate it.

He was too late. After a few months of writing and cabling Egypt to suggest a variety of schemes—that he auction Farouk's collection at the upcoming American Numismatic Association convention, or that he fly to Cairo and buy the coins outright—Kosoff finally got word that Sotheby's, the British auction house, had been quicker than he. A scant few months after Egypt's rampant hatred of British rule led to Farouk's abdication, the brilliant and dashing Peter Wilson, on track to become Sotheby's chairman, went to Cairo to wangle introductions to the new minister of justice and other representatives of the revolutionary government. Negotiations continued for several months, but finally Wilson and another Sotheby's official, Tim Clarke, secured a contract to catalogue and sell Farouk's Palace Collections. A shrewd marketer, Wilson saw to it that the signing of the contract was announced at a press conference in Cairo on February 26, 1953. The BBC broadcast its report of the signing ceremony throughout Europe and the Middle East.[4]

A team from Sotheby's spent the spring and summer of 1953 in Egypt, sorting and cataloguing Farouk's collections. The British set up operations in the king's bedroom at the Koubbeh Palace—his thousands of ties and suits still filled the closets—and marveled at the vastness of Farouk's accumulations. Some of his pieces were exquisite: ". . . every type of luxury article made by master craftsmen from all countries and periods," wrote Sotheby's historian Frank Hermann. "The gold boxes often encrusted with jewels, the two thousand magnificent gold watches, . . . the enamel pieces by Fabergé including several of his famous Easter eggs, the silver and glass." As Sotheby's experts inventoried Farouk's holdings, dealers operating in tiny niches—not just stamps and coins, but clocks and automata and snuffboxes—nervously awaited the tsunami about to crash over their markets. Farouk had, for instance, been the world's foremost collector of intricately crafted glass and crystal paperweights, singlehandedly driving paperweight prices to multiples of their previous records. Anticipation of the sale of his collection drastically changed the economics of the paperweight business. "A person taking a paperweight along to a minor antique dealer these days will almost certainly be told that there is no longer any market for it now," noted *The Times of London*.[5]

Others of Farouk's collections were shockingly banal. Cataloguers roaming through the Koubbeh Palace found "an immense collection of early aspirin bottles, paper clips and even razor blades. Rumor had it that Farouk had dispatched agents to find rare examples of such things to remote villages as far away as Persia and Argentina,"[6] Hermann wrote. Farouk's pornography and erotica filled twenty rooms at Koubbeh and occasioned quite a bit of debate. The British Museum was interested in purchasing certain items, and Sotheby's believed that if the erotica were offered at auction, it would find buyers. The revolutionary government, however, wanted to use Farouk's rooms of pornography to discredit the king. The government ultimately decided to set up an exhibit of Farouk's naughty toys, books, and pictures, and offer tours to anyone who spent more than £5,000 at the auctions.

Negotiating the fate of Farouk's pornography was not the only complication Sotheby's encountered. The new Egyptian government was so unstable that even General Neguib feared for his presidency. Senior Egyptian officials working with Sotheby's were maddeningly erratic. Either they refused to take responsibility for decisions or they changed their minds about which items were to be withheld from the sale after catalogues had been written and collectors alerted. Questions from Sotheby's staffers were often misinterpreted as political slurs, and every time the auction house finally established trust with an Egyptian, it seemed as though he was transferred out of the palace. Other auction houses, meanwhile, were working throughout 1953 to undermine Sotheby's standing with the new government. They were effective enough that Sotheby's was forced to agree to permit a consortium of French auctioneers to handle sales to the French market.

Farouk's stamp and coin collections were simply too enormous and valuable for Sotheby's to catalogue without help from specialized experts. Fred Baldwin, a respected London coin dealer, was engaged to impose order over Farouk's 8,500 coins and medals. He was widely considered to have botched the job. Baldwin went to Cairo in the summer of 1953. By October he had produced a telephone-book–size catalogue that grouped coins into large lots, seemingly without regard for the value of individual pieces. The most glaring example was Farouk's 1913 Liberty Head nickel, the Fred Boyd specimen that Abe Kosoff had sold to the king. Baldwin's catalogue lumped it in with a batch of ordinary-date five-cent pieces. Baldwin made oblique excuses for the catalogue's deficiencies in his two-page introduction. "With so vast an array of important coins and medals in one sale, encumbered by such an *embarras de richesse*, it has been found difficult to select those lots most suitable for special emphasis, and a catalogue has been prepared which is deliberately conservative in style and presentation," Baldwin wrote. "Good wine needs no blush." The catalogue included only seventy-two photographic plates to illustrate the coins, Baldwin explained, "because those responsible for the preparation of the plates found that the taking of accurate plaster casts of coins was impossible in Cairo for technical reasons," and so coins had to be photographed directly. "Though not ideal for illustrating extremely fine coins," Baldwin temporized, "[the direct photography] has produced results not unsatisfactory in the circumstances."

Hundreds of Baldwin's hardcover catalogues were sent to coin dealers and collectors in the fall of 1953. Dealers, for the most part, were astonished by the quality of Farouk's collection but full of scorn for the catalogue. It "was not an example of expertise or even of good organization," Abe Kosoff later wrote, complaining especially about the photographs Baldwin had taken pains to defend.[7] A young New York dealer named John Ford was even more scathing. "The man who catalogued Farouk's coins spent a great deal of time chasing all the available Anglo Saxon women in Cairo rather than concentrating on the coins," Ford claimed in a 1988 interview. Baldwin, a respectable-looking fellow with a big, bald head, a brush mustache, and round glasses, was in his sixties when he catalogued the Farouk collection, Ford noted, but that didn't slow his skirt-chasing. "In fact, there is supposedly a famous cablegram from Sotheby's in Cairo: 'Get this guy out of here. He's seduced every white woman in Cairo,'" Ford continued. "Anyhow, apparently because of his extracurricular activities, he really screwed up the Farouk catalogue."[8]

Baldwin's curatorial deficiencies aside, the Farouk sale was the talk of the coin world at the end of 1953. Spink & Son, the venerable British coin house, began its advance advertising in the October issue of *The Numismatist*. "A Most Important Forthcoming Auction Sale," the Spink's ad heralded. "Progress on the cataloguing of the FAROUK COIN COLLECTION indicates the sale will take place, as previously anticipated, at the end of February and the beginning of March, 1954." Fred Baldwin's advertising started the following month. By December 1954, a Baltimore coin dealer was advising readers of *The Numismatist* that he was planning to go to Cairo and would execute purchases there for a commission of seven and a half percent. (A crafty dealer named Charles Foster ran a counter-advertisement in the magazine's February issue: "When the cats are away the mice will play," it said. "While many of the 'boys' are concentrating their interest and money on what is happening in Egypt, I am ready and willing to assist the King of them all, Mr. Average Collector.")

Abe Kosoff and Hans Schulman both made plans to travel to Cairo for the Farouk sale. Schulman had no choice. He needed to recover the hundreds of thousands of dollars he was owed. The revolutionary government had at first indicated that it did not intend to honor Farouk's debt to Schulman. Then Schulman put out word to his fellow coin dealers that he would file claims against purchases at the auction unless the Egyptians paid him for the coins he had sent Farouk on credit. At the beginning of 1954, Schulman took his American lawyers to Cairo. He also hired an Egyptian lawyer and filed suit in the Egyptian equivalent of the Supreme Court. Schulman won from the court a declaration that the coins he'd sent Farouk on credit were still American property. With that leverage, he began negotiating with the military officers overseeing the disposition of Farouk's coins. Ever the charmer, Schulman befriended the pair of officers, Colonel Younes and Major Gaafar, who were in charge of the coin auction. The Egyptians still refused to pay Schulman outright, but they agreed to give him a credit of more than $300,000 to use at the auction. Schulman hurriedly arranged with other dealers to make purchases on their behalf. He'd then resell them the coins at a slight discount.[9]

Kosoff went to Egypt to buy. He had obtained an early draft of the Baldwin catalogue, which left him convinced that he had to attend the sale in person and that he had to get to Cairo early enough to inspect every coin that interested him. Baldwin's catalogue warned that Farouk's silver and copper coins had been recently cleaned, "often leaving the surface somewhat, though not irrevocably, stained." With so few of Farouk's coins photographed—and those done poorly—Kosoff didn't want to rely on Baldwin's descriptions. He decided to make a family adventure of the trip to Cairo, taking along his wife, his daughter, and his best friend and fellow coin dealer, Sol Kaplan of Cincinnati. Kosoff ran an advertisement in the January 1954 issue of *The Numismatist*. "Cairo February–March," it said. "Collectors desiring representation at the forthcoming Auction Sale of the Numismatic Collection of former King Farouk may commission their bids to us." As rumors flew—Farouk had enjoined the sale, the Bank of England was buying the whole coin collection, Jews wouldn't be permitted to enter Cairo without special visas—the Kosoffs traveled from their home in California to New York, collecting commissions for the sale.

NEWS OF the upcoming Farouk auctions penetrated even the popular press in America. On December 2, 1953, an article entitled, "Farouk's Treasures Going, Going, Gone," appeared in the *Washington Daily News*. The article quoted an official of the Egyptian Embassy predicting that Farouk's magnificent collection of gold and silver objets d'art might bring half a billion dollars when it was sold off. "There'll be bidding, too," the story noted, "on the 8,500 17th, 18th, 19th, and 20th century coins and gold and platinum medals, considered one of the most complete modern coin collections in the world."

Russell Daniel, a Secret Service inspector, saw the *Daily News* clipping. The Secret Service, it seemed, had not forgotten about its connection to King Farouk: the 1933 Double Eagle. On December 3, 1953, Daniel wrote a memo on the 1933 Double Eagle for his boss, Chief U. E. Baughman, describing the history of the Secret Service's investigation and seizure of the coins:

> Our files do not show that any attempt was ever made to recover the Farouk coin. Now that the Farouk collection is to be auctioned, it would appear to me that we are obligated to place the Egyptian embassy on notice that the coin is stolen, and that title remains in the United States. To fail to do so might place the Secret Service in an embarrassing position should some collector within the limits of the United States purchase the coin and we should then attempt to recover it. We would also be subject to criticism from the nine collectors whom we have previously dispossessed of their coins if we fail to attempt to recover the Farouk coin.

Daniel's memo occasioned a diplomatic minicrisis. The Secret Service alerted Secretary of the Treasury George Humphrey, who in turn sent a letter to Secretary of State John Foster Dulles about the 1933 Double Eagle. Treasury wanted State to tell the Egyptian revolutionary government about the peculiar history of this coin, "and request whatever cooperation is possible in the matter." Though the language of the letter is polite to the point of impenetrability, the treasury secretary finally came to the point at the end. Farouk's 1933 Double Eagle was believed to be the only one of its kind that wasn't in the hands of the U.S. government. The Treasury Department wanted the Egyptians to give it back.[10]

The State Department responded quickly. On December 10, 1953, Dulles's office sent a cable to Ambassador Jefferson Caffery in Cairo, briefly sketching the story of the 1933 Double Eagle and directing Caffery to "take the matter up with the Egyptian Government with a view to recovering the coin." The State Department even included a letter drafted by the Treasury Department for Caffery to present to the Egyptians.

The embassy in Cairo didn't reply right away, so the State Department sent another communiqué on January 27, 1954. This one was more declarative. Farouk's 1933 Double Eagle was listed in the catalogue of coins to be auctioned in February. The U.S. government did not want the coin to be sold. "The embassy is requested to bring the matter to the attention of the appropriate Egyptian authorities," the State Department again instructed. "The embassy should request that the coin be withheld from sale and that it be returned to the United States Department of the Treasury." If the Egyptians balked, the memo continued, the "seriously concerned" Treasury Department was planning to issue a press release in Washington and Cairo advising Americans not to buy the 1933 Double Eagle unless they wanted it to be seized upon return to the United States.

The controversy leaked to newspapers in Cairo, which quoted Egyptian officials as saying that they planned to hold the coin in escrow. Nevertheless, as of February 10, Farouk's 1933 Double Eagle remained on display in the coin showcase at the Koubbeh Palace.

CAIRO WAS a dangerous place in the weeks leading up to the Palace Collections auctions. The Farouk era was unquestionably over. A revolutionary tribunal was wrapping up trials of Farouk's former cronies and politicians who had been loyal to him. The ex-king's chauffeur was stripped of all his property. Farouk's valet was sentenced to fifteen years of hard labor, as was a once-powerful cabinet minister. But the revolutionary government's own hold on power was tenuous. The military tribunal's next investigation, once it finished the Farouk trials, involved a plot to overthrow the revolutionary regime and establish a Soviet state.[11] Even the group that had led the revolution was splintering. General Neguib, a popular favorite, was engaged in a power struggle with Nasser, the revolt's mastermind. Trucks full of machine-gun-toting soldiers filled the city's streets. The morning after David Spink of the eponymous British coin house arrived in Cairo for the Palace Collections auctions, he awoke to the sound of airplanes overhead: General Neguib had been ousted, and Nasser was in charge.[12] The situation remained so chaotic that within days Neguib had regained the presidency.

Abe Kosoff and his party arrived in Egypt bristling with wariness, worried about political unrest but more concerned with reports of thieves drawn to Cairo by the international conclave of rich coin, stamp, and art dealers and collectors. The Kosoffs and Kaplans had been warned never to travel alone and always to leave word at their hotel of their whereabouts. On one of his first days in Cairo, Kosoff noticed a man he described as "a slick-looking character" sitting in the lobby, eyeing him and his friends, one after the other. The man appeared to be reading a paperback, but when Kosoff walked past, he noticed that the book was upside down. The slick-looking character turned up again at a restaurant where the Kosoffs were dining, and then again at the Koubbeh Palace. A frightened Kosoff appealed to Hans Schulman for help. Schulman talked to his new Egyptian friend, Major Gaafar, and a member of the secret police was detailed to guard the Kosoffs.

John Pittman, a longtime Eastman Kodak engineer and coin collector, was so convinced of the danger of going to Egypt that he took out extra life insurance before making the trip to Cairo. He went anyway, part of a small American coin contingent that included, in addition to Schulman, Kosoff, and Kaplan, a Texas coin dealer named Robert Schermerhorn and Ambassador and Mrs. R. Henry Norweb, a formidable pair of collectors. "I was willing to take the chance," Pittman said, "because having known about the overthrow of the French monarchy under Louis XVI and Marie Antoinette and the sale in London later of their material, I knew this sort of sale doesn't happen but once every hundred or two hundred years. You have to take a chance because if you don't take a chance you don't benefit."[13]

THE KOUBBEH Palace, where the auctions were staged, was a haven of tranquility in the tension of post-revolutionary Cairo. Its manicured lawns, bougainvillea gardens, and acres of ponds had never looked more beautiful than they did for the Palace Collections sales, despite the beggars who congregated outside the six-mile-long wall surrounding the grounds. Sotheby's had turned the Koubbeh into the setting of the most sumptuous garden party in history. "Guests strolled around," wrote Sotheby's historian Frank Hermann, "pausing to sip cool drinks from glasses tinkling with ice, served by courteous servants in the familiar tarboosh and white galabaiya. A brass band played military music and Viennese waltzes in the gardens throughout the sales."[14] Food was bountiful, with catering tents and bars set up in the gardens. For dessert every day after lunch, a Swiss baker turned out delicate pastries that were handed around by the caftan-clad servants.

Thousands of Egyptians came to the Koubbeh and paid $1.40 to tour the treasures displayed in the Palace Library. Intended to convince the Egyptian people of their former king's profligacy, these included a solid gold soda-bottle holder (Farouk, a Muslim, did not drink alcohol) and a diamond-encrusted flyswatter.[15] The soldiers guarding Farouk's Fabergé eggs were said to be so giddy amid the hoopla at the Koubbeh that they tossed around the priceless eggs like footballs.

The sales opened on February 12, 1954, with a short speech by a young Egyptian Army officer. Standing on Farouk's onetime throne, before the marble staircase in the Koubbeh's main reception room, the officer told an audience of more than a hundred dealers and collectors that these auctions would restore to the people of Egypt money that Farouk had diverted for his own pleasure. Then the auctioneer, a Sephardic Jew named Moishe Levi (he had anglicized his name to Maurice George Lee), took charge. A jauntily dressed fellow who stood less than five feet tall, Lee had lived in Egypt for more than forty years, rising to the head of the country's leading art and auction house. He spoke seven languages, most of which he employed in the auctions; for the stamps that were sold in the auctions' first sessions, Lee accepted bids in French, Arabic, and English.

The stamp sales brought even more money than expected. Dealers were especially eager to snap up the older parts of the collection, which had been assembled by Farouk's father, King Fuad, a discerning philatelist. Poor Farouk did not measure up to his father's standards, even in stamp collecting. "Farouk's contribution is just a mixed-up accumulation," sniffed Jack Minkus, the stamp buyer for Gimbel's department store, who was in Cairo for the sale.[16] Even for Farouk's stamps, though, the bidding was intense, bringing prices that seemed outrageous.

While the stamp sales were under way, Abe Kosoff and the other coin dealers in Cairo plotted strategy for the coin auctions, which would come next. Kosoff and his friend Kaplan were certain that the Egyptians were spying on American dealers, hoping to learn enough about their plans to drive up the prices of especially desirable coins. One afternoon when Kosoff was telephoning from the lobby of his hotel to Hans Schulman at another hotel, he noticed that the operator used a two-wire connection, plugging someone else into his conversation. "So careful were we that our pre-sale meetings were held in different locations each time, with those decisions being made as close to the last minute as possible," he later wrote. "Are we sure we were weren't bugged despite our precautions? Not in the least."[17]

The Americans also occupied themselves inspecting Farouk's coin holdings. It was a tedious process thanks to Fred Baldwin's grouping of the coins in enormous lots but necessary because of Farouk's questionable cleaning techniques. John Pittman, the Kodak engineer, concluded, after examining the coins, that Farouk's conservator had applied nitrocellulose lacquer to the coins but had not damaged the gold and silver.[18] Pittman resolved to bid actively.

THE AMERICAN Embassy, meanwhile, was still trying to persuade the Egyptian government to withdraw the 1933 Double Eagle—included in a lot with sixteen other double eagles—from the auction and surrender it to the United States. On February 17, 1954, Consul Basil Macgowan cabled the State Department: An Egyptian newspaper was reporting that President Neguib himself had approved the withdrawal of "an American coin" from the auction, but the embassy had not yet received any official word on the 1933 Double Eagle. Appeals to Egypt's Foreign Ministry continued. On February 23—the day before the coin sales were to begin—Ambassador Caffery was informed that the 1933 Double Eagle would not be sold at the auction; it was "to be held pending final decision re disposition," according to a cable Caffery sent to the secretary of state. Caffery remained skeptical. There had been no public announcement, and the 1933 Double Eagle was still on display in the auction room. The embassy,

Caffery noted, was prepared to issue a press release on the coin if so ordered by the State Department.

The 1933 Double Eagle was part of lot 185, which was to be sold on the first day of the coin auctions. Though the rows of brocade chairs set up for bidders weren't as crowded as they had been for the stamp sales, the auction opened briskly, with Farouk's Mexican and Hawaiian gold coins the first lots sold. Maurice Lee began the bidding for each coin in Arabic, then kept prices moving in English, French, German, and Italian, depending on who was bidding. The U.S. gold coins began with lot 180, which consisted of thirty-six double eagles from the 1850s and early 1860s. Abe Kosoff bought that lot as well as the next two, acquiring a trove of double eagles from the late 1800s, all in excellent condition, from all the mints that produced the $20 pieces.

Lot 185 came up without any fanfare. Auctioneer Lee calmly announced that the 1933 Double Eagle was being withdrawn. He provided no additional explanation. Both Kosoff and John Pittman assumed that the withdrawal resulted from the urging of American bidders, who were aware the coin couldn't be imported into the United States. Pittman, who knew nothing of the high-level diplomatic contretemps over the 1933 Double Eagle, later told an interviewer that he was responsible for the withdrawal of the coin.[19]

But at the sale that day, the audience spent no time considering the implications of the withdrawal of the 1933 coin—they were concentrating on the coins that remained. Fred Baldwin's large, ill-catalogued lots meant unbelievable bargains for bidders who knew American coins. Spink bought the 1933 Double Eagle's erstwhile lot, which still included major Saint-Gaudens double-eagle rarities, for a paltry $8,400.[20] John Pittman bought another lot of rare proof-finished coins for less than $600.

The U.S. Embassy didn't send a representative to the coin sale but received briefings immediately afterward from two Americans who had attended the auction. Both confirmed that the 1933 Double Eagle had been pulled from lot 185. Consul Macgowan cabled the news to the State Department, following up the next day with the official Egyptian Foreign Ministry confirmation that President Neguib had ordered the coin withdrawn from the auction. But the Egyptian government didn't consider the matter closed, Macgowan reported on February 25. The Foreign Ministry promised only that the 1933 Double Eagle wouldn't be sold at auction "until a definitive decision shall have been reached on this subject."

For the next ten days, Kosoff, Pittman, and the rest of the American coin contingent trooped to the Koubbeh every morning, taking their places in the brocade chairs for the dispersal of Farouk's coin collection. At each day's three-hour lunch break, they drank at the bar and ate the Swiss pastries served outside the throne room. Every night, at the conclusion of the afternoon session's bidding, buyers stepped up to the podium to pay, in cash, for their purchases. Hans Schulman whittled down his $300,000 credit. Abe Kosoff bought back some of the pattern coins he'd sold to Farouk, many of which had once been owned by Fred Boyd and, before him, William Woodin. Sol Kaplan bought Farouk's 1913 Liberty Head nickel, then immediately sold it to Kosoff, who was acting as an agent for Ambassador and Mrs. Norweb. John Pittman bought carefully, picking up so many underpriced treasures that he cemented his reputation as the shrewdest collector of his day. The coin sales ended on March 6, producing totals that disappointed Sotheby's and the revolutionary government. (The Egyptians later refused to pay Sotheby's most of its commission for the Palace Collections sales.) Coin dealers tried to figure out how to ship their purchases home without paying extortionate rates, and auctioneer Maurice Lee moved on to the sale of Farouk's jeweled snuffboxes and Fabergé eggs.

THE 1933 Double Eagle wasn't forgotten, however. The American Embassy was desperately trying to find out what had become of the coin. An embassy officer was "in constant touch with Dmitri Rizk Hanna, acting director of the administrative department of the ministry of foreign affairs, on the subject of the return of the $20 gold coin," Macgowan reported to the State Department on March 31, 1954, but the embassy couldn't get a definitive answer. The Egyptians were still considering the matter. "Mr. Rizk Hanna notified the report-

ing officer today that he hoped to have some information within two
or three days," noted Macgowan at the end of his March 31 telegram.

That was the Egyptian Embassy's final communication to the State
Department on Farouk's 1933 Double Eagle. As of May 11, 1954,
when Secret Service agent Harry Neal wrote a memo for the file on
the 1933 Double Eagle, the embassy had "received no word yet from
the Egyptian Government that the coin will be returned."

In 1956, when the last of the cases challenging the United States
government's seizure of 1933 Double Eagles finally whimpered to an
end, the Treasury Department decided that it was at last time to end
the troublesome matter of these 1933 Double Eagles. One coin, the
Eliasberg specimen, was locked in a safe in the office of the Philadelphia Mint superintendent. On August 17, Leland Howard ordered
that coin to be destroyed. To ensure that this time there would be no
mistakes, he instructed the superintendent of the melting department
to execute his order in the presence of the Mint assayer and Mint
superintendent.

The other eight coins that had been seized by the Secret Service
were stored at the Treasury Department building in Washington. Four
days after the Mint's last 1933 Double Eagle was melted, four Treasury Department officials gathered to witness the destruction of those
eight coins.

The only 1933 Double Eagles still known to exist were the two in
the National Numismatic Collection at the Smithsonian—and one
coin whose whereabouts no one in the United States knew. For the
Egyptian government never did turn over Farouk's 1933 Double Eagle
to the U.S. Embassy after the Palace Collections auctions. The
embassy never found out what had happened to the coin. Farouk's
1933 Double Eagle had simply disappeared.

Chapter Nine

Surfacing

ONE DAY IN THE early part of 1993, an Egyptian trader named Mohammed Ezzadin showed up at Spink & Son, the renowned coin house on King Street in London. He asked to see Andre de Clermont, the head of Spink's world coin department. De Clermont had been dealing with Ezzadin for years. The Egyptian ran a tourist business in Cairo, but he made extra money by foraging in the city's bazaars, searching the antiques stalls of the souk for coins and jewelry to resell in London. De Clermont had little fondness for Ezzadin, whom he considered greedy, disloyal, and impatient. Most of what the Egyptian brought to Spink was junk—cheap fakes from Indonesia or the Philippines, or coins damaged from use as jewelry. Every once in a while, though, Ezzadin came up with something good, so de Clermont usually agreed to meet with him, albeit grudgingly, when he turned up at Spink.[1]

Andre de Clermont was a rarity in the coin business: a dealer with no particular affection for coins. He had never bought a coin in his life when he first went to work at Spink in 1967, but he needed a job. His degree from the University of East Anglia and his postgraduate travels around the United States didn't lead to the media position he wanted, so he turned to his uncle, a director at the coin house, for help. De Clermont started as a packer, making sure that coins were properly packaged for delivery to buyers. He moved up to become a runner, which meant that he greeted customers who came into the shop, conveyed their coins to Spink's experts for appraisal, and watched to make sure that none of them pocketed specimens. Finally he was promoted to dealer, buying and selling English tokens, the least expensive of the items Spink handled. "I suppose I was lucky to find I enjoyed doing it," de Clermont said. "It could bore a lot of people." Eventually, de Clermont, like his uncle, was named a Spink director, in charge of all of the auction house's non-British coins.

Dealing with unsavory characters like Ezzadin was an unfortunate necessity of the job. "Here we go again, a few more bits and pieces from Mohammed," de Clermont thought to himself as Ezzadin laid out his offerings that day in 1993. Then de Clermont looked down at the coins the Egyptian had brought. There before him were twenty-five or thirty gold coins—American $10 eagles from the mid-1800s—all in brilliant condition. The Spink dealer was taken aback. Ezzadin had never brought him coins like this before. These hadn't come out of some rickety stall in the souk. De Clermont knew he had to be careful in handling Ezzadin. He didn't want the Egyptian to know how eager he was to buy these coins, but nor could he risk having Ezzadin pack up and take the gold eagles to another dealer. He asked Ezzadin to leave the eagles with him for a day. "I need to look a few up, to check it," he told the Egyptian.

After Ezzadin left the gallery, de Clermont consulted his *Red Book*, the standard reference guide to American coin prices. As he had suspected, this was quite a valuable haul. None of Ezzadin's eagles was a true treasure, but they were all highly desirable coins worth several thousand dollars apiece. When the Egyptian returned to Spink the next day, de Clermont bought all of the eagles for about $50,000—by far the most he'd ever paid Ezzadin.

Then, on a hunch, he fetched another book from his personal library—a 1953 hardcover catalogue of the Palace Collections sale of King Farouk's coins. Fred Baldwin's catalogue, whatever its deficiencies, had become a collectible rarity itself, a necessary item in any respectable library of numismatic literature. De Clermont had browsed through his copy before, imagining what Farouk's coin collection would be worth all these years after the sale. Now, though, he had a more specific purpose. De Clermont wanted to see if the eagles he'd bought from Ezzadin could somehow have come from the Farouk collection. No one else in Egypt, he speculated, could have owned such a cache of valuable American coins in such impeccable condition.

Sure enough, de Clermont was able to match all of the coins he'd just bought from Ezzadin with lots from the Farouk sale. The hardcover catalogue that de Clermont owned, purchased through Spink's book department, had originally belonged to a dealer who had attended the sales sessions back in 1954. In the book's margins, that dealer had noted who purchased each lot, and for how much. De Clermont recognized some of the famous names written in the book—Abe Kosoff and Sol Kaplan and Baldwin all appeared—but he noticed that there were no names written next to the lots that included the Ezzadin eagles. These coins, de Clermont concluded, must have been pulled from the 1954 auction, or else bought by some unknown Egyptian collector. Either way, de Clermont was reasonably sure that the gold American eagles he'd just bought had once belonged to King Farouk. This, he thought, was an exciting development. Maybe Ezzadin had a line to more Farouk coins.

In August 1993, de Clermont took the Farouk eagles to the convention of the American Numismatic Association, held that year in Baltimore. The ANA convention is a three-day festival of coins, during which devotees of every obscure offshoot of the hobby—and they are obscure indeed, from whole societies determined to preserve the legacy of otherwise-forgotten Mint engravers to clubs dedicated to the fine points of numismatic literature—meet up with fellow zealots. For dealers of American coins, the ANA convention is one of the year's signal events, the coin-world equivalent of spring break in Fort Lauderdale. De Clermont knew he'd be able to get a good price for his coins there. On the first day of the convention, he took a break from the Spink stall on the bourse floor and, Ezzadin eagles in hand, walked over to the table of an American dealer named Ed Milas, the head of RARCOA

(Rare Coin Company of America) and a partner with Spink in a coin venture in Switzerland. De Clermont showed Milas the eagles. Milas immediately bought them all for about $100,000, a very nice return on de Clermont's $50,000 investment.

DE CLERMONT intended his deal with RARCOA to be a secret, but keeping a secret on the bourse floor, with sharp-eyed dealers monitoring who's talking to whom, isn't easy. Word of de Clermont's sale to Milas quickly spread to a British coin dealer named Stephen Fenton, also attending the convention. Fenton knew de Clermont well. The coin world is small to begin with, and Fenton's shop, Knightsbridge Coins, was just around the corner from de Clermont's office at Spink. Fenton was in and out of Spink so often, buying foreign coins (particularly American ones) from de Clermont, that he sometimes joked he should just move into the auction house.

Fenton and de Clermont had actually entered the coin business at about the same time in the late 1960s, though from quite different directions. De Clermont had been an aimless university graduate when his uncle got him that first job at Spink. Fenton was a teenaged high-school dropout who never wanted to be anything but a coin dealer. He started collecting coins as a child—but he always regarded them with a businessman's cool, not a collector's passionate attachment. Fenton was fourteen when he bought his first really good coin with a pound of his father's winnings from the racetrack. It was a beautiful Victoria penny that caught his eye at an antiques store in London's West End. The coin cost £2, but the shopkeeper agreed to sell it to Fenton for seventy-five pence, as long as he promised to hold onto it. Fenton promised and took his penny home. When he showed it to his mother, she was appalled that he had spent so much. Fenton bet her that he'd get his money back. The next day, he scraped up bus fare back to the West End, where he sold the Victoria penny to a different dealer for a £1 profit. From that moment, Fenton considered himself a coin dealer. Within two years, using money he made trading coins, Fenton had assembled a good collection of specimens from the reign of King Charles II. That was his last coin collection. When he sold it, he felt no regret in giving up the coins, only exhilaration at the price they fetched: £56, more than he made in a month at his day job.

At sixteen, Fenton talked his way into an apprenticeship with a vest-pocket London coin dealer. He liked his boss, a grumpy realtor who dealt coins on the side, but after several years it became obvious that Fenton's talent exceeded his boss's ambitions. Moreover, Fenton's then-wife kept reminding him that he was never going to get rich working for someone else. Fenton borrowed money from his shop-keeper father, took over a corner of his uncle's rug store, and launched his own business. "I ate, slept, and read about coins non-stop," he said. "My life was coins, coins, coins." Within a year, Fenton had paid back his father, and by the time he was twenty-five years old, he was the owner of a thriving one-man coin operation. De Clermont, with whom he lunched regularly, considered Fenton to be the top dealer of American coins in England. His specialty was acting as a middleman between dealers, rather than selling to collectors, whom he considered more trouble than they were worth. Fenton had no patience for coddling indecisive clients, no interest in stoking their ardor. Coins were strictly business with him.

ON THE bourse floor in Baltimore, after hearing about de Clermont's sale of the Ezzadin eagles to Milas, Fenton confronted his friend from Spink. "What's this I hear, that you've sold these amazing coins?" he said. "How come you didn't offer them to me?"

De Clermont promised that the next time he bought a cache of American coins—if there were a next time—he would call Fenton first. He also showed Fenton the eagles he'd sold to Milas and told Fenton about checking the Palace Collections catalogue. "I really think they were once part of the Farouk collection,"[2] de Clermont said.

Fenton didn't ask how de Clermont had gotten his hands on the coins. He didn't much care, and besides, he knew de Clermont wouldn't tell, for fear another dealer, even his friend Fenton, would try to steal his source. That's the way the coin business worked. Dealers gossiped about transactions with other dealers, but if you wanted to make money, you kept your mouth shut about your clients. "Well, if you get other U.S. coins I'd like to be involved," Fenton repeated.

IN EARLY 1994, Mohammed Ezzadin once again appeared in London to see Andre de Clermont. This time, de Clermont was no longer working at Spink. The venerable coin house had been sold to Christie's, which had installed a young stamp dealer as de Clermont's managing director. De Clermont decided to quit Spink and venture out on his own, though not without considerable unease. The coin business had changed drastically in the twenty-five years since he had first gone to work at Spink, and dealers were finding it increasingly difficult to make a decent profit on their sales. Coins aren't like paintings. Most of them aren't one-of-a-kind, and specimens turned up on the market often enough that as information became more easily accessible, buyers became savvier about prices—and less dependent on dealers to find and evaluate coins for them. De Clermont believed that rapid turnover and high volume were the only ways for a dealer operating on his own to make money, but with so many good coins selling at auction, he would be competing for inventory with well-informed dealers from all over Europe. Nevertheless, de Clermont took out a second mortgage on his house, set up a home office, and told his contacts that he was open for business.

Ezzadin was more faithful than de Clermont would have guessed. In 1994, just as he had in 1993, Ezzadin brought American coins to show de Clermont. And as before, they were excellent pieces: a rare U.S. trade dollar, a few unique pattern coins, and a handful of gold double eagles. Ezzadin also brought with him a man he introduced as his colleague, an Egyptian businessman named Khalid Hassan.[3]

Ezzadin told de Clermont that Hassan was his source for the American coins. De Clermont studied Hassan. He was younger than Ezzadin, and much more refined. When Hassan spoke, de Clermont felt none of the distaste he always had to swallow when he bought from Ezzadin. Hassan told de Clermont that he was not a coin dealer, just a jeweler who happened to have access to a magnificent collection of rare coins. De Clermont thrummed with curiosity—he was sure that Hassan was talking about the Farouk collection. He sensed, however, that Hassan wasn't yet ready to disclose anything more, so he didn't press.

The Egyptians wanted more than £10,000 for the coins they had

brought,[4] which was more than de Clermont, with his fledgling operation, could comfortably afford. De Clermont remembered Fenton's
request to be involved if any other high-quality American coins made
their way to him. So de Clermont called his friend.

For this first deal, de Clermont told Fenton only that he had a connection in Egypt, a jeweler who could supply him with outstanding
coins. The jeweler was in London right now, offering some good
pieces—all of which, de Clermont had determined, were listed among
Farouk's holdings in the Palace Collections catalogue. Was Fenton
interested?

He was indeed. The two British dealers discussed what Hassan's
coins were worth and how to structure the deal. In the end, de Clermont bought the pieces outright from Hassan and Ezzadin and
shipped them to Detroit, the site of the 1994 American Numismatic
Association convention. At the convention, de Clermont sold the
whole lot to Fenton.

Less than a month after Fenton and de Clermont completed the
Detroit transaction, Hassan returned to London. This time, he was
alone. (Ezzadin would still turn up occasionally with Hassan, but from
August 1994 onward, de Clermont dealt directly with the jeweler.)
Hassan had five more coins to show de Clermont, all rare American
pattern trade dollars. A smarter businessman than Ezzadin, he had
researched the value of these coins in the *Red Book* and was asking a
considerable sum for them. As before, de Clermont called Fenton to
discuss how to proceed.

This time, the dealers decided to split the cost of the coins and
then split the profits when they were sold. It was a comfortable
arrangement. De Clermont needed Fenton's capital to buy Hassan's
coins and Fenton's contacts in the American market to sell them. Fenton, in turn, needed de Clermont's connection to the Egyptian jeweler. In all the deals that followed over the next fifteen months,
Fenton never met Hassan, never even knew the Egyptian's name until
their final transaction. Fenton would sometimes try to imagine what
de Clermont's source looked like, but that was the extent of his
curiosity. He didn't ask de Clermont for details. To Fenton, de Clermont's shadowy source was known only as "the jeweler chap."

Between August 1994 and November 1995, Fenton and de Clermont completed nine transactions with Hassan. They bought dozens of coins from all over the world from the Egyptian jeweler. In September, in addition to more U.S. pattern coins, Hassan brought them a pair of Italian pieces and a valuable old Russian ruble. In November, the Egyptian sold them a trove of rare German and Austrian coins worth £10,000, as well as an 1872 pattern quarter-dollar worth almost £4,000. There were occasional disappointments in Hassan's offerings—Fenton was particularly upset about a mint-state 1921 double eagle that had been cleaned inexpertly—but more often the Egyptian brought wonderful coins: Bavarian ducats and pfennigs, Saxony thalers, Italian lire, and all manner of American rarities.

After the first couple of deals, Fenton suggested to de Clermont that the accounting would be cleaner if Fenton put up all of the money to make purchases. Fenton and de Clermont would divide the coins—American coins to Fenton, coins from other countries to de Clermont—and sell them. After Fenton had been paid back the purchase price, they'd split profits. The deals all proceeded in more or less the same way. Hassan would call de Clermont from Egypt and tell him he was coming to London, or else he'd call from his London hotel and say he was in town. Usually he brought the coins to de Clermont's office, though once in a while de Clermont would go to Hassan's hotel. Then de Clermont would call Fenton and they'd calculate what the coins were worth. Fenton would advance de Clermont the money and de Clermont would pay Hassan, in cash, as the Egyptian preferred.

Fenton's true ownership of the coins was reflected in the sales invoices de Clermont drafted. The two dealers kept a running account of their profits on the Hassan pieces, treating each other like the old friends they were. They figured up their splits only occasionally, each trusting the other to report sales truthfully. De Clermont estimated that his share of profits was about £40,000.

Fenton, who didn't think provenance counted for much in the coin market, always said he didn't care where de Clermont's source was getting the coins. De Clermont, though, continued to check the Palace Collections catalogue every time Hassan brought another delivery. He wanted to know the story of Hassan's coins, and he worked assiduously to build Hassan's trust. When, for instance, de Clermont and Fenton resold one of Hassan's coins for more than they expected, de Clermont gave a cut of the windfall to the Egyptian. "I was very keen to have a very close relationship with [Hassan]," he said.

De Clermont's careful cultivation paid off with an extraordinary story, revealed in dribs and drabs over the months of 1994. Years before, Hassan told de Clermont, his father, who was also a jeweler, had befriended a high-ranking officer in Egypt's Revolutionary Army, a man descended from a wealthy and important Egyptian family. The officer had been a coin collector, so when Sotheby's came to Egypt to sell Farouk's coin collection, he followed events closely. The officer attended the Palace Collections auctions, where he purchased some of Farouk's coins. Then, after the sales ended, Hassan told de Clermont, he somehow acquired additional Farouk coins. The officer treasured his Farouk specimens, maintaining them carefully and never revealing that he owned them.

When the Egyptian officer died, he left his entire estate, including his piece of the Farouk collection, to his six adult children. The children had no interest in coins, and, through the family connection to Hassan's father, had engaged Hassan to dispose of their father's collection. The family, Hassan told de Clermont, decided when and what to sell. Hassan was merely their agent.

Just as Fenton didn't ask de Clermont to disclose Hassan's name, de Clermont never asked Hassan to tell him the officer's name. Hassan was careful to refer to his clients only as "the family," and de Clermont didn't want to endanger his friendship with Hassan by demanding more details. De Clermont called the Egyptian Army officer "the Colonel," although he didn't know the officer's rank. Nor did he know whether, after the Palace Collections auction, the officer had purchased Farouk coins that hadn't sold, or had been given the coins by an ally in the revolutionary government. All de Clermont knew about the officer was that "he was one of the people close with Nasser who had instigated the overthrow of Farouk." And that he had a hoard of unbelievable coins.

For de Clermont, Hassan's story of the Egyptian officer erased any questions about whether the coins he and Fenton were buying had once been Farouk's. No other explanation made sense. The odds were infinitesimal that Hassan could have concocted the story of the Egyptian officer and then bolstered it through the purchase of a broad assortment of extremely rare and expensive coins to match the Farouk catalogue. The coins Hassan had sold to him and Fenton were too hard to find. Only Farouk had had them all.

From studying his copy of the Palace Collections auction catalogue, de Clermont had identified particular Farouk rarities he wanted Hassan to bring him. He didn't ask Hassan straight-out for the coins, though. Their relationship demanded more subtlety. So during one visit, when Hassan was telling de Clermont that the family had shown him some banknotes that he considered unimportant, de Clermont suggested that Hassan might want to consult with him if he was unsure. "If you see things, you should check with me first," de Clermont said.

"What are you looking for?" Hassan asked.

"Anything interesting or rare," de Clermont replied. He told Hassan, by way of example, about a set of Brazilian gold ingots—individually numbered and coveted by collectors—that Farouk had owned. On a subsequent trip, Hassan brought the Brazilian ingots. The Egyptian also managed to come up with a rare Venezuelan coin from the Farouk collection that de Clermont had requested. Hassan always said he could only deliver what the family chose to sell. But the family seemed to be listening when Hassan conveyed de Clermont's requests.

One day in 1995, when he and Hassan were discussing rarities from the Farouk collection, de Clermont asked Hassan about a coin from a lot marked as "withdrawn" in his copy of the Palace Collections auction catalogue. It was a famous rarity, a coin whose story had grown to legendary proportions in the years since the auction. Everyone in the coin world knew about the 1933 Double Eagle—its questionable legality, and its disappearance after the Americans demanded its withdrawal from the Farouk sale. The 1933 Double Eagle was a sacred relic of coin collecting.

"There is a '33 twenty-dollar, a rare one, in the Farouk collection," de Clermont said to Hassan. "Have you seen that coin?"

The Egyptian shrugged. "If it comes, it will come," he replied.

•   •   •

AT THE end of September 1995, Andre de Clermont received a phone call from Hassan, who asked de Clermont to meet him at his hotel in London. De Clermont went right over. As usual, he had no idea what coins would be in Hassan's latest batch, only that they'd be worth the trip.

Hassan laid out the coins, pointing to one in particular. "Here it is," he said.

And there it was: The 1933 Double Eagle. The Egyptian officer's family had agreed to part with the coin, Hassan told de Clermont, but only for a high price. They knew how valuable this coin was. Not only had Hassan seen the *Red Book* description of the 1933 Double Eagle, but the Egyptian officer had written "very rare" on the envelope in which he stored the coin. The price, Hassan said, was $325,000.

De Clermont left the hotel and rushed directly to Stephen Fenton's shop on Duke Street. The 1933 Double Eagle was in London, he announced to Fenton. Hassan wanted $325,000 for it. To Fenton, his businessman's mind calculating, that seemed like too much money. The most expensive American coin he had ever handled had been a 1796 half-cent that he had sold for about $100,000. Sure, the 1933 Double Eagle—the *Farouk* 1933 Double Eagle—was a much more exciting coin, much more glamorous. But the mystery that lent the 1933 Saint its glamour wasn't necessarily a good thing for a coin dealer. Fenton had heard too many stories of 1933 Double Eagle sightings over the years to feel secure about this coin's rarity. Once he bought the coin de Clermont had seen, three or five or ten more might pop out of hiding. And even if this coin was the only 1933 Double Eagle outside of the Smithsonian, Fenton thought, would he be able to find a buyer? Fenton was doing quite nicely in the coin business, clearing a few hundred thousand dollars a year in profits, but he didn't like the idea of tying up more than $300,000 of capital in a coin he couldn't sell. Fenton told de Clermont he needed a couple of days to think about Hassan's deal.

First he checked prices. The 1907 ultra-high-relief Saints—the rare specimens produced at the command of Theodore Roosevelt on the Mint's hydraulic presses—were bringing several hundred thousand dollars apiece on the rare occasions when they appeared at auction. That was auspicious. So were the prices fetched by 1927-D Saints, and there were a dozen or so of them in circulation among collectors. Maybe the 1933 Double Eagle would sell in that range if Fenton could find a buyer for whom the romance of the coin's history outweighed questions about its legality.

Fenton also asked de Clermont if he could see the 1933 Double Eagle. De Clermont went to Hassan, who granted permission. De Clermont took the coin to his safe-deposit box in a repository on Lower Regent Street. Fenton met him there. When de Clermont removed the 1933 Double Eagle from his box and handed it to Fenton, the dealer (despite the nonchalance he prided himself on) was dazzled. The coin looked like an ordinary mint-state double eagle, with a few nicks here and there—but only until he glanced toward Liberty's upraised left foot and saw the date. "That magical date," he called it. Fenton picked up the coin and felt almost dizzy, as if he had just bolted an espresso. "I'm holding the Farouk 1933 Double Eagle," he said to himself, "a coin that has been missing for forty years."

Fenton wanted it, but at his price. De Clermont shuttled between Fenton and Hassan with offers and counteroffers. After a few rounds of negotiation, Fenton agreed to buy the 1933 Double Eagle and some other American gold coins from Hassan—whom he still hadn't met— for $220,000. On October 3, 1995, Fenton's company, Knightsbridge Coins, wired the money directly to an account Hassan had set up at the Notting Hill branch of the National Westminster Bank. (De Clermont was cut out of the purchase but understood that Fenton would give him a share of the profits when he sold the coin.) The invoice Fenton wrote up for the deal wasn't as complete as de Clermont's inventories in previous transactions with Hassan. It did not specifically mention the 1933 Double Eagle but simply indicated that Fenton had bought what was described as a "group of U.S. gold coins" from Hassan.

Once he had taken possession of the coin, Fenton immediately locked it in his safe-deposit box. The 1933 Double Eagle was his. Now he just had to find someone to sell it to.

The 1933 Double Eagle:

An ounce of gold like no other.

(Photograph courtesy of Sotheby's)

LEFT The famed sculptor Augustus Saint-Gaudens was invited to redesign the nation's coinage by Theodore Roosevelt in 1905. "I suppose there will be a revolt about it!" Roosevelt predicted. Saint-Gaudens accepted the President's commission, albeit with trepidation. (*Dartmouth College Library*)

BELOW Saint-Gaudens created his gold coin designs at his colonnaded studio in Cornish, New Hampshire. Midway through the project he was diagnosed with cancer, and had to rely on a devoted assistant to fight his battles at the U.S. Mint. (*Dartmouth College Library*)

ABOVE Exhausted from days of
heroic bill-drafting, Secretary of
the Treasury William Woodin
watched President Franklin
Roosevelt sign the law that saved
the U.S. economy—and paved
the way for America to abandon
the gold standard. A noted numismatist, Woodin made sure coin
collectors were protected from
restrictions on gold ownership.
(*Bettmann/CORBIS*)

RIGHT Abe Kosoff was one of
the coin dealers who traded 1933
Double Eagles in the late 1930s.
He later went to Egypt to attend
the Palace Collections auction
from which one of the coins disappeared. (*Photograph courtesy of the
American Numismatic Association*)

LEFT Frank Wilson, chief of the United States Secret Service during the Double Eagle investigation in 1944, was the most celebrated detective of his era. Wilson took a personal interest in the case, sending agents in pursuit of Israel Switt's financial records. (*Photograph courtesy of United States Secret Service*)

RIGHT AND BELOW B. Max Mehl revolutionized coin collecting in the first half of the 1900s. With advertisements such as his call for 1913 Liberty Head nickels—of which only five are known—Mehl inspired thousands of coin enthusiasts. He handled three 1933 Double Eagles, including the only coin known to have eluded the Secret Service in 1944. (*Photographs courtesy of the American Numismatic Association*)

OLD MONEY WANTED. WILL PAY FIFTY DOLLARS FOR NICKEL OF 1913 WITH LIBERTY HEAD (NO BUFFALO). I pay cash premiums for all rare coins. Send 5¢ for Large Coin Folder. May mean much profit to you. B. MAX MEHL, 150 Mehl Bldg., Fort Worth, Texas.

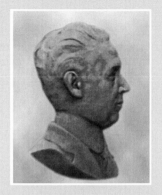

LEFT F.C.C. Boyd displayed his 1933 Double Eagle at the American Numismatic Association convention in 1939. He surrendered it to the Secret Service in June 1945. "I do not care to have in my possession anything that has been embezzled or stolen," wrote Boyd, an executive of the Union News Company, in a letter to the agency. "However, as a collector, I should like to keep his coin." (*Photograph courtesy of the American Numismatic Association*)

RIGHT King Farouk of Egypt assembled a peerless coin collection, including the 1933 Double Eagle he exported to Cairo only weeks before the Secret Service began seizing the coins. After Farouk was forced to abdicate after a revolutionary coup, he left behind palaces full of the treasures— and the junk—he'd accumulated. (*Bettmann/CORBIS*)

LEFT London coin dealer Stephen Fenton couldn't resist when a friend and fellow coin dealer located a 1933 Double Eagle in 1995: Fenton bought the coin that had been missing for forty years. After the 1933 Double Eagle landed Fenton in jail in New York in 1996, his live-in girlfriend, Sheryl TK, flew over from London with bail money. (*Photograph courtesy of Stephen Fenton*)

ABOVE Retired truck driver Jack Moore was the unlikely buyer of Fenton's 1933 Double Eagle. He would later say that the coin ruined his life. (*Bryan Christy*)

RIGHT Secret Service agent R. David Freriks led the agency's second 1933 Double Eagle investigation. He prided himself on "taking a case nobody else was interested in and turning it into something." (*Bryan Christy*)

RIGHT Barry Berke represented
Stephen Fenton in the 1933
Double Eagle case. When Fenton
first told him the story of the coin
Berke called it "the most absurd
criminal case" he'd ever heard of.
*(Photograph courtesy of Kramer Levin
Naftalis & Frankel)*

LEFT Assistant United States
Attorney Jane Levine took over the
government's case in 1999. Though
she had no living witnesses, she
vowed to prove a sixty-five-year-old
theft from the U.S. Mint.
(Jennifer M. Moore)

RIGHT Sotheby's vice-chairman
David Redden was determined to
win the contest to auction the
1933 Double Eagle. He promised
Fenton and U.S. Mint officials that
he would attract bidders who
weren't coin collectors—and he
did. *(Photograph courtesy of Sotheby's)*

ABOVE On July 30, 2002, Redden presided over the sale of the 1933 Double Eagle. When it was over, the coin was the most valuable in the world. (*Photograph courtesy of Sotheby's*)

LEFT In August 2005 the Mint announced the recovery of ten additional 1933 Double Eagles from the family of Israel Switt. There is still, however, at least one 1933 Double Eagle the government doesn't know about. In the 1980s a prospective buyer of the secret coin took this photograph of its face. Its current whereabouts remain a mystery.

Chapter Ten

The Deal

STEPHEN FENTON HAS A ROUND, rubbery, comfortable face, with a flyaway fringe of brown hair and merry brown eyes. He looks like a man who laughs a lot, which he does. His voice, soft and lightly accented, falls easily on the ear, which is no small asset in a business that depends so heavily on phonework as coin dealing. When he was a boy, Fenton used to lunch alone at restaurants instead of eating with his schoolmates. Now he is popular at coin shows all over Europe and the United States. Other dealers are happy to grab a bite or make a deal with Fenton, who is known to be trustworthy and well connected. "Stephen has his ear to the ground," one dealer told me.

He is also discreet. Fenton is so engaging, so full of amusing stories told with a self-deprecating, eye-crinkling smile, that one doesn't notice at first how adept he is at avoiding questions he doesn't care to answer, spinning diversions from awkward facts. Fenton has never said exactly what he knew of the legality of the 1933 Double Eagle at the time he bought the coin from Hassan in October 1995. He did not consult a lawyer before or after the deal, nor did he call his insurance carrier to increase his coverage once he took possession of the coin. He told only his longtime assistant, Jim Brown, that he'd bought the coin. Then he locked it in his safe-deposit box.

Over the next couple of weeks, Fenton thought about the best way to sell the 1933 Double Eagle. An auction, he decided, was out of the question—not because he feared the coin would be seized by the U.S. government but because it might not bring the price he wanted. If it didn't sell, the coin would have a taint of undesirability. In this case, smart business meant operating more warily. But that was Fenton's usual approach, anyway. A good boutique dealer like Fenton makes his money one coin at a time, quietly searching among his dealer clients for just the right buyer. There was no reason, he concluded, to handle the 1933 Double Eagle any differently, even if it was the most expensive piece he'd ever bought. This coin, more than any other Fenton had sold, demanded circumspection.

So Fenton's first call, in the fall of 1995, was to Mark Emory, an old friend and a dealer with Heritage Rare Coins, a major U.S. coin house. Fenton had known Emory, an American who lived in Germany, since the 1970s, and he was sure he could trust him. Fenton told his friend that he'd acquired a 1933 Double Eagle. "Do you think you can help me find a buyer?" Fenton asked.

"I'll see what I can do," Emory promised.[1]

Emory made a few calls himself and returned to Fenton with a name: Jasper "Jay" Parrino, the owner of a Kansas City coin business called The Mint. If Fenton wanted to sell his 1933 Double Eagle, Emory said, Jay Parrino was his man.

IN THE fall of 1995, there was no American coin dealer with more swaggering braggadocio than Jay Parrino, a tough-guy contestant in coin dealing's long-running pageant of self-aggrandizement. With Parrino, everything had to be the biggest and the best. He bought the most in-your-face tables at coin shows and proceeded to display coins that left convention-goers gasping—$10 or $20 million worth of rarities, laid out for everyone to see. He ran advertisements in coin newspapers crowing about his own triumphs of buying and selling, featuring advice from—and, of course, photographs of—the master. Parrino demanded prices that other dealers considered to be absurdly high, yet he somehow got people to pay them. He boasted of his "millionaires list," which in his case wasn't just the usual coin dealers' roster of customers with more than $1 million in net worth; Parrino's list was of customers who had *spent* more than a million dollars buying coins from him.

Parrino's swagger brought him a fair share of enemies in the coin business. One collector told me that when he resisted paying Parrino's price for an extremely rare coin he needed for his best-in-the-world set, Parrino unleashed a stream of insults over the phone. "You're a pissant," the dealer said. "You can't buy this coin." Parrino was trying to provoke the collector's ego, and his trick worked; the collector ponied up. He never bought from Parrino again, though. There were a lot of coin people who had questions about Parrino. Could he possibly own the spectacular inventory of rarities he claimed? And if he did, where exactly had he obtained the millions to buy it?

Parrino told me that he always just laughed at the gossip he heard about himself, though he made that assertion with sufficient bitterness that I wondered whether it was true. I was surprised, when I interviewed Parrino at a coin show in Orlando in 2004, by how small and apparently mild a man he is. From the stories I'd heard and the photographs I'd seen, I had imagined him to be a bruiser. In pictures, his face is strong and fierce—piercing eyes; dark, heavy brows; mouth set in a thin, unsmiling line. His stance is defiant, almost challenging, as if he had to remind himself to unclench his fists for the camera. In person, though, Parrino seemed more like a pudgy gray grandfather than an enforcer. He unfolded a pair of reading glasses to examine a coin someone walked up to show him, and he paused in the middle of our conversation to take a call from his wife, who was waiting on the Space Mountain line at Disney World with one of their granddaughters. Parrino's talk was as full of bravado as I had expected—he told me about a cent he claimed to have sold for $12 million and a client for whom he'd built a $150 million coin collection—but in person, the boasting seemed more a mark of insecurity than of menace.

Parrino offered a humdrum explanation of his sudden arrival at the top of the coin business in the 1980s. He began collecting coins, he said, as an eight-year-old Boy Scout trying to earn a merit badge. His father, a plumber, had a friend who owned a drugstore and used to allow Parrino to look through the coins in his cash register. Parrino quickly found most of the pennies, nickels, and dimes he needed to fill his sets. Then he had the same lightning-bolt revelation that strikes so many of the boys who grow up to become coin dealers: The few coins he had trouble finding were the same few that all the other Boy Scouts needed to complete their collections. Parrino, an entrepreneurial kid, figured he'd go looking at coin shops for those relatively rare pieces, buy as many as he could find, and resell them to other Scouts at a profit—an elementary-school version of the same philosophy he later embraced as a big-time dealer. Parrino's childhood ambition, he told me, was not to become a firefighter or a baseball player, but to be the first person to pay $1 million for a rare coin.

By the time he was attending the University of Missouri in the early 1960s, Parrino was making $50,000 a year selling coins. (He also told me that he and his roommate, a math scholarship student, devised a card-counting system and took in $500 a day on trips to Las Vegas.) Right after college, Parrino said, he went to school to become a casino dealer and worked on the Las Vegas Strip for a couple of years. Then he returned to Missouri and coins. In the 1970s, Parrino and his mentor, Ed Wirth, expanded their coin operations in the Midwest, opening a string of small shops that sold coins, stamps, and jewelry. Parrino told me that he once owned twenty-seven coin shops, though he's been quoted elsewhere as saying that he had twenty-seven employees.[2] Another big part of his business, Parrino said, was buying coins as investments for union pension funds.

In the early 1980s, with his pension investment business in decline after a change in tax laws, Parrino decided to sell off all his coins. He had devised a new approach to coin dealing. Instead of relying on an enormous inventory of ordinary coins, he'd reverse the equation and carry only a few extremely valuable pieces. That way, he wouldn't have to worry about dishonest employees and robberies at far-flung shops, nor about the bookkeeping headaches of thousands of coins. Parrino sold his shops and his inventory and invested the money in ten great rarities. Telling his wife he'd work from home, he gave the experiment six months. The second week, Parrino told me, a client called. "He said, 'I'm flying my son down on a private jet.' I sold him the Panama Pacific $50 piece in the original frame from the Exposition. I made $10,000 and I said, 'This is the way to go.'" (Parrino told coin investment newsletter writer Maurice Rosen a different version of the story, in which the unnamed client bought a 1797 half-dollar in Parrino's third week of business.[3])

Parrino's new business scheme depended on the quality of the coins he held. If he was going to carry only a limited inventory, he had to be able to realize big profits on each piece. That meant buying and reselling the most highly desirable coins on the market. "I realized I was dealing with people who have a lot of money," Parrino told Maurice Rosen in 1996. "When these people want something badly enough they simply buy it. That's what caused me to specialize in rarities, super conditions, finest knowns."

Parrino began showing up at important coin auctions, a rare unfamiliar face in the usual-suspect lineup of dealers. Coin auctions, for the most part, are grubby affairs, scented with coffee and sweat and populated by unkempt, bespectacled men whispering to one another. They have the feel of a reunion of the high school chess club—a gathering in which everyone has known everyone else for years and they all speak a language not entirely comprehensible to outsiders. Strangers at coin auctions always get stares. Unwary strangers sometimes get duped. Parrino was no mark, though. When he played the Midwestern rube at those early auctions, it was to lull the prominent dealers from whom he was now buying. "I took advantage of it," he told me. "They were like, 'Kansas City, what's that?' I said, 'Fine, you think I'm a hayseed, I'll be a hayseed.' The coin business is very cliquey. To be quite honest, I was shocked when I started buying topquality coins. Dealers I had read about and looked up to—when I met them I realized I probably knew more at age twelve than they did now. I thought, 'Hmmm. I can compete with these guys.'"

Parrino moved quickly from the shadows of the coin business to the spotlight. Once he was known, he made a show of bidding high to scare off competitors. He sent out missives to collectors, preaching his "Box of Twenty" philosophy, in which he advised clients to abandon their hard-earned sets and sell everything but the twenty rarest coins they could afford, because only the rarest, hardest-to-find coins would consistently appreciate. Parrino himself carried far more than twenty coins in his inventory, but he told collectors that he followed his own ideology rigorously, only dealing true rarities, never commodity coins they could buy from any clown on the bourse floor. "And when I was hitting the auctions and buying rarities through the eighties and nineties," Parrino told me, "it was all my own money. Never borrowed. It was all mine." Parrino knew that other dealers badmouthed him to their clients. He dismissed the talk. His wife once overheard a couple of Parrino's rivals disparaging him at a restaurant during a coin show. "Forget them," Parrino sniffed. "It's just jealousy."

BEFORE THE fall of 1995, when Mark Emory told Stephen Fenton to sell his 1933 Double Eagle through Jay Parrino, Fenton had bought one coin from Parrino's stock, a $100 George III shilling, at a show in the early 1990s. He didn't know Parrino, though, so he asked Emory to act as an intermediary. Only in late November, when Emory abruptly informed Fenton that he was withdrawing from the deal, did Fenton call Parrino himself.

"I have a client who has the 1933 Double Eagle," Fenton said in their initial conversation. Fenton didn't want Parrino to know that he actually owned the coin outright. His reference to a fictitious client gave him leeway to bargain over price and terms. "Would you be interested?"

"I might have somebody," Parrino said. "Let me make a call."

In the weeks that followed, after Parrino reported that he did, indeed, have a buyer for the 1933 Double Eagle, Fenton and Parrino talked on the phone several times. They arrived at a purchase price for the coin with relatively little negotiation. Fenton told Parrino that he was buying the 1933 Double Eagle from his client for $800,000 and he wanted Parrino to buy it from him for $850,000, netting Fenton a profit of $50,000. Fenton, of course, wasn't telling Parrino the truth, since he had paid Hassan only $220,000 for the 1933 Double Eagle and some other U.S. gold coins. If Parrino paid him $850,000 for it, he'd clear more than $600,000.

Parrino lied right back to Fenton. "I'm not going to make much on this deal," he told Fenton when he agreed to pay Fenton's asking price. In fact, he expected to take home several hundred thousand dollars from the deal he arranged. Neither Fenton nor Parrino took seriously the other's protestations of how little he'd earn from the transaction. Both had been coin dealers long enough to expect several layers of deception in a deal this big. As long as both of them were satisfied with their profits, the lies didn't matter.

The particulars of how the deal would be executed proved tougher to settle than the price of the coin. Parrino kept telling Fenton that he had a client in Amarillo, Texas, but for all Fenton knew, Parrino's client was as illusory as his own. Fenton had little history with Jay Parrino, and he didn't know whether to trust the American dealer. Maybe Parrino's client was plotting to steal the 1933 Double Eagle. Best not to endanger the coin. "Why don't you come to London?" Fenton asked Parrino.

"My client wants to do it here," Parrino said. The back and forth continued for weeks. Fenton suggested Switzerland, where a big international coin show was held every winter at the end of January. Parrino said no, Fenton had to come to the United States. His client, he told Fenton, was flexible about how he'd pay, acceding to the overseas wire transfer that Fenton preferred. He was willing to capitulate on Fenton's one inviolable condition—that Fenton be in the room while Parrino's client examined the coin. He was even prepared, Parrino said, to consider any United States location Fenton wanted, including Puerto Rico. But he absolutely wouldn't travel to Europe to do the deal. As of the third week in January 1996, Fenton and Parrino weren't sure they would be able to pull off the sale of the 1933 Double Eagle.

FOR ALL of Fenton's suspicions, most of what Parrino told him in their series of telephone conversations in December 1995 and January 1996 was true. Parrino did have a buyer for the 1933 Double Eagle, and he was conducting contemporaneous negotiations with him. Parrino's buyer did live in Amarillo, Texas, and he absolutely did insist on executing the deal in the United States.

Parrino's client was a paunchy, middle-aged man named Jack Moore, a retired truck driver devoted to coins, guns, his wife, Marty, and their three pet parrots. About four years before the 1933 Double Eagle deal, Parrino had met Moore at a coin show in California, after which the dealer kept bumping into Moore on the coin circuit. "He was no different from other rummies I'd see at shows," said Parrino, who believed that big-money collectors at coin shows were as rare as wheat pennies in pocket change. "He'd bring coins over, I'd give him advice." Moore considered himself a coin expert; Parrino privately derided him as a rank amateur. Moore usually turned up at shows with his best friend, Kent Remmel, who, as far as Parrino could tell, knew even less about coins than Moore. Parrino could hardly believe it when he first heard that these men he considered bumblers had somehow landed an enviable assignment. Remmel and Moore were building a complete set of Saint-Gaudens double eagles for a collector with more cash than coin expertise.

The collector, John Groendyke, was Remmel's cousin and Jack Moore's boss, the multimillionaire owner of one of the biggest trucking operations in the United States. Parrino might not have taken Moore and Remmel seriously, but it was obvious to him that they had serious money behind them. Moore and Remmel kept Groendyke's identity a secret, but they emphasized to dealers his determination to build a complete Saints set—which made them popular men with the coin trade. Set builders are a dealer's dream. They need to acquire particular coins, and the closer they get to filling all the holes in their collection, the more they're usually willing to spend. Moore and Remmel were deluged with offers of mint-quality Saint-Gaudens double eagles.

In less than a year, they had acquired all but seven or eight of the hardest-to-find Saints for Groendyke. They had become fixtures at the big coin shows, where they'd stay at the same hotels as important dealers like Parrino. Moore and Remmel made friends easily among the dealers, as buyers with tens of thousands of dollars to spend are wont to do. Remmel always had the air of a kid on a toy-store shopping spree, someone who couldn't believe his luck. Moore was less ingenuous, but he flattered and bluffed his way into the confidence of such dealers as Charles Karler of Southwestern Gold and even David Akers, the renowned gold expert. Akers, who supplied several of the coins for Groendyke's Saints collection, liked Jack Moore enough that he even invited Moore and Remmel to sell some of their own coins—bought as a sideline while they collected for Groendyke—from his table at shows.

The first coin that Jay Parrino sold to Moore and Remmel was a 1909 Saint stamped from an altered 1908 die. He later sold them three or four more Saints of increasing rarity: the 1926-D, the 1926-S, the 1929. Parrino snickered about Moore behind the Texan's back, but as long as Groendyke's wire transfers went through, he was perfectly happy to sell him coins.

Moore and Remmel completed Groendyke's Saints collection at the end of 1992, supplementing the standard fifty-two coins of the set with a rare high-relief 1907 Saint with a special satiny "proof" finish. Groendyke was so proud of the collection that he permitted Remmel and Moore to reveal his identity and take his coins—now known as The Groendyke Collection—on the road to display at shows. In the summer of 1993, Groendyke even accompanied Moore and Remmel to the American Numismatic Association convention in Baltimore. (That was the convention, coincidentally, at which Stephen Fenton and Andre de Clermont first discussed de Clermont's Egyptian connection.) Their exhibit billed The Groendyke Collection as a complete set of Saint-Gaudens double eagles.

Jay Parrino, also at the Baltimore show, went to look at Groendyke's coins and then walked over to Moore. The set, Parrino gibed, wasn't really complete: Groendyke didn't have a 1933 Double Eagle. He draped an arm over Moore's shoulders and said, "How would you like to have a 1933 to go with that set?"[4]

"It'd be real neat, but you couldn't display it," Moore said. "It's illegal to own one."

Parrino ignored Moore's objection. "Your man would have the only complete set outside of the Smithsonian," he said.

"Nah, I don't think so," Moore answered.

Parrino next tried Remmel. Did Remmel think Groendyke wanted to buy a 1933 Double Eagle? Remmel said probably not, but he'd check with Groendyke. When he confirmed that his cousin didn't want the coin, Remmel told Parrino no and dismissed the incident.

Parrino and Moore kept talking about the 1933 Double Eagle, though. When Parrino would see Moore at a coin show, he would remind Moore that Groendyke's set wasn't complete without the 1933 Saint. If Parrino didn't mention the coin, Moore would bring it up.[5] "How's that '33?" he'd say. Moore had the coin on his mind, it seemed to Parrino. He'd sometimes even call Parrino at home to talk about the 1933 Double Eagle. Once he asked how much the coin would cost. "I know where three of them are," Parrino responded. "It just depends on which one you want to buy."

Parrino liked utterances like that. They showed Moore that Parrino knew the secrets of the coin world—secrets to which Moore would never be privy. The truth was, Parrino felt a little sorry for Moore, who would always be small-time, his nose pressed up against the window that separated him from the real money. Guys like Moore reminded Parrino of how big-time he was.

IN THE fall of 1995, when Parrino first heard about Stephen Fenton's 1933 Double Eagle, he ran through a list of collectors in his head. There were dozens he could call, and any one of them to whom he didn't sell the coin might never talk to him again. He thought about Jack Moore and all the times they'd talked about the 1933 Saint. Maybe he thought also about John Groendyke's millions and Moore's apparent naïveté. Years later, even Parrino couldn't explain exactly why he selected Jack Moore, of all the clients he might have called. But he did. At the beginning of December, Parrino picked up the phone and dialed Moore in Amarillo. He told Moore that he had a rock-solid lead on a 1933 Double Eagle that had surfaced in Europe. This was no joke. Was Moore in?

He might be, Moore said. He had to talk to someone. He'd call Parrino back.

A day later, he called Parrino. Moore said he had a buyer.

The next several weeks were a coin-dealing tour de force by Parrino, a master class in the tedious plotting and cajoling necessary to set up a million-dollar coin sale. He alternated transatlantic conversations with Fenton to negotiate the price at which Fenton was willing to sell the 1933 Double Eagle with calls to Jack Moore in Amarillo, probing to find out how much Moore's buyer would pay for the coin.

In his first conversation with Moore, Parrino said the asking price was $1.5 million. It was a brash demand; no one as of then had ever paid even $1 million for a coin at auction. Moore countered with an offer of $750,000. He also told Parrino that his buyer insisted on doing the deal in the United States, in cash. Parrino thought the first restriction was strange and the second a deal-breaker. "I don't do cash transactions," he said flatly. Moore asked Parrino to call him back after he'd talked to the seller.

Parrino didn't respond for a couple of days. On December 15, 1995, Moore called him, sounding apprehensive. "I assume you haven't found anything out 'cause you haven't called me," Moore said. "Was that price agreeable? If not, maybe I could do something else."

"I don't know," Parrino said. "Actually, all I said to them was that we'd like to buy it a little cheaper." A bigger issue at the moment, Parrino said, was that the seller wanted to do the deal overseas. "[The coin] is okay over there, but it's not okay over here," he told Moore.

"Well," Moore said, "I'll see what I can do. I don't know if I could get my person to go overseas or not. I know he wants the coin. . . . And he's got the money. But I don't know if he'll go [overseas] to pick it up."

"Let me see what I can find out," Parrino responded.

In their next conversation, on December 18, Moore raised his offer to $950,000 and intimated that his client could go even higher—all the way to $1.5 million if Parrino insisted. Moore also said the buyer was now willing to execute the deal by wire transfer. Moore's client would wire the money to Parrino's account, and Parrino would in turn wire money to the seller. Moore said he assumed that Parrino's commission would come from the $1.5 million his client was paying. He wanted to be sure, however, that Parrino planned to take care of him, too.

"Are you in there to make some money?" Parrino asked him.

"Well, I wouldn't be doing this if I wasn't going to try and make something on it," Moore answered. "I can get my guy to wire a million and a half if somebody—and I don't care who—hands me a briefcase with some cash in it."

"Well," said Parrino later in the conversation, after Moore repeated his "briefcase with some cash in it," demand, "you have to tell me how much, because that's not an easy thing to do."

"I'd rather tell you that in person," Moore said.

"I know what this represents," Parrino said. "I may have to get involved somewhere so that you could get what you want."

THE DEAL remained stalled for two weeks, with Fenton insisting on Europe and Moore swearing to Parrino that his client wouldn't leave the United States. Then on January 5, 1996, Parrino reported a break-through. He and Moore had agreed to meet at the Orange County Convention Center in Orlando, where Florida's big annual coin convention was to begin the next day. Parrino was setting up his booth, and Moore walked over. "We basically got it done," Parrino told Moore. As long as Moore's client was willing to wire the money to the seller's overseas account, the seller would bring the coin to New York, where Moore had said his client traveled frequently on real-estate business. Everything was going to work out, Parrino said. The seller would transport the coin into the United States secretly, maybe hidden in the middle of a roll of gold coins, or maybe mislabeled as a 1932 double eagle. The coin transfer would take place among the seller, Parrino, and Moore, with Moore's client waiting in another room. "[The seller doesn't] want to know you," Parrino told Moore. "And they don't want you to know them. And they [don't] want to ever know where this coin went. They just want the money."

So did Moore, as he reminded Parrino. "I'll let you know about the deal we talked about," he told Parrino. "I'll let you know before the week is done."

There were still land mines to clear. First, Fenton balked again about coming to the United States. "They're just afraid they have been scammed," Parrino told Moore. Parrino wheedled Fenton back in, but then he got stuck trying to find a date that suited Fenton and Moore's buyer.

Moore's client canceled a tentative date at the Waldorf-Astoria on January 24, leaving Parrino to relay alternative dates and locations to an irritated Fenton. Finally, on January 21, Parrino had the arrangements in place. They'd all meet at the Waldorf on February 8. Parrino and Fenton, still known to Moore only as "the seller," would go up to Moore's room. Moore would check the coin, and, if he approved it, would call for his client and his client's coin expert to enter. Once Moore's client okayed the deal, he would wire $1,650,000 to Parrino.

Now ALL that remained to be negotiated was Moore's fee for bringing Parrino a buyer. He'd been thinking about it, Moore told Parrino on January 17. "I'm not going to pay taxes on what I do, so I want cash," he said. "Is that a problem?"

Parrino laughed. "I don't have the cash. We'll work it out. You and I aren't going to have a problem."

Five days later, Moore got in his pickup truck and drove out of Texas, headed northeast for Parrino's office in Missouri. He spent the night in Wichita and arrived at the Mark Twain Bank in Independence on the morning of January 23. Moore stood in front of the two-way mirror Parrino had told him about and pushed the buzzer. He heard a click, walked through the door, and headed down the stairs to Parrino's basement headquarters, a garage-size room with a big rectangular table in the middle. There were no coins in sight.

Parrino was on the telephone. He waved to Moore and motioned for him to sit down. Moore looked around, trying not to eavesdrop. Finally Parrino hung up. He greeted Moore with a handshake and they settled down to business. Moore had said that he wanted a commission of $150,000 for the deal. Parrino had promised he'd take care of Moore, but he didn't want to get burned if the sale fell through.

So Moore handed Parrino a coin: John Groendyke's beautiful satin-finished, high-relief 1907 Saint, worth at least $150,000. The coin would serve as collateral for the commission Parrino had promised Moore. Parrino would advance Moore the $150,000 but would hold onto the 1907 Saint. If the 1933 Double Eagle deal was completed successfully, Parrino would return the 1907 Saint to Moore at the Waldorf. If the deal fell apart, Parrino would keep the other coin until Moore returned his money.

Then Parrino wrote two checks to Moore for $25,000 each. Moore, in turn, wrote out an invoice for an extremely rare coin, a silver twenty-cent piece minted in Carson City, Nevada, in 1876, one of only ten of its date and mint mark. The invoice—on which Moore duly recorded the numbers on the checks Parrino had given him—indicated that Parrino had paid Moore $50,000 for the rare twenty-cent piece, though in fact no such sale had taken place. In a firm hand. Moore signed his name, *Jack R. Moore*, just below his notation of Parrino's check numbers. He held onto the invoice and the two checks.

Parrino also gave Moore $20,000 in cash and about $50,000 worth of South African gold Krugerrands. Between the checks, the cash, and the coins, Moore now had $120,000 of the $150,000 he had requested from Parrino as a commission on the 1933 Double Eagle deal. The rest, Parrino said, would come in a package of coins he promised to mail to Moore's home in Amarillo.

Moore left Parrino's office, climbed back into his truck, and made a call from his cell phone. "The meeting is over," he said. "I need to sit down with you."

Moore was calling his mystery client, the buyer whose name he hadn't revealed to Jay Parrino. Parrino thought it was John Groendyke. It wasn't.

Moore's buyer was Agent R. David Freriks of the United States Secret Service.

Jack Moore, the Amarillo truck driver, was a government informant. The United States wanted its 1933 Double Eagle back.

Chapter Eleven

"It's Not Okay Over Here"

IN THE WHOLE UNLIKELY assemblage of characters who populate the tale of the 1933 Double Eagle, Jack Moore is the unlikeliest—not because of who he is but because of what he did. This round-bellied retiree managed to deceive people who should have known better, succeeding, at least for a while, in outsmarting Jay Parrino and half a dozen agents of the United States Secret Service. In the end, Moore's betrayals cost him almost everything, but in the strange twistiness of reality, they also led to the revelation of the 1933 Double Eagle's story. It was only because of Jack Moore that the history of this coin—its seventy-year legend of art and greed and passion—didn't simply end in the darkness of some rich collector's safe-deposit box.

That's small consolation to Moore. I met Jack Moore in Amarillo in March 2004, eight years after the end of his stint as a government operative. He was sixty-five but looked much older. Beneath the base-ball cap he wore, his face was puffy and sallow, his eyes clouded. Moore was elaborately polite, in the style of Southwestern men raised to pull out chairs for women and confer enthusiastic hellos upon strangers. In happier times, he was a regular at Logan's, the roadhouse where we had lunch, so he spent fifteen minutes asking after old friends on the restaurant staff. To me he offered friendly counsel on the proper way to crack Logan's peanuts on the table and throw their shells on the floor. He was trying hard, but we both knew that his heartiness was hollow. The last eight years had been hell for Moore, mostly through his own doing.

Jack Moore was born and raised in Borger, Texas, a dusty, onetime boomtown in the state's panhandle. Boys in Borger—whose founder and foremost citizen, land speculator Asa Borger, was shot to death by the county treasurer in 1934—grew up messing with guns, working in the oil business, and expecting to live out their days in Borger. Moore left only because Phillips Petroleum laid him off in 1960 and he got a job as a truck driver out of Amarillo.

Moore's first wife died in 1968, leaving him with four daughters and a drinking problem. A year later, he met a spitfire named Marty Stewart. "I fell in love the minute I saw her," he told me. On their first date, Marty informed Moore that she hated men and had shot her first husband. He was hopelessly smitten. Marty turned Moore's life around. He and his four children moved in with her and her three. Jack and Marty got married and started driving trucks together, leaving the kids with her aunts. "We'd haul loads of beef—Clovis or Cactus—to Florida. We hauled grapefruit from Florida up to British Columbia. We'd load up with apples and pears and haul them back to here," Moore said. "Everything was going fine."[1]

Inevitably, in a life as punctuated by dramatic incidents as Moore's, those halcyon days ended suddenly. On December 31, 1975, Moore was driving by himself, hauling a load of ruby grapefruit out of Vero Beach, Florida. When he got to Tallahassee and switched from the Interstate to U.S. 90, one of his tires blew out. Moore's truck and trailer rolled into the river below. He survived only because a deputy sheriff happened to have been driving behind him. The sheriff pulled him out of the river and saved his life.

Moore's knee was too badly damaged in the accident for him to go back to driving a truck. A lifetime member of the National Rifle Association, he started working in a gun shop in Amarillo. He also sued the company that manufactured the tire that had blown out. In 1979, he won $125,000 at trial. With his windfall, Moore revived his boyhood interest in coin collecting, buying copper pieces and silver dollars. He figured he'd deal a little, have some fun, maybe make a bit of extra money. Marty indulged him. "She ended up doing most of the dealing," Moore said. "She was real good at stuff like that." Moore and Marty were on the road together again, now visiting coin and gun shows instead of hauling steaks and grapefruit. "We didn't go very far," Moore said. "And we didn't make much money."

In 1982, Moore went to work as a dispatcher for John Groendyke, the transport magnate whose trucks were as ubiquitous as squashed armadillos on the highways of the Southwest. Two years later, Moore met Kent Remmel, Groendyke's cousin, when Remmel's construction company was building a new Groendyke depot in Amarillo. Remmel was also a coin collector and gun enthusiast. He and Moore struck up a friendship, then created an informal partnership called R&M Rare Coins. Remmel bought a couple of safes for R&M holdings—guns, gold, and silver that they stored at Moore's house. They also rented three safe-deposit boxes at Stout Safe Storage in Amarillo. Moore and Remmel and their wives traveled together to coin shows within easy driving range: Oklahoma, Texas, New Mexico, Nevada. Moore still wasn't clearing much profit in the coin business, but with Remmel he was buying more expensive pieces, making bigger bets. For both men, R&M became a consuming enterprise. "We'd talk on the phone six or eight times a day," Remmel told me. "We were closer than most brothers."

It was through Remmel that Moore befriended John Groendyke and embarked on the series of coin transactions that changed his life. One day in 1989, Remmel and Moore were visiting Groendyke in his office in Enid, Oklahoma, when Moore noticed that Groendyke had a 1908 double eagle in a holder on his desk. "That's real neat," Moore said, picking up the coin. "Why did you choose a 1908 gold piece? They started making these in 1907."

Groendyke explained that his father, the founder of Groendyke Transport, had been born in 1908, and he liked to collect memorabilia from that year to honor his dad. "Do you think it's a nice coin?" Groendyke asked Moore.

"It's uncirculated," Moore said. "I don't know how high it would grade, but it's uncirculated."

"How many Saint-Gaudens gold pieces are in a set?" asked Groendyke, who was a coin dabbler.

"Hell, I don't know," Moore answered. "We can find out, though." Groendyke said that he had a *Red Book*, the bible of American coin collectors, on a shelf in his office. Moore checked the book. "A complete set runs from 1907 to 1932," he told Groendyke. "With the mint marks, it's fifty-two coins."

"I want a complete set," Groendyke said.

"Do you have any idea how much that will cost?" asked Remmel. "You're talking about hundreds of thousands."

"I don't care what it costs," Groendyke said. "I want a complete set. I want you all to start putting together a complete set."[2]

Groendyke promised that he would pay for Moore and Remmel to travel to all the major coin shows. They were to get to know dealers and find the highest-quality Saints on the market for Groendyke's set, without worrying too much about prices. Moore would be the coin expert and dealmaker. Remmel would handle finances. When they were ready to buy a double eagle for the collection, Groendyke would wire Remmel the money, plus a commission of four or five percent for him and Moore to split.

Moore began the Groendyke collection with a stunt intended to attract the attention of the top strata of dealers, the men who buy and sell the finest Saint-Gaudens double eagles. Moore drove to Portales, New Mexico, and, according to him, traded $160,000 of John Groendyke's cash for two briefcases of gold coins.[3] He and Remmel took the gold-filled briefcases to a coin show in Long Beach, California, and found a $20,000 1920 Saint from the San Francisco Mint that they wanted for Groendyke. To pay for it, Moore opened his briefcases and began counting out common-date gold pieces. Dealers swarmed around; after that, Moore said, they never left him and Remmel alone. "It's a pretty small world," said Remmel, "and we were privileged to be doing this on a real serious basis."

Moore and Remmel did all of their buying for Groendyke's collection at coin shows, never at auctions. Almost every month of the year, there's a major coin show somewhere in the country, and Moore and Remmel happily joined the troupe of dealers who spend their days tramping a circuit of concrete convention halls. Coin shows are a strange sort of drama. The audience for whom the conventions ostensibly are staged—ordinary collectors buying and selling moderately priced coins—have little idea of the transactions humming just out of their sight. The big-money action isn't usually with the collectors sitting at dealers' tables on the bourse floor with jeweler's loupes. It's more often between dealers, buying for their own inventory or acting on behalf of clients who would never deign to attend a coin show. Jack Moore was once among the uninformed, trying to scratch out a couple of hundred bucks of profit on undistinguished coins, never penetrating the aristocracy of the coin world. But thanks to John Groendyke, at last, he was doing business he considered worthy of him.

Every succeeding purchase for Groendyke's set became a chance for Moore to show off his cunning. He'd find a Saint, negotiate the price, then once in a while set up a side deal. Moore had become friendly enough with some dealers that he would ask them to write invoices inflating the purchase price of Groendyke's coins by several thousand dollars. When Groendyke wired the money to buy the coins, Moore would keep the difference between the invoice price and the price he paid the dealer. Moore claimed that he skimmed $40,000 or $50,000 from Groendyke this way.[4] Once, a couple of days after Moore and Remmel had purchased a coin for Groendyke, Moore received an offer from someone who wanted to buy the coin for $10,000 or $15,000 more than Groendyke had paid. "Have you already told Groendyke we have the coin?" Moore asked Remmel. If not, they could resell the coin, pay Groendyke back the purchase price and pocket the $15,000. "No," Remmel said he told Moore, "but we're here for John. We're supposed to be doing this for him."

Moore and Remmel's September 1992 deal for the 1927-D Saint-Gaudens double eagle—one of only a dozen or so 1927-D Saints in the world—seemed, at least to Remmel, to be the height of coin-world intrigue. Moore got word from one of his dealer friends, Charlie Karler of Southwestern Gold, that Karler had a line on a 1927-D Saint, a coin that very rarely surfaces on the open market. Moore told

Karler that Groendyke was interested, but that Moore had to check the piece first. Karler said he'd arrange to bring the coin to a hotel in Baltimore, the site of a big annual coin show. "We went to a secure room with an armed guard at the door," Remmel said. Karler showed Moore the coin, and Moore pronounced the 1927-D genuine. Groendyke wired $475,000 to Remmel to buy it. Remmel and Moore took their $5,000 commission from the wire transfer, then sent the money on. By then, they had learned enough to know that the rest of the purchase price wasn't all going to the coin's owner, whose identity they could only guess at. "On a deal like this," Remmel said, "when the coins go from hand to hand, everyone has his hand in."

THERE WAS only one important coin dealer Moore didn't like to do business with, though he happened to be a dealer Moore couldn't avoid: Jay Parrino. Moore was prepared to dislike Parrino even before he bought a single coin from him. He had heard stories from other dealers about Parrino's arrogance, his outrageous prices, his obscure beginnings in the business. "Everything I'd heard about him was negative," Moore said, "but we wanted to get the set together and he was the only one who had the coins." Moore's first two or three deals with Parrino went surprisingly well, but as Groendyke's set neared completion, Moore began to suspect that Parrino was inflating prices on the few coins Groendyke still needed. That's a typical dealer tactic when a collector is trying to finish a set, but Moore considered Parrino's prices a personal affront. He set up a test. He asked a confederate to negotiate to buy a 1927-S Saint from Parrino. Parrino priced the coin at $45,000. Then, when Moore asked Parrino about the same coin, the price shot up to $54,000. "He jacked up the price to us on everything," Moore said. "I got tired of it."

Moore hated to think of Parrino making a fool of him, though he was no innocent himself when it came to nasty disputes among coin dealers. In the early 1980s, he'd been accused by a Texas dealer of stealing more than $30,000 worth of silver; and in the early 1990s, he raised a ruckus with another dealer, whom he claimed had failed to pay for fifty or sixty gold coins Moore had sold him.[5] With Parrino, however, pride was at stake, not just money. Moore was convinced that Parrino was not only arrogant but also outright crooked—that Parrino was using coin deals to launder money for the Mafia. It galled him that Parrino had become rich and respectable in the coin business, and he hadn't.

Moore tried complaining to Groendyke about Parrino's price-gouging, but Groendyke said he was more concerned about buying quality coins than what they cost. "Just pay the price," Groendyke would say.[6] Moore gritted his teeth and kept buying from Parrino, until Groendyke's Saints collection—which included a mint-quality example of every Saint-Gaudens double eagle produced between 1907 and 1932—was finished at the end of 1992.

Then Parrino started talking to Moore about acquiring a 1933 Double Eagle. From the first time he mentioned the coin, at that 1993 convention in Baltimore, Moore believed that Parrino was trying to entrap him and Remmel in an illicit purchase—somehow scheming, in ways Moore couldn't even explain, to force them to sell Groendyke's collection to him. "He was trying to set us up by getting us this coin," Moore insisted. "He was trying to set us up to get our whole set."[7]

Every time Parrino mentioned the 1933 Saint at coin shows in 1993 and 1994, Moore became more certain he was plotting something, maybe blackmail. Moore's resentment built until finally, sometime in 1995, he made his first attempt to ruin Jay Parrino. According to Moore, he was contacted by Internal Revenue Service agents who were conducting an audit of Parrino and had seen Moore's name in Parrino's records.[8] Moore gave the agents his paperwork on the purchases he'd made from Parrino. He also told them about his suspicion that Parrino was connected to organized crime. The IRS auditors referred Moore to Colin Scott, an FBI agent in Kansas City. Moore called the agent, and kept calling him regularly, even after Scott was transferred to Branson, Missouri.[9] To Moore's frustration, Scott never seemed interested in opening an investigation based on his allegations of Parrino's money laundering.

•   •   •

BUT THEN fate—in the golden shape of the 1933 Double Eagle—intervened. In December 1995, Jay Parrino called to offer Moore Stephen Fenton's coin, not a hypothetical specimen to speculate about at coin shows, but a genuine 1933 Double Eagle. "Are you interested?" Parrino asked. "I might be," Moore said, calculating his revenge on Parrino before he even hung up the phone.

Moore called Agent Scott, who brushed him off again. This time, though, Moore didn't give up. He called a friend in Amarillo, a retired FBI agent working as an investigator for the district attorney of Randall County, Texas. Moore had come to know the agent in the 1970s through undercover work he'd done for law enforcement. (In Moore's telling, he starred as the ice-blooded hero of sting operations for the FBI that involved "everything from turning in murderers to setting up a [candidate running to become] a U.S. Senator." When I asked his friend, the retired agent, about Moore's account, he laughed. "He's done work for me," the agent said. "He's provided information in a few cases, one I considered real important. [But] I won't say he's done a buy [undercover]. He hasn't. He's provided information.")[10] Moore told his FBI friend about Parrino and the illegal 1933 Double Eagle. The retired agent didn't know anything about coins, but he had received enough good information from Moore to trust Moore's judgment. So he, in turn, called a friend in Lubbock, a Secret Service agent with whom he had worked on a few cases.

R. David Freriks, the agent in charge of the two-man Secret Service office in Lubbock, Texas, was the next unlikely addition to the list of characters in the 1933 Double Eagle story. Freriks had spent most of his long Secret Service career far from the glory of the White House detail, working in outposts such as Indianapolis and Grand Rapids, with only a short stretch in the intelligence unit in Washington in the 1960s. For almost twenty years, Freriks had been stationed in Lubbock, covering the northern third of Texas—the gritty, small-town part of the state. But Lubbock suited Freriks just fine. An imposing, sandy-haired six-footer, he worked mostly on the usual run of Secret Service cases: counterfeiting, stolen government checks, bank and credit-card fraud. Occasionally he got an assignment that demanded more creativity, such as the months he spent monitoring an inchoate militia movement in Snyder, Texas. Those were his favorite kinds of cases. Freriks once cracked a ring that was counterfeiting Krugerrands and then laundering them with the cooperation of a bank president who accepted the fake coins as collateral for loans. Another case involved a Palestinian caught writing bad checks; Freriks traced him back through sixteen years of forgeries. "In thirty-two years I never lost a case," Freriks said. "I had a knack for taking a case nobody else was interested in and turning it into something."[11]

Freriks was seven months from retirement on December 8, 1995, when Moore's friend, the retired FBI agent, called to tell him about Jack Moore and the 1933 Double Eagle. Freriks had never heard of the coin, but he trusted his buddy from the FBI. "If he said it was something," Freriks said, "I took his word for it." Besides, this was the kind of case Freriks looked for, the kind other agents might turn down but that he could make something of. So right after talking to the retired FBI agent, Freriks called Jack Moore and set up a meeting with him for later that day. No time like now, he figured. He got in his car and drove 120 miles to Amarillo, pulling up at lunchtime at the place Moore had chosen, the Santa Fe Restaurant & Bar on 34th Street.

Moore was waiting for the agent in the parking lot, arms full of reference materials that mentioned the 1933 Double Eagle. The two went inside and took a booth in the back. Moore started talking. He told Freriks about Jay Parrino, about how Parrino was always trying to get him to buy this coin, the 1933 Double Eagle. "What's so bad about the coin?" Freriks asked. Moore showed him David Akers's book about double eagles and told him how the 1933 coins had been confiscated and melted down by the Secret Service back in the 1940s and 1950s. As Moore rattled on, Freriks scribbled notes in his spiky handwriting. "US $20 St. Gaudens gold 1933," he wrote. "Made and destroyed. 8–12 got out. USSS seized all but four." The coins were illegal to own, Moore told Freriks, but this dealer, Parrino, claimed he had one lined up for Moore to buy.

"He's trying to set me up," Moore told the agent. Parrino was a Mafia henchman, Moore said. He'd appeared out of nowhere in the 1980s and begun spending millions on coins—laundering money, Moore told Freriks, for organized crime. Freriks kept writing. This was a new world for him. "A guy connected with OC in KC travels to coin shows," he wrote. "Wanting to sell above coin for $1.5 million."

Freriks wasn't sure what to make of Jack Moore's bizarre story, but he was more impressed with Moore than he'd expected to be. He'd met a few coin dealers on the job, and he didn't think much of the trade. "Flat-out shady," was how he regarded the other coin dealers he knew, but Moore didn't seem shady to Freriks. He seemed like an expert, extremely knowledgeable about both the 1933 Double Eagle and the workings of the coin business. Moore's description of Parrino also tantalized Freriks, who wondered fleetingly if Parrino might be enrolled in the federal witness-protection program.[12] Parrino sounded like a target worth pursuing. If what Moore was saying was true and Parrino really did have a 1933 Double Eagle, at the very least he was in possession of property stolen from the United States. And even if the coin was a fake, Parrino was culpable for dealing with counterfeit goods.

Three days after that first meeting, Freriks returned to Amarillo for another lunch with Moore, this time at Dyer's Barbecue. He had good news. "We want you to work for us," Freriks told Moore. He assigned Moore a confidential informant number, 324–15, authorized him to offer Parrino $750,000 for the 1933 Double Eagle, and instructed him to start taping his calls with the Kansas City coin dealer. Moore was to set up a deal to buy the 1933 Double Eagle. He had to insist on doing the deal in the United States, so the Secret Service would have jurisdiction to arrest Parrino. "Otherwise," Freriks told Moore, "conduct the transaction like coin dealers do. Do what you need to do to get the deal done."

IN THE three days between his meetings with Moore, Freriks had obtained permission from the Secret Service chain of command to conduct the undercover 1933 Double Eagle investigation, first from his supervisor in Dallas, then from Washington. Headquarters was admittedly perplexed by the case. When Freriks called Washington, he was transferred to three different divisions as the Secret Service brass tried to figure out where this oddball of an investigation belonged. Finally, Freriks ended up on the phone with Agent Richard Ensminger of the Special Investigations Division, a short, square man known as "Rock."

"Okay, why are we doing this?" Ensminger asked.

"It's a stolen coin," Freriks said, and launched into the story of Jay Parrino and the 1933 Double Eagle, as he'd heard it from Moore. He played up Moore's assertions of Parrino's Mafia ties and his supposed money-laundering operation.

Ensminger was hooked, agreeing with Freriks that Parrino sounded like a suspicious character.[13] The Washington agent told Freriks to proceed with the 1933 Double Eagle investigation—Ensminger would get authorization from higher up—and to check with other law-enforcement agencies about Parrino. Freriks made inquiries in Kansas City. The FBI's Kansas City Strike Force, Freriks learned, had once investigated Parrino in connection with some stolen coins in the 1970s but had determined that Parrino was not connected to the stolen coins or to organized crime. Nor was Parrino known to the Kansas City Police Department. There was no evidence, in other words, to support Jack Moore's tales of Parrino's underworld operation.

But by the time Freriks learned of Parrino's clean record, Moore had already begun bringing in tapes that, in Freriks's view, justified the continuation of the 1933 Double Eagle case. Moore recorded his calls with his own equipment, using a suction cup and a microcassette recorder. Freriks provided the cassettes. After every taped conversation with Parrino, Moore would call Freriks, who would drive to Amarillo and meet with Moore in a hotel or restaurant for a debriefing.

In almost all of Parrino's discussions with Moore, Parrino said something that Freriks considered incriminating. On December 15, for instance, Parrino noted that the seller wanted to do the deal in Europe because, "It is okay over there, but it's not okay over here." That sounded to Freriks like a man planning an illegitimate sale. To keep Parrino talking, Freriks kept authorizing Moore to raise the price Moore told Parrino his client would pay for the 1933 Double Eagle— first to $950,000, then to Parrino's asking price of $1.5 million.

In January 1996, the Secret Service's 1933 Double Eagle investigation expanded to Florida. Moore had told Freriks that he and Parrino planned to finalize the details of their deal in person at the big coin show in Orlando right after New Year's. Moore wanted to wear a wiretap to the meeting, which would take place at the show. Freriks called the Orlando Secret Service branch and made the arrangements. On January 3, Moore arrived in Orlando, a few days before the coin show was to start. He went to the Secret Service field office, where an agent named John McKenna fitted him with the wiretap and showed him how to turn it on and off. Moore practiced a few times, then assured McKenna he'd be fine.

Two days later, at about five-thirty in the afternoon, Moore met McKenna at their designated rendezvous in the parking lot of the Orange County Convention Center. He handed the agent his tape-recording equipment and climbed into the backseat of McKenna's car for debriefing. As they drove around the parking lot, Moore told McKenna that Parrino had just dug himself a deeper hole than ever. He'd taped Parrino saying that he was going to write a falsified receipt for the 1933 Double Eagle, and admitting that the coin would have to be smuggled into the country in a roll of common-date Saints or in a type set with a fake date. Moore hadn't been able to coax Parrino into a crystal-clear admission that he planned to break the law by brokering the coin, but Parrino's comments were only an inferential step away.

Dave Freriks was so confident that Moore had caught Parrino incriminating himself in Orlando that later in January, when Moore and Parrino were stuck in the seemingly interminable negotiations over exactly where and when to do the deal for the 1933 Double Eagle, Freriks told Moore he didn't need to keep taping. The Secret Service had what it needed to make a case against Parrino.

MOORE'S COIN-DEALING partner, Kent Remmel, had been with him in Orlando when Moore sidled up to Jay Parrino to talk about the 1933 Double Eagle. Remmel knew what Moore was up to and wanted nothing to do with it. Remmel could see the kick Moore got from his cloak-and-dagger adventures—he was also in the backseat of Agent John McKenna's car while Moore fed the Secret Service highlights from the Parrino tape—but he didn't understand what Moore thought he would accomplish. "It will ruin your reputation in the coin trade," Remmel warned. Side deals and secrets are the essence of coin dealing. No one, not even Jay Parrino's enemies, was going to thank Moore for inviting the Secret Service to scrutinize the business.

"I know what I'm doing," Moore told Remmel. "I'm going to make a lot of money off this deal." Remmel thought that Moore was just talking big, that this was another one of his partner's grandiose schemes. He'd heard Moore talking to Parrino in Orlando about his cut of the 1933 Double Eagle money, but Remmel thought Moore was playing his undercover role. The Secret Service, Remmel figured, wouldn't let Moore keep a commission on a coin transaction that was really a sting operation. Would it?

Jack Moore believed it would—but only if the Secret Service didn't realize that his payment from Parrino *was* a commission on the 1933 Double Eagle deal. Money had been a sore point for Moore from the beginning of the 1933 Double Eagle operation. He first started nudging Freriks about it after their second or third meeting in Amarillo. Moore wanted the Secret Service to pay him $75,000 for setting up this deal, he told Freriks. Freriks laughed. Government informants didn't get that kind of money, he said. Three thousand was more like it. Moore argued. Freriks finally said that he might be able to get Moore a little more money, but it would be on the order of $5,000—$7,500 at the outside. Seventy-five thousand just wasn't going to happen.

Moore kept scheming. Parrino had said in an early phone conversation that he was willing to pay Moore a commission on the 1933 Double Eagle deal. "What if the money came through Parrino?" Moore asked Freriks on Friday, January 12, when he was in Lubbock to go over the Orlando tapes with Freriks. The Secret Service wouldn't have to pay Moore directly, Moore explained. Instead, the government could offer to pay Parrino extra money, more than the $1.5 million asking price for the 1933 Double Eagle. Then Parrino could transfer the difference to Moore.

No way, Freriks said. Totally improper. The agent, disturbed that Moore would even suggest such deception, delivered a lecture to his informant. Freriks couldn't have been more forceful. Moore was just supposed to *act* like he was making a deal with Parrino. He could talk to Parrino about a commission for the sake of realism, but he couldn't actually take money from Parrino for the 1933 Double Eagle deal. That would wreck the case against Parrino. Moreover, if Moore did accept Parrino's money in connection with the 1933 Double Eagle, Freriks said, the service would find out and seize it. Moore, Freriks later reported to his bosses, "was instructed not to offer any more money, not to charge [Parrino] any more for a fee, and that if a deal could not be completed . . . at the Waldorf in NYC, the deal should be terminated."[14]

But Moore saw a crack of opportunity in Freriks's lecture. What if he were to make a *separate* deal with Parrino? What if, he asked Freriks, he made a sale to Parrino that didn't involve the 1933 Double Eagle?

"It's not related to this sale?" Freriks asked.

"No," Moore answered.

"Well, I don't want to get into your business," Freriks said.

As long as the side deal with Parrino had no connection to the 1933 Double Eagle, the agent shrugged, Moore could do whatever he wanted.

Moore stopped giving Freriks recordings of his conversations with Parrino in the middle of January 1996. Once he told the agent that his recorder's batteries had failed. Besides, Freriks had told him that the Secret Service had enough evidence against Parrino. Moore and Parrino were just working on details, Moore said, and Freriks didn't need to hear all that. He'd tell Freriks when everything was in place.

ON JANUARY 23, Moore called Freriks on his cell phone. He was in his truck, he told the agent, in Independence, Missouri. He had just left Jay Parrino's office in the basement of the Mark Twain Bank and was headed back to Texas. He needed to see Freriks right away to tell him what had happened. Moore hadn't taped the meeting, he told Freriks, but he had plenty to show the Secret Service.

The next day, Freriks and Moore met at the Days Inn in Amarillo. First Moore dispensed with the basics. The 1933 Double Eagle deal was all set for the morning of February 8 at the Waldorf in New York. The price was up to $1,650,000—the extra money, Moore said, a sweetener to reassure the seller about coming to the United States.

Then Moore fed Freriks a fantastical tale. Parrino, he told the agent, was even more crooked than Moore had imagined. He had all kinds of safe-deposit boxes stuffed full of gold ingots, gold coins, and cash he was sheltering from the IRS—$25 or $30 million worth, Moore claimed. Parrino was also hiding a stash of stolen and illegally held rare coins, Moore told Freriks. He had seen the list on Parrino's computer, where it was accessible only with a secret code.

Parrino, Moore claimed, had actually asked him to run money to Las Vegas for him, laundering $10 or $15 million at the casinos every three months. Moore said that Parrino had promised to pay him $100,000 a trip because the job was so dangerous; according to Moore, Parrino's last bagman had been murdered. Then Moore tossed in one more irresistible detail. Parrino, he said, was also running cash to antigovernment militia and tax-protest groups in Kansas and elsewhere. "Parrino," Moore told Freriks, "intended to funnel money into these groups as he strongly believed in their objectives."[15]

As evidence of Parrino's cache of suspect coins, Moore showed Freriks the invoice he'd written for Parrino's rare Carson City twenty-cent piece; Parrino, he claimed, had asked him to write the false invoice to give Parrino cover on how he'd obtained the coin. Moore showed the agent the two $25,000 checks Parrino had written. And to support his account of safe-deposit boxes stuffed with hidden money, Moore also displayed the $70,000 in cash and gold Krugerrands that Parrino had given him.

But Moore assured the Secret Service agent that all the money Parrino had paid him was unrelated to the 1933 Double Eagle sale. It wasn't a commission, he told Freriks. He'd made a side deal with Parrino, a deal involving another coin, not the 1933 Saint.

In fact, Moore continued as Freriks photographed the money and checks from Parrino, Moore had a request to make of the Secret Service. During the sting at the Waldorf, Parrino was going to hand Moore a coin, a high-relief 1907 Saint, and an invoice. That coin,

Moore told Freriks, was part of his side deal with Parrino. Before the Secret Service arrested Parrino, Moore needed to get that high-relief 1907 Saint back from Parrino.

Freriks said he'd take care of it, and he was as good as his word. "BEFORE THE ARREST," he later informed New York Agent Don Dillard, who was finalizing plans for the sting, "[Moore] is to retrieve from Parrino an original coin and its accompanying invoice."

When he said goodbye to Freriks at the Days Inn on January 24, 1996, Jack Moore was sure he'd pulled off the greatest deal of his life. Jay Parrino, who believed he was holding John Groendyke's 1907 high-relief Saint as collateral on the commission he'd paid Moore for the 1933 Double Eagle sale, was going to return the 1907 coin to Moore. The Secret Service, which believed that the 1907 coin had nothing to do with the 1933 Saint, would never know that Parrino's payment to Moore was in fact a commission on the 1933 Double Eagle deal. John Groendyke wouldn't ever realize that Moore had used his 1907 Saint as collateral, Jay Parrino would be under arrest, and Moore would be a hero—a hero richer by a well-earned $150,000. The 1933 Double Eagle seemed like the best thing that had ever happened to Jack Moore.

Chapter Twelve

The Sting

In all the hours he spent with Jack Moore, Dave Freriks was never sure he really understood why Moore had become a government informant. Moore talked a lot about Jay Parrino being a black mark on the coin business, but Freriks had never known small-time coin dealers like Moore to be overly scrupulous about the integrity of their profession. Moore also told Freriks that Parrino had once cheated him out of a $5,000 commission, an explanation Freriks found somewhat more credible. Occasionally Moore would drop some hint about trouble at home, usually when he was trying to persuade Freriks to request more money for him from the Secret Service. Moore's wife, Marty, had begun to suffer one medical crisis after another, and Moore, who had retired from Groendyke Transport in 1994, worried about doctor and hospital bills. Freriks put in Moore's request for a higher confidential-informant payment but otherwise kept his distance. Moore's motives didn't matter to him. "I never got to know Jack that well," he said. "I'm not Oprah. I don't care about problems in his life unless it's going to affect the case."

And on the case, Moore was solid. When Freriks reviewed the tapes of Moore's conversations with Parrino, the burly agent shook his head in admiration. Moore was so smooth, so calm. It was as if Moore actually believed he was making a deal for the 1933 Double Eagle, not just playacting for the government.

Even on the trip to New York for his final performance as an undercover operative, Moore seemed to Freriks to show no nervousness. On Tuesday, February 6, 1996, Moore drove from Amarillo down to Freriks's headquarters in Lubbock. Together they went to the Lubbock airport and boarded a plane for Dallas, then flew on to New York. It was a long day of enforced proximity. Mostly Moore and Freriks read and chatted about nothing—the weather, traveling, New York. They talked only briefly about what would happen on February 8. Moore reminded Freriks that he needed to complete his side deal before agents arrested Parrino. He also said he'd need the Secret Service's protection from Parrino afterward. Parrino was connected, Moore insisted to Freriks. After he was arrested, he might be willing to give up all kinds of stuff, not just talk about the 1933 Double Eagle.

New York Secret Service Agent Don Dillard met Moore and Freriks at the airport and drove them to their hotel in Manhattan. They were not staying at the Waldorf. There was a $500-a-night Waldorf suite reserved in Moore's name, but it was for the sting. Moore and Freriks would be staying a few blocks away at the Kimberly Suites, where the room rate was an un-Waldorfian $140 a night. Dillard, a bright young agent barely thirty years old, told Moore and Freriks that he'd be back in the morning to drive them to the big planning meeting downtown at the Secret Service offices. Then he left them. On the loose in New York, Freriks and Moore blew their $38 meal per diem on dinner at a midtown steak house.

THE NEXT day at the planning session, Moore realized just how important the Secret Service considered the case of the 1933 Double Eagle to be. Until that morning, he'd worked only with Freriks and the Florida agents who had helped him tape Parrino at the Orlando coin convention. Now, seated at the Bank Fraud Division conference table on the tenth floor of Seven World Trade Center, he saw that an entire platoon of Secret Service agents had been pulled deep into the coin investigation. He and Freriks met Margaret Flanagan, head of the Asset Forfeiture Division in New York and the first New York agent Freriks had consulted about transacting the 1933 Double Eagle deal in Manhattan. Flanagan had handed the case down to Don Dillard, who was also at the table. Dillard was the New York case agent, responsible for making arrangements at the Waldorf. In the weeks of uncertainty over the specifics of the deal, Dillard had conferred repeatedly with Freriks and with Rock Ensminger, another of the Secret Service agents at the planning session on February 7.

Ensminger was the Washington-based special investigations agent who had first given Freriks permission to proceed with the 1933 Double Eagle investigation. In the beginning, Ensminger had approved the case because he liked Parrino as a target,[1] but he had since been captivated by the history of the coin. Ensminger had visited the National Archives with Secret Service historian Michael Sampson and lawyers from the Mint, locating the records of the agency's 1944 investigation and the litigation that followed. He had read the old Treasury Department legal opinion confirming that private ownership of the 1933 Double Eagle was unlawful. He'd visited the Smithsonian to examine the museum's two 1933 Double Eagles. Ensminger knew more about the coin than anyone else in the Secret Service. In the sting the next day, an agent named Charles Haas was slated to play Moore's client, mostly because the buyer was supposed to be a rich Texan and Haas looked and sounded the part. Ensminger would act as the buyer's coin expert because he *was* an expert—at least on the subject of the 1933 Double Eagle.

Before the agents reviewed with Moore and Freriks the details of how the sting would proceed, Don Dillard was anxious to quiz Jack Moore, the informant on whom the entire operation depended. Dillard was about to commit a dozen members of the Secret Service— undercover operatives Haas and Ensminger, technical experts who'd set up the video surveillance, arresting agents who'd rush into the hotel room to handcuff Parrino and the seller—to the 1933 Double Eagle sting. He wanted to assure himself that Moore was trustworthy enough to justify the risk the Secret Service was taking. "How were you originally approached by Parrino?" Dillard asked. "What made you take this information to the authorities?"

Moore told Dillard what he'd already told Freriks so many times. Parrino had first spoken to him about the 1933 Double Eagle after Moore finished assembling John Groendyke's Saints set. Moore didn't trust Parrino, whom he considered a smirch on the coin business, so he took the matter to the government. As usual, Moore was smooth and convincing. He'd be fine, he told the agents. He could do this, he said, and Dillard believed him.

For the next few hours, the New York agent briefed the team. Everyone would report to the Waldorf at seven-thirty the next morning, February 8. The sting would take place in Room 22K of the Waldorf Towers section of the hotel. Agents would be stationed in the adjoining suite, 22K2, watching and listening to what was happening next door through audio and video surveillance. Haas and Ensminger, playing the buyer and the buyer's expert, would be stationed in a third room, so that when Moore called them on the phone from 22K, Parrino and the seller wouldn't hear ringing in the adjacent room.

Moore would at first be alone in the "sting suite" to greet Parrino and the as-yet-unknown seller. He would evaluate the coin. If Parrino and the seller had a real 1933 Double Eagle, Moore was to telephone Haas and Ensminger and say, "It's here." If the coin was a fake, he was to say, "I've got something for you." And if something was wrong, Dillard told him, Moore was to say, "We've got a problem."

After receiving Moore's call, Haas and Ensminger would enter the sting suite. Ensminger, if possible, was surreptitiously to slip the dead bolt so the door would remain slightly ajar. Arresting agents, known as takedown teams, would assemble silently in the hallway outside the door, armed and ready to burst in on cue. Ensminger would look over the coin, and once he'd concluded it was time to make the arrest, he'd say, "My work is done." He'd go to the door as if to leave the room, but instead of exiting, he'd open the door to admit the takedown teams.

Arresting agents were to use the service elevators to take Parrino and the seller to 49th Street, where Secret Service transport cars would be waiting.

"Keep in mind," Dillard told everyone at the end of the long February 7 meeting, "Haas, Moore, and possibly Ensminger are in the room. Watch where you point your weapon."

THURSDAY, FEBRUARY 8, the day of the sting, was cold and crisp in New York. At the Kimberly Suites, Moore and Freriks woke up before sunrise, ate a quick breakfast, and walked the three blocks to the Waldorf. Dillard, Haas, Ensminger, and the takedown teams were already massed in the lobby. Dillard asked Moore to wait outside for a few minutes while he and the agents went up to the sting suite to make sure that the surveillance work was underway. Moore left the hotel and stomped around impatiently in front of St. Bartholomew's, the brick-and-limestone church on 50th Street, scowling at a tourist—or maybe, he fumed, an agent sent to babysit him—who kept bumping into his briefcase. This was supposed to be his show, Moore thought. He was the one risking his life. So why was he out here in the cold, waiting?

Finally, Freriks retrieved Moore and took him up to the sting suite, a spacious corner room with a separate sitting area. Since the suite was supposed to look as though it was Moore's, agents had fetched Moore's suitcase from the Kimberly, and now some of his clothes were strewn across the foot of the bed, which was mussed to appear that Moore had slept in it. Moore calmed down when he saw his jeans and shirts on the bed; staging the room with his clothing had been his idea, and he felt vindicated to see that the Secret Service had accepted his suggestion.

The technical squad had finished wiring the room, and Dillard showed Moore where the main microphone was located, in the base of a table lamp in the sitting area. The video camera was hidden in a clock radio. Moore and Freriks rehearsed the sting scenario, moving furniture around so that Moore, without maneuvering unnaturally, could keep the action within the range of the microphone and the camera. Next door, Secret Service technical experts ran sound and video checks.

At about nine o'clock, Moore's cell phone rang. It was Parrino, who said the seller was on his way to the Waldorf. What was Moore's room number? "I'm in twenty-two K," Moore said. Ten minutes later, Parrino called again. "I'm down here in the lobby," he said. "The seller's here. Are you ready?"

"I'm ready," Moore said, as Freriks and Dillard slipped out of the room to take their places next door. "Come on up."

JAY PARRINO was more excited about the 1933 Double Eagle deal than he liked to admit. He'd told Jack Moore that he'd seen other 1933 Saints—in particular, a coin that he said belonged to a collector in New Jersey. But that was just Parrino braggadocio. He'd really never seen a 1933 Double Eagle, and even after years of buying and selling great rarities, Parrino was still passionate enough about coins to be a little breathless at the prospect of holding a 1933 Saint—on top of the $600,000 he was going to clear in a deal in which he hadn't even had to risk any of his own money. This whole trip to New York felt celebratory to Parrino. He'd been bumped up to first class on the flight out—a good omen—and the Waldorf, where he was staying for the first time, was every bit as deluxe as he'd hoped. The hotel was a kick. Who'd have guessed they'd have high-tech surveillance equipment for sale at the Waldorf-Astoria?

More important, the deal so far was running as smoothly as a mint production line. Stephen Fenton had turned up in the lobby just as he was supposed to do. He'd brought along his cousin, Barry Castelete, but that wasn't a problem. Fenton said he had the coin, and that was all that really mattered to Parrino. And Moore said his buyer was ready to go. "It's going to be a wonderful deal," Parrino told Fenton as he, Fenton, and Castelete headed for the bank of elevators that would take them to the twenty-second floor of the Waldorf Towers.

"Yes, it is," Fenton replied. The elevator doors closed.

MOMENTS LATER, Parrino knocked at the door of Room 22K. Moore opened it. "Hey, Jack," Parrino said.

"Hey, Jay," Moore answered. He turned to Fenton and Castelete and stuck out his hand. "Nice to meet you. How are you guys?" He didn't ask their names. Parrino had told him the seller didn't want to reveal his identity.

Moore was wearing fancy ostrich-skin boots, pressed jeans, and a Western-style shirt. Fenton couldn't take his eyes off Moore's belt buckle, which bore a National Rifle Association insignia that was as big as two fists. This fellow really is a Texan, Fenton thought.

Moore ushered the three men over to a table by the window in the sitting area, where he had set up an electronic scale next to the lamp. "Those are the scales, and the real one weighs 33.4 [grams]," Moore said. He held up a 1908 Saint he'd brought to check the scale.

"It's funny you say the real one," Fenton said, reaching into his pocket. He held up a common-date Saint-Gaudens double eagle. "You brought an extra one, too?" Moore said. "Yeah, just in case," Fenton answered. Everyone laughed.

THE AGENTS next door weren't laughing. They had been expecting only Parrino and a seller to come to the sting suite. Who was the third guy? Dave Freriks squinted at the video monitor. There was something black stuffed in the third guy's back pocket. Three agents pointed to the screen at the same instant. "Damn," Freriks said. "Is that a gun?" The agents looked at each other nervously.

Freriks kept watching as Moore walked over to the table with the scale and the microphone-implanted lamp. Maybe it wasn't a gun. Moore didn't seem worried. Freriks was. He felt a lot of pressure to see this operation come off. He'd taken Moore's word about the coin, and had convinced the Secret Service to pour all these resources into the sting. On the video monitor, Moore appeared to be unimaginably cool, but Freriks wasn't going to relax until he saw the 1933 Double Eagle on the video monitor.

There it was. Freriks watched the seller take a gold coin out of his shirt pocket and hand it to Parrino. "Well, this sure is a pleasure," Freriks heard Parrino say as the dealer held the coin up to his glasses. "I thought I'd handled everything."

Freriks nodded to the other agents. Parrino thought the coin was real. They had a real 1933 Double Eagle in the room next door.

•   •   •

JACK MOORE had never seen Parrino so edgy. First he had dropped one of the common-date Saints on Moore's scale; then, when the seller took the 1933 Double Eagle out of his shirt pocket, Parrino fumbled to pull it out of its plastic envelope. What was bothering him? Moore attempted a joke. "Well, it's a nice coin but it's not worth over $500," he teased when Parrino handed him the 1933 Saint. Parrino seemed to loosen up a little. The seller, meanwhile, retreated to a spot near the armoire, against the wall. Moore understood what he was doing; the seller considered Moore to be Parrino's buyer, so he was going to let Parrino handle things from here. Standard procedure, Moore thought. Everything was going the way it should.

Then, out of the blue, Parrino said, "They have a spy shop downstairs."

Spy shop? Moore told himself to stay calm. "What do you mean?" he said. "Where you can buy spy stuff?"

"Yeah, right in the lobby," Parrino said. "I mean, you should see it. They have a phone, and if someone lies on the phone it will tell you."

What was going on? Moore's head whirled. Was Parrino taping him? Had he been recording their phone conversations? Did Parrino know Moore was setting him up? No, Moore reassured himself. He was the government informant. If Parrino had somehow found out about the sting, he would never have come up to the room with the seller and the 1933 Double Eagle. This spy-shop talk must be just a weird coincidence. Moore fussed with the scale to buy himself a couple of seconds. "Lay it there on the scale," he told Parrino.

NEXT DOOR on the video monitor, Freriks saw Parrino place the 1933 Double Eagle on the scale and then show Moore yet another Saint-Gaudens double eagle. How many gold coins were in that room, anyway? Freriks heard Parrino talking about "proof twenty," words that meant nothing to the agent until he realized that Parrino was holding the other coin Moore had told him about—the high-relief 1907 coin for which Moore and Parrino had negotiated a separate deal. Well, Moore must be glad Parrino brought it, Freriks thought.

The 1933 Double Eagle hit the right numbers on the scale. "You can make your call," Parrino said, picking up the legendary coin. "I'm just soaking this in."

Freriks watched as Moore made the crucial phone call to Haas and Ensminger. "You all just might as well come up," Moore said into the phone. "It's here and it's real." Freriks sighed with relief. Damned if Jack Moore hadn't pulled it off.

Freriks kept staring at the monitor, waiting for Haas and Ensminger to show up. Moore seemed almost to be showing off now, sharing at Parrino's expense a private joke with Freriks and the other Secret Service agents watching next door. Moore teased Parrino about the coin expert who was supposed to come in and evaluate the 1933 Double Eagle, the part Rock Ensminger was playing. "I want to prove [something] to the son of a bitch," Moore said. "This guy that you are going to meet is really an eccentric guy, so don't pay any attention to him. I just met this coin expert last night. He's a Yankee." Moore riffed about the "five grand" the coin expert was going to pay him because he'd never seen a 1907 proof high-relief Saint. Just chatter, Freriks thought. Where were Haas and Ensminger?

But Moore wasn't done with Parrino yet. Freriks sat up straight when Moore asked Parrino a question. "If we need to do this," Freriks heard him say, watching Moore gesture at the 1933 Double Eagle, "can't we do the deal that you were talking about? Make [the 1933 Double Eagle] legal?"

"Well, that's a very interesting thing," replied Parrino, who had once told Moore that it might be possible to remove legal barriers to ownership of the 1933 Saint. Parrino glanced at the seller leaning against the wall. "What would you feel would happen to the value of this if it was legalized? I have someone who could do this for $50,000."

"Double," Freriks heard the seller say.

In Room 22K2, Freriks and Dillard looked at each other and grinned. Moore was unbelievable. He'd gotten Parrino to admit the coin was illegal—and the seller, too, whoever he was. Prosecutors couldn't ask for a better piece of tape than the one Jack Moore had just managed to produce. "Parrino's history," Freriks whispered. Come on, Rock, he thought to himself; let's wrap this up. Moore had been in there with Parrino and the seller for only about five minutes, but to Freriks it felt like much, much longer.

NEXT DOOR, Moore still had one last bit of business to transact. "I talked to Marty," he told Parrino. "She said she didn't get the little package. You send it off?" The package that Parrino had promised to send to Moore's home was supposed to contain the rest of Parrino's payment to Moore—his commission on the 1933 Double Eagle deal.

"You'll have it today," Parrino said. "[My wife] mailed it out last night."

As Haas and Ensminger entered the room, Moore turned his back to the camera, momentarily blocking the picture of Parrino handing him John Groendyke's 1907 high-relief Saint. Then Moore moved out of the way again.

Ensminger and Haas played their parts quickly and efficiently. Ensminger took out a loupe to examine the 1933 Double Eagle, bantering with Moore. "You didn't think a country boy like me could have one," Moore taunted him. "I didn't think you had that kind of wood," Ensminger replied.

In a matter of moments, Ensminger was satisfied. "I'm happy," he said to Haas.

"Then I'm happy," Haas said. He picked up the telephone, pretending to initiate a wire transfer to Parrino's bank account.

"Well then, I'm going down to the lobby," said Ensminger, walking to the door. "Good luck, Jack. See you again."

SOMETHING IS not right here, Stephen Fenton thought to himself as the buyer's coin expert began his exit. That guy is too nervous. When the expert—if that's who he really was—had picked up the 1933 Double Eagle, Fenton had started to say, "It's a fantastic piece." Then he noticed the supposed expert's hand trembling. A real coin dealer wouldn't be shaking, Fenton thought. Something is about to happen. This is a setup. I'm going to be robbed.

The next thing Fenton knew, the hotel room door banged open and eight people wearing body armor rushed in, pointing guns at him, his cousin, Parrino, Moore, and Haas. "What is this?" Castelete demanded. "Don't say anything," Fenton instructed. He felt as if he were floating, as if he were on top of the armoire looking down at what was happening. He couldn't believe how relaxed he was—nor that he was detached enough to notice how relaxed he was.

"Shut up," one of the gunmen shouted. "Don't say another word. You're all under arrest." In what seemed like an instant, all of them—Fenton, his cousin, Parrino, Moore, and Haas—were handcuffed and ordered to lie down on the floor. "We're from the United States Secret Service," one of the agents said. "We're taking you downtown."

UNTIL THAT moment, Jay Parrino thought someone was playing a joke, and not a funny one. Guys in body armor? With guns drawn? This was a coin deal, for god's sake, not a drug sale. But as soon as he heard the words, "You're all under arrest," Parrino knew: Jack Moore had done this. He didn't know how or why, but he was sure Moore was responsible.

One at a time, each flanked by a pair of Secret Service agents, Fenton and Castelete—who, when agents frisked him, turned out to have only his black knit cap, not a gun, in his back pocket—were escorted out of Room 22K and into the service elevator. Next was Parrino. "Don't you tell them anything," he said to Moore, who was still lying on the floor in handcuffs, as agents pushed him out of the room.

With overcoats draped over their handcuffs, Fenton, Castelete, and Parrino were placed in separate cars and driven downtown to the Secret Service offices.

BACK IN the sting suite at the Waldorf, agents celebrated. A petite female agent had been assigned to "arrest" the strapping Haas, and she sat on the floor laughing with him. Dave Freriks unlocked Moore's handcuffs and pumped his hand in congratulations. "Pat yourself on the back, Jack," Freriks said. "Man, you did a good job." Dillard retrieved the 1933 Double Eagle from the scale, and he, Freriks, Moore, Haas, and Ensminger passed it around, carefully. For fifty years, this coin had eluded the Secret Service. It wasn't getting away now, and neither was Parrino.

Jack Moore rode down to Seven World Trade Center with Freriks and Dillard in Dillard's Chevy Suburban. He clutched the 1933 Double Eagle the whole way.

Chapter Thirteen

"I Was Just Selling a Coin"

THERE IS NO CONVENTIONAL cosmology in the story of the 1933 Double Eagle, no easily divided list of heroes and villains. Gray is the predominant color of the rare-coin world, and the people whose lives changed because of the 1933 Double Eagle all lived in that gray haze in which fate has little to do with morality. Consider the example of Israel Swift and George McCann, the original confederates, according to the Secret Service, in the theft and sale of the coins. Swift's business began to flower at precisely the time he started selling those illicit 1933 Double Eagles. He died a rich old paragon of respectability; McCann, on the other hand, lost his money, his job at the U.S. Mint, and his freedom, ending up as a lonely office clerk with a criminal record. The same divergence of destiny was eventually true of Jack Moore, Jay Parrino, and Stephen Fenton, though it wasn't immediately apparent on February 8, 1996.

Jack Moore was received at the Secret Service headquarters at Seven World Trade Center with handshakes and congratulations. Twenty agents lined up to greet him and Freriks. Even Mary Jo White, the chief federal prosecutor in Manhattan, was on hand to thank Moore for a job well done. Don Dillard gave Moore the honor of placing the seized 1933 Double Eagle in a Secret Service safe, and then Moore and Freriks retreated into an interview room, out of sight of Parrino and Fenton, for Moore's debriefing. It was really more of a revel than an interview, an abbreviated session because Moore and Freriks had to get to the airport. They flew home to Texas later that afternoon, exhausted but elated. Throughout the trip, Moore could not stop talking about his performance in the hotel room. Freriks grew tired of hearing him, but the agent had to give Moore his due. He had been brilliant.

"What about my informant fee?" Moore said on the plane ride to Lubbock.

"We'll get you the $7,500," Freriks promised.

"And the protection?" Moore asked.

"I'll call the police department in Amarillo and make sure they post guards at your house," Freriks said.

JAY PARRINO spent much of the day in a holding cell at Seven World Trade Center, stunned and horrified at his arrest. In the afternoon, two agents, William Whiteside and Scott Alswang, pulled him out of the cell for questioning. They prodded Parrino to talk, baiting him with Jack Moore's wild accounts of safe-deposit boxes full of cash, connections in Las Vegas, and suitcases of illicit coins smuggled to Europe. "We know all about it," the agents said to Parrino. "It will be a lot easier for you if you tell us now."[1]

Parrino was still paralyzed with disbelief. "I was just selling a coin," he told the agents, again and again. "I'm just a coin dealer."

After what felt like hours of questioning, Parrino agreed to write a statement. He admitted nothing about Jack Moore's outlandish allegations, describing only his involvement with the 1933 Double Eagle: Moore's pestering over the years, the call from Mark Emory about Fenton's coin, the negotiations with Moore and Fenton. "I knew of the controversy with the coin," Parrino conceded in his statement, "but really don't know of the particulars. I have never seen one before except in photographs. There was a rumor a few years ago about another one but it was never confirmed. I did not know this was government property, just [that it was] not legal to own one. Again, I never knew why."

Late that evening, Parrino at last called a lawyer, a friend of his in Connecticut named David Krassner. "I'm in jail," Parrino told Krassner.

"Yeah, sure," said Krassner, a coin collector so devoted to Parrino that he once left his law practice to apprentice with the dealer in Kansas City for six months. "What did you do, jaywalk?"

Then Krassner heard someone shout at Parrino, "You have thirty seconds left."

"My God! You really are in jail!" Krassner said. "What's going on?"

Quickly Parrino explained what had happened. He'd just been arraigned before a magistrate, he told Krassner, and his bail was set at $500,000. Krassner needed to arrange for his bail and get him out. Krassner promised he'd take care of it as soon as he could, first thing in the morning.

Parrino was returned to the holding cell. He spent the night lying on a bunk with a roll of toilet paper for a pillow.

FENTON WAS treated a little more gently than Parrino. The two agents assigned to transport him from the Waldorf to the Secret Service offices, Betty Conkling and Timothy Kerrigan, took him directly to an interview room and left him there, alone. Fenton could hear people moving around in adjoining rooms, but he couldn't see what was happening. He sat in the interview room for two hours, confused and disoriented.

Around noon Conkling and Kerrigan returned. "We need a statement from you," they said. "If you just give us a statement, everything will be fine."[2]

"What about my coin?" Fenton asked.

"You can't have it."

Conkling started asking Fenton a lot of questions. Who was he? Was he a coin dealer? Did he own the 1933 Double Eagle or was he representing someone else? Where had he gotten the coin?

Fenton wondered if he should ask for a lawyer, but he figured that would only delay his release. Once he told the agents that he was just a coin dealer, he thought, they'd surely let him go. So he agreed to write a statement answering Conkling's questions.

Fenton's statement, signed that afternoon, was not entirely ingenuous. There was no mention of Andre de Clermont, Khalid Hassan, or King Farouk—just a vague account of an unremarkable coin deal. "Anywhere from five to ten years ago, to the best of my recollection, I purchased a miscellaneous group of gold coins, which could have included hundreds of foreign and British coins," Fenton wrote. "This purchase was made from an individual seller at my store in London. This was a routine transaction, one of possibly dozens made monthly. It was not until after the purchase, upon reviewing the lot of coins, that I realized I had a 1933 $20 gold coin, which I knew to be a better date, an unusual date. Anything in the 1930s is considered unusual."

He had arranged to sell the coin through Jay Parrino, Fenton wrote, without researching whether it was legal in the United States. "As far as I knew, ownership of this coin—1933 $20 gold coin—was no problem in England," he said. "But I was not sure of the ownership restrictions in the United States. I never inquired with anybody about any restrictions, if any. Mr. Parrino never offered to me any information about problems with ownership of this coin in the United States."

By the time Fenton signed his statement, it was dark outside. He was taken to another room for his arraignment before a magistrate judge. The prosecutor from the U.S. Attorney's office, a young woman named Mei Lin Kwan-Gett, told the magistrate about the 1933 Double Eagle's unique history; Fenton, in a fog, heard little of what she said. His attention clicked into focus only when she mentioned the coin's purchase price. Kwan-Gett said that Parrino had arranged to sell the 1933 Double Eagle for $1.5 million.[3] That was a lot of money, Fenton thought, more than he thought the sale price would be. It would have been a nice profit for Parrino. Then he heard another number: $250,000. That was the bail set by the magistrate. Fenton could be released, the judge said, if he promised to return to court with $50,000 in cash—half due within the week, the other half by February 19. In the meantime, Fenton would have to surrender his passport to the Secret Service and would not be permitted to leave New York.

A pair of Secret Service agents arrived to escort Fenton back to his hotel, where he'd left his passport. On the ride uptown to the Hilton, Fenton sat stonefaced, even when the agents tried to talk to him. "Sorry about this," they said. "Guess you never thought things would work out this way." Fenton said nothing.

The agents accompanied Fenton to his room but stopped at the doorsill. "My passport's inside," Fenton said. "You'll have to come in while I get it."

"We'll wait out here," they told him.

When he stepped back out with his passport, Fenton noticed that the agents had their hands on the handles of their guns, as if they half-expected him to emerge with barrels blazing. Fenton gasped, so loudly that his cousin—who had been released earlier that afternoon by the Secret Service after explaining that he wasn't involved in the coin deal—heard the commotion and stepped into the hall from his own room. "What's going on?" Castelete demanded, for the second time that long, long day. "He doesn't have a gun," he snapped at the agents.

Shaking, Fenton handed over his passport and promised he'd return to court with the bail money. The agents left. Fenton's cousin took his arm. "We're getting some dinner," Castelete said.

"You'll have to pay," Fenton said. "They took everything—my money, my credit cards, my wallet. All I have is what I'm wearing." He walked beside his cousin like a zombie. At dinner, he couldn't eat. Afterward they went to the movies. Castelete thought *Get Shorty*, a comedy, might cheer his cousin, but Fenton just stared at the screen seeing nothing.

THE NEXT morning, Fenton took a slip of paper from the pocket of the jacket he'd worn the day before. Written on it was a name—Barry Berke—and a telephone number. Barry Berke was a lawyer, a criminal defense lawyer. Fenton didn't know him, but he'd been recommended by the public defender who had accompanied Fenton to his arraignment the previous day. When the public defender told Fenton he couldn't represent him because Fenton could afford to pay for a lawyer, Fenton had pleaded for help. "I don't know any lawyers in New York," Fenton had said. "I don't know who to call." The public defender said he had a suggestion: a former colleague, a professor of criminal law, Harvard-trained, now working at a big firm. "How old is he?" Fenton had asked, as he wrote down the name and number. "Some old guy?" "No," the public defender had answered. "He's only thirty-two."

Fenton picked up the phone and dialed the number. Okay, Mr. Barry Berke, Fenton thought. Let's see what you have to say. Berke didn't pick up, but Fenton liked what he heard on Berke's answering machine—a strong voice, reassuring, friendly, and confident. He left a message describing his predicament. Berke called right back, inviting Fenton to come to his office on Third Avenue. Fenton grabbed his cousin and went to meet the lawyer. "That was the biggest stroke of luck," he told me years later, "the best thing that could have happened to me."

On the day he met Stephen Fenton, Berke was indeed only thirty-two years old, and just five months into his career as a lawyer at Kramer Levin Naftalis & Frankel. Kramer Levin had a long and impressive history of white-collar criminal defense, but Berke wasn't the typical big-firm New York litigator. He grew up in a small town in Florida. When he enrolled at Duke University, he became the first person in his family to attend college. Berke had a political awakening at Duke when students rallied for the resignation of an administrator accused of racism. For Berke it was a lesson in the power of idealism. Before college, he had always intended to be a corporate lawyer and get rich. After Duke, he headed to Harvard Law School, determined to become a criminal lawyer—not representing people who could pay for his Harvard credentials but helping accused criminals who couldn't afford their own lawyers. He wanted to be a public defender.

Berke stuck to his plan even when everyone he knew tried to talk him out of it. He'd done well at Harvard and had earned a prestigious clerkship with a federal judge after law school. He was tall and handsome, with wavy dark hair and a broad, open face. He could join the litigation department at any big firm he wanted, friends told him, and in a few years move to the U.S. Attorney's office to pick up trial experience and valuable connections as a prosecutor. Then he could go back to private practice. That was the usual résumé of a Manhattan defense lawyer. Berke's idea—to go to work as a public defender in the federal system right after his clerkship—was career suicide.

Berke wasn't dissuaded. He didn't like to sound grandiose about it—he's not much for oratory—but he believed fundamentally in what he was doing. "You're standing between a person and the worst thing that will happen to them in their lives," he said. "You are the gladiator." As a federal public defender in Manhattan, Berke represented everyone from illegal immigrants who didn't speak English to a bond-fund president and a lawyer charged in a fraud case. He was single in those days, with nothing to distract him from his cases, so he logged endless hours at the office. His results reflected that dedication. In almost four years of battling federal prosecutors accustomed to winning more than ninety percent of their cases, Berke won complete acquittals for his clients in ten of his eighteen trials. Only five of his clients were convicted at trial. "I do believe I've represented many people who are innocent," Berke said. "And I always take the view that I represent people with full lives. I don't just represent the [accused] embezzler—I represent the husband, the father, the son."

Berke's confidence is quiet but inviolable. The same faith that led him to the public defender's office against the advice of his friends also accompanied him into private practice at Kramer Levin in September 1995, after four years as a public defender and a year teaching criminal law at New York University. Though the firm was home to Gary Naftalis, one of the city's best-known criminal defense lawyers, Berke said he didn't want to work as an assistant on Naftalis's cases. He was a young man in a specialty that places a premium on gray-haired wisdom, but he assured the Kramer Levin partners who hired him that he could develop his own practice, with his own clients referred by lawyers who had seen his work as a public defender. As usual, Berke's certitude was well founded. When Fenton called in February 1996, Berke had already begun to justify the partners' trust with a caseload of clients who had sought him out.

Berke showed Fenton and Castelete into one of Kramer Levin's conference rooms; his own office was too small for an important client meeting. Fenton poured out his story. Berke kept stopping him, asking him to back up and explain. Berke has a deliberative style. He speaks slowly, but only because he doesn't like to show how fast he is thinking. As the coin dealer answered his questions, Berke absorbed Fenton's account of the 1933 Double Eagle and the sting at the Waldorf. At the same time, he evaluated Fenton. The man was obviously traumatized, Berke thought, but credible, a likable guy. And what a story he was telling. Berke always thought of his cases as novels, but he'd never had material like this before. For trying to sell a coin—a *coin*—Fenton was in danger of spending the next decade of his life in prison. This is a good case, Berke thought. I'm going to help this guy.

When Fenton finished answering his questions, Berke looked at the coin dealer sitting across the table. "This is the most absurd criminal case I've ever heard of," he announced. "I think the government's judgment is seriously skewed. I would love to represent you."[4]

AFTER HIS horrible night in the holding cell, Jay Parrino fled back home to Kansas City, his release secured by his lawyer friend, Krassner, who then began searching for a criminal defense specialist to represent Parrino. He needed someone who could get the criminal charges dropped, and soon. Within days of the sting at the Waldorf, news reports of Parrino's arrest and the seizure of the 1933 Double Eagle began appearing not only in coin newspapers but also on the front page of *USA Today* and in Parrino's hometown paper. Parrino's business evaporated. Even clients who believed in his innocence didn't want their coin deals examined by the government as agents investigated Parrino. Moreover, not everyone stood by Parrino: The American Numismatic Association informed the dealer that he wouldn't be allowed to buy tables at upcoming conventions. Unless Parrino cleared his name fast, he'd be ruined.

The first few criminal lawyers whom Krassner called offered him little hope. There was no way, they all said, that the government would drop the criminal charges; the Secret Service had spent too much time and money on the sting and had received too much press coverage to walk away. Parrino was in for a long fight, they said. Krassner kept looking. One of the people he'd consulted on Parrino's behalf was Harvey Stack, the longtime coin dealer who had been a teenager at his family's New York auction house when the Secret Service launched its first 1933 Double Eagle investigation back in 1944. It was Stack, a loyal friend to Jay Parrino, who told Krassner to talk to a New York lawyer named Alan Mansfield, who had represented Stack's in a few coin disputes.

Krassner called him. "I think we *can* get this knocked out," Mansfield said, after listening to Krassner's description of the 1933 Double Eagle story. "It's a historical quagmire. How can the government possibly prove the case? There are all kinds of issues here that are so inconsistent with putting on a case they can prove beyond a reasonable doubt—and that's before you even get to the normal issues," Mansfield said. "Why is this coin contraband? That's an easy question if you're talking about a bag of heroin, but this is an American coin. Why is it contraband? And even if it is, how's anyone supposed to know that?"[5]

Mansfield was telling Krassner exactly what he wanted to hear. With Parrino's consent, Krassner and Mansfield dug into the case. Krassner was in charge of coin research. He sent Freedom of Information Act (FOIA) requests to the Bureau of the Mint and consulted with coin-world luminaries. Mansfield, who had good contacts within the U.S. Attorney's office, would turn Krassner's research into arguments to present to prosecutors.

BERKE'S FIRST priority for Fenton was winning permission for his client to leave New York and the United States. A couple of days after the sting, when Secret Service agents arrived at Fenton's hotel to inventory the dozens of coins Fenton had stored in the Hilton's safe, Berke was there to negotiate a deal. He arranged to have Fenton's coins evaluated by a government-approved expert, who concluded that the coins were worth about $100,000. At Fenton's court hearing on February 13, five days after his arrest, Berke told the magistrate that Fenton was willing to leave his coins in escrow with the coin expert in exchange for the return of his passport. The magistrate agreed to permit Fenton to return to London, on the condition that on arrival he surrender his passport to U.S. Secret Service agents stationed in London. Fenton and his live-in girlfriend, Sheryl Steen, who had rushed to the United States with bank drafts for Fenton's bail, flew home that afternoon. As instructed, Fenton went straight to the American Embassy to turn in his passport.

"What is this nonsense about a coin?" an embassy official asked him. "I've never heard of anything so ridiculous in my life."

Fenton shrugged. "What can I tell you? I'm supposed to give up my passport, so here I am."

WITH FENTON sprung from New York, Barry Berke turned his attention to the crux of the case: how to persuade prosecutors that the 1933 Double Eagle affair didn't belong in criminal court. The government's complaint against Fenton and Parrino had been drafted by Assistant U.S. Attorney Kwan-Gett, working with Secret Service Agent Don Dillard. It described, in the broadest strokes, the history of the 1933 Double Eagle, the negotiations between Parrino and Moore (in the complaint, Moore was called only "a confidential informant"), and the sting at the Waldorf. The complaint listed only one criminal count against Fenton and Parrino—the same crime that Treasury lawyers had used as a bludgeon fifty years earlier to compel collectors to return their 1933 Double Eagles to the government. A person could not knowingly receive, conceal, or retain property stolen or embezzled from the United States. Fenton and Parrino, Kwan-Gett asserted in the criminal complaint, "unlawfully, willfully, and knowingly did combine, conspire, confederate, and agree together and with each other to commit a crime against the United States"—a crime that carried a sentence of up to ten years' imprisonment.

Berke saw two avenues of attack. First, he could attempt to show that Stephen Fenton's 1933 Double Eagle was not, in fact, rightly the property of the United States. That wasn't going to be easy, at least not without a lot of research. Berke's quick search of legal databases turned up Judge Marion Boyd's ruling in the 1947 case brought by

1933 Double Eagle owner L. G. Barnard. In no uncertain terms, Judge Boyd had concluded that Barnard's 1933 Double Eagle had been wrongfully removed from the Mint and thus belonged to the government. Moreover, Judge Boyd had ruled that *no* 1933 Double Eagles could have left the Mint by legal means. Parrino's lawyer, David Krassner, was eager to test that finding, but a couple of weeks into the case, Berke had already logged enough hours in the stacks at the American Numismatic Society library to realize that intensive research into the history of the 1933 Double Eagle would take more time than he had if he was going to persuade prosecutors to drop the charges against Fenton.

A faster way to end the criminal case, Berke believed, was to challenge the government's assertion that Fenton and Parrino *knew* the coin rightfully belonged to the United States. That was the second critical element of the crime with which the men were charged. Fifty years earlier, when Treasury Department agents forced collectors to surrender their 1933 Double Eagles, it was after Treasury's general counsel had sent out letters informing collectors that the coins had been stolen from the Mint. Those collectors couldn't pretend to be unaware of the government's ownership claim. But since then, the 1933 Double Eagle had become the stuff of coin-world mythology, not legal argument. Mei Lin Kwan-Gett was going to have a hard time, Berke reasoned, proving exactly what Fenton and Parrino knew of the coin's history.

Kwan-Gett was confident, at least at first. She was a novice prosecutor with only a few months' experience in the U.S. Attorney's office, but from the first time Secret Service agent Dillard described to her the 1933 Double Eagle deal that Jack Moore had engineered—a secret meeting at the Waldorf, a mysterious unnamed seller, a million-dollar wire transfer—she was convinced it was crooked. "Had it all been on the up-and-up," Kwan-Gett said, "they wouldn't have conducted things the way they did." The mere circumstances of the sale, Kwan-Gett believed, proved that Fenton and Parrino knew the coin was illegal. "This isn't the way normal people conduct business," Kwan-Gett said.[6]

Besides, the government had Parrino on tape, plotting with Jack

Moore. During the Orlando meeting taped by Moore, for instance, Parrino had talked about sneaking the 1933 Double Eagle into the United States in a roll of common-date Saints. He'd called the coin, "okay [in England] but not okay over here." And, of course, there was the tape from the Waldorf sting, which captured Moore asking Parrino how much the coin would be worth if it were legal. Parrino hadn't said, "It is legal." He'd brought Fenton into the discussion, and Fenton had said the price would double. There was incontrovertible proof, in Kwan-Gett's eyes: Both Fenton and Parrino knew the 1933 Double Eagle was illegal to own.

It wasn't, however, proof that the men knew the coin was rightfully the property of the United States. That was what the government's criminal case required, and for that, Berke and Mansfield kept telling Kwan-Gett, she had no evidence. In their statements to the Secret Service, neither Parrino nor Fenton had admitted knowing that 1933 Double Eagles had been stolen from the U.S. Mint. Fenton had said he was unsure of ownership restrictions in the United States; Parrino had said he didn't know why the coin was considered illegal to own. Jack Moore had taped a dozen conversations with Parrino, but he never caught Parrino conceding that the 1933 Double Eagle belonged to the government. In fact, when the defense lawyers reviewed the transcripts of Moore's tapes, they noticed that Parrino had once contradicted Moore when Moore tried to bait him about the coin's illegality. "I'm talking to you on a completely clean line," Moore had said to Parrino on January 17. "You and I both know it's illegal to own or possess this coin, right?"

"Well, that's not true," Parrino had answered. "As a matter of fact, there's legislation now to have this all done." (Parrino may have been referring to talk in coin circles that then-Congressman Jimmy Hayes of Louisiana, a noted coin collector himself, would introduce a bill to declare the 1933 Double Eagle legal to own.)

Moore had persisted. "Right now, as we talk right now, it's illegal to possess it, isn't it? If someone knew about it?"

"I don't think so," Parrino had said. "I mean, I thought so, but now I don't think so."

Kwan-Gett was going to have to come up with more evidence than she had. Secret Service agents were instructed to continue investigating Fenton and Parrino.

BERKE ORGANIZED his arguments against prosecuting Fenton in an enormous black binder, a habit he'd developed in his public-defender days. As the control date approached—the date by which, under the law, Kwan-Gett had to obtain an indictment against Fenton and Parrino or else dismiss criminal charges—Berke requested what he calls a "black binder" meeting with Kwan-Gett and her boss, Karen Seymour, deputy chief of the Criminal Division. Berke had spent six weeks learning everything he could about Stephen Fenton and the 1933 Double Eagle. Everything he now knew confirmed his initial impression: Prosecutors would be crazy to indict in this case.

Kwan-Gett had been impervious to all of the lobbying Berke had done so far, though. When Fenton visited Berke's offices in March, having received permission from the court to attend a coin convention in Chicago, Berke had warned him that indictment still seemed likely. The black-binder meeting at the U.S. Attorney's office, which Alan Mansfield would attend on Parrino's behalf, would be the defense lawyers' last, best chance to persuade Kwan-Gett and Seymour to drop the charges against Parrino and Fenton.

Berke began the meeting with a flat declaration. "Whatever you believe about the tapes," he said as he opened his binder, "you're never going to be able to convict." He and Mansfield laid out their arguments. The government was going to have to prove that Fenton's 1933 Double Eagle was stolen sixty years earlier. "How many were there to begin with?" Mansfield asked. "And which one was this particular coin? How are you going to prove *this* coin was stolen?" Prosecutors would then have to establish that Parrino and Fenton had guilty knowledge, when even the government's tapes were ambiguous on that point. And they couldn't just show that Parrino and Fenton had a vague idea that the coins were illegal to own—but would need proof that the two men knew that 1933 Double Eagles rightfully belonged to the United States.

Finally, Berke said, "There's the fairness question. Nobody could reasonably expect that owning coins might lead to his arrest." Berke ran through a list of other coins with dubious histories. Had anyone been arrested for attempting to sell a 1913 Liberty Head nickel or an 1804 silver dollar? How about all the pattern coins that were supposed to have been melted down but instead found their way into the rare-coin market? No one had ever been arrested for buying and selling pattern coins. Berke repeated to Seymour and Kwan-Gett what he'd told Stephen Fenton when he first met his client: "This is the most absurd criminal case I've ever heard of."

After the meeting, Berke called Fenton in London. "I have no sense of what they're going to do," he said. "They asked some questions, but they didn't say much. You should prepare to be indicted."

Despite her stoicism at the meeting, Kwan-Gett was beginning to have qualms. Not about the guilt of Fenton and Parrino—she never believed their avowals that this was an ordinary coin deal—but that she'd be able to prove their guilt beyond a reasonable doubt. The Secret Service's post-arrest investigation wasn't helping. Agents in London ran checks on Fenton but found nothing in the criminal records on him or Knightsbridge Coins. A Minneapolis agent was dispatched to interview a coin dealer who once briefly worked for Parrino, but the former employee offered no leads. "He did not remember ever having a discussion with Parrino about the 1933 Saint-Gaudens $20 gold coin," a Minneapolis agent reported to Rock Ensminger in Washington. "[He] also advised that he had no information whatsoever about [a] fortune accumulated by Parrino in an attempt to hide it from the IRS."

Word of Kwan-Gett's doubts leaked out to the Secret Service in early April of 1996. Don Dillard was furious when he heard that the U.S. Attorney's office was considering dropping the charges. The Secret Service had worked hard to assemble a good case. Agents had put their lives on the line, and they'd brought in the coin and the guys trying to sell it. What was the prosecutors' problem? Dillard scoured his files and asked other agents to scour theirs, searching for any bit of 1933 Double Eagle history they hadn't already sent to Kwan-Gett.

Nothing turned up, but when Dillard talked to Kwan-Gett, he urged her to proceed with the indictment. "Don't you see what I see?" he pleaded.[7]

On April 5, 1996, Barry Berke received a phone call from Paul Gilkes, the *Coin World* reporter covering the 1933 Double Eagle case. William Whiteside, the Secret Service spokesman, had just informed Gilkes that the government was dropping the criminal charges. "Can I get a comment from you?" Gilkes asked.

This was the first Berke had heard of the news. He'd been waiting for word from Kwan-Gett, and he wasn't happy that *Coin World* knew what was happening in the case before he did. "I have to call you back," Berke told Gilkes. He dialed Kwan-Gett.

"Mei Lin, what's going on?" Berke demanded. "I just got a call from a reporter who says a Secret Service agent told him you're dropping the charges."

"He shouldn't have said that," Kwan-Gett answered.

"What do you mean? Are you going to indict or not?"

"There's no final decision," Kwan-Gett said. But from the tone of her voice, Berke knew it was true. The government was abandoning the criminal case. "I'm calling my client," he told Kwan-Gett. She didn't tell him not to do so.

Berke called Fenton and reached his answering machine. He left a message: "Stephen, it's Barry. Call me right away. I have very big news."

It was a bank holiday in Britain, and Fenton and his girlfriend had been out with friends, returning late in the afternoon. Fenton played Berke's message, and his heart started pounding. He paced through the house as he dialed Berke's number. When Berke answered, Fenton was standing in his dining room, which he thereafter called his "lucky room."

"They're dropping the charges," Berke told him. "You're free."

Fenton almost dropped the phone. "This is the greatest news I've ever gotten," he told Berke. "Thank you. I don't know how you did it, but thank you."

Chapter Fourteen

"All Right, Then. Let's Fight"

JAY PARRINO WAS EUPHORIC when Alan Mansfield called to tell him that the criminal charges had been dropped. His name was cleared, his wife and kids could finally relax, and he could begin to resuscitate his business. Parrino took the opportunity of a May 21, 1996, auction at the St. Moritz Hotel in New York City to dispel any lingering doubts about his place in the coin world. The legendary collection of Louis Eliasberg was up for sale, and all the important dealers were there. The climax of the night was the bidding for Eliasberg's 1913 Liberty Head nickel, the finest of the five known specimens of the coin. Parrino, who'd dreamed as a child of being the first person to pay $1 million for a coin, shut out competitors with a bid of almost $1.5 million—the first time a coin sold at auction for more than $1 million. Parrino was welcomed back into the exclusive fraternity of the coin trade as if the Waldorf sting had never happened. Wearing a Hawaiian shirt and a face-cracking grin, he shook hands, posed for pictures, and even autographed auction catalogues. When the *Kansas City Star* reported on the record-setting bid of Missouri's most famous coin dealer, there was no mention of the humiliating arrest the news-paper had covered three months earlier.

Through 1996 and 1997, Parrino kept buying and selling coin rari-ties: a Brasher doubloon, a 1927-D Saint, a rare 1921 half-dollar. He resumed advertising in trade newspapers and behaved, at least pub-licly, with more aggressive ostentation than ever before. The Secret Service gnashed its teeth. After the 1913 Liberty Head nickel auction, Agent Rock Ensminger sent a note to Margaret Flanagan, head of the Asset Forfeiture Division in Manhattan. "Thought you might like an update on the commercial side of the 1913 nickel story," Ensminger wrote. "It was sold at auction for $1.485 million. The purchaser was none other than your old pal, Jasper 'Jay' Parrino. . . . Oh well, another sad tale of lost opportunity."[1]

For all of his bravado, though, Parrino never forgot the horror of being locked in a jail cell, and he never forgave anyone who hadn't stood by him during the criminal case. He boycotted American Numismatic Association conventions and avoided dealers he sus-pected of having talked to the government. His bitterest enmity, of course, was reserved for Jack Moore, whom he called "a piece of scum." When I spoke to Parrino at a coin convention in Florida in 2004, a full eight years after his arrest, Parrino still flashed fury at the mention of Moore's name. "They opened this gigantic can of worms because of Jack Moore," he said bitterly, "and he double-crossed everybody."

Moore heard about prosecutor Mei Lin Kwan-Gett's decision to abandon the criminal case from Dave Freriks. Both were crushed. Freriks had talked to Moore on the phone a couple of times since the sting at the Waldorf, and had met with him in person to deliver Moore's $7,500 informant fee on March 21. Neither of them had any inkling there were problems with the case. "It seemed like everything was fine," Moore said. "They had the coin, they had the people." So when Freriks told him that Kwan-Gett had dropped the charges, Moore felt as though the government had abandoned him as well. He had placed himself in danger—Amarillo police officers were still guarding his house weeks after the sting—and had delivered every-thing he promised, everything Freriks said prosecutors needed to convict Parrino. Now Parrino was vindicated, and Moore couldn't even go to coin shows. A couple of dealers had called to congratulate him after they found out he was responsible for Parrino's arrest, but many more shunned him, just as his onetime partner Kent Remmel had predicted they would. Moore had violated an unspoken code of the trade: What happens in the coin world stays in the coin world. "He's a scumbag," said one dealer who had once worked closely with Moore but didn't like to be reminded of the association. "I don't have anything else to say about him."

And Jack Moore was soon to discover that his isolation from the coin trade was only the beginning of his problems as the saga of the 1933 Double Eagle continued. For it did continue, in its inimitable spinning, lurching fashion, like the haphazard course of a toddler or a drunk. The coin's legal travails, instigated by Moore in the fall of 1995, did not end with the dismissal of criminal charges against Fenton and Parrino six months later. The coin dealers were free, but the 1933 Double Eagle was not. The government expected to keep the coin it had expended such effort to seize, but Stephen Fenton wanted it back. It was their struggle for possession that led to the excavation of the 1933 Double Eagle's history in all of its dusty detail—and also, almost incidentally, to Jack Moore's ruin.

ON THE same day that Fenton learned the criminal charges had officially been dropped, Barry Berke told him that the U.S. government was suing to retain possession of the coin. Fenton was taken aback. He'd had only a couple of days to savor Berke's news that Mei Lin Kwan-Gett wasn't going to seek his indictment, and now came this sour development. To Fenton, the government's suit seemed utterly unjust. The 1933 Double Eagle was his. He had paid good money for it. If prosecutors were admitting he hadn't done anything wrong, then he deserved his coin back.

"What can we do?" he asked Berke.

"We can fight them for it," Berke said. The litigation would undoubtedly be long and expensive, Berke warned, but based on what he had learned about the 1933 Double Eagle in the six weeks of the criminal proceeding, he believed Fenton had a reasonable chance of winning.

"All right, then," Fenton said. "Let's go ahead. Let's fight."

The government's action, *United States of America* v. *A $20 Gold Coin*, was called an in rem proceeding, which meant that it was a civil lawsuit to determine the status of a piece of property—in this case, the 1933 Double Eagle. The coin itself was named as the defendant, and if the government prevailed, Fenton's 1933 Double Eagle would be forfeited forever to the United States. The grounds for forfeiture, as outlined by prosecutor Evan Barr in the initial complaint, were twofold. The first, which came as no surprise to Berke when he read the complaint, was the government's contention that the coin had been stolen from the Mint in Philadelphia, and was thus contraband, illegal for anyone to possess. Berke already knew enough about the coin's history to believe he could mount a convincing challenge to an argument that depended on proving a sixty-year-old theft for which no one had ever been prosecuted.

The complaint's second assertion, however, was new and extremely unwelcome. Prosecutor Barr claimed that Fenton had filed a fraudulent customs declaration to bring the 1933 Double Eagle into the country. By making such false statements, the complaint stated, Fenton forfeited title to the coin.

This new accusation worried Berke. If prosecutors could prove that Fenton had lied, that he had intentionally smuggled the 1933 Double Eagle into the country, the case was over. Fenton would lose the coin. Berke reviewed the complaint carefully. It appeared that on February 8, the day of Fenton's arrest, an agent from the Secret Service had been sent to check Fenton's customs declaration. According to the U.S. Customs paperwork the agent found, Fenton had declared the total value of all the coins he was bringing into the United States to be $742,000—which was less than what he intended to receive from Parrino just for the sale of the 1933 Double Eagle. Moreover, Fenton's customs agent, Lawrence Baker, from a company called Jet Air Service, had filed a letter with the U.S. Customs Service at JFK Airport that contained problematic language. The letter stated that Fenton was importing "legal tender U.S. gold coins minted by the United States government between 1830 and 1932." It made no mention of the one coin that fell outside of those chronological parameters—Fenton's 1933 Double Eagle.

When Berke told Fenton about the new false-statement allegations, Fenton felt almost as frustrated and angry as he had when he'd first been arraigned in the criminal case. Was this some kind of vendetta? Fenton thought his reputation had been restored when prosecutors dropped the criminal charges, but now they were accusing him of fraud. These prosecutors, Fenton told Berke, obviously had no idea of how coin dealers handled their imports. Lawrence Baker of Jet Air was Fenton's longtime customs broker. Before every coin-dealing trip to the United States, Fenton or his assistant, Jim Brown, would fax Baker a general description of the coins Fenton planned to bring in. For this trip, Brown had prepared the inventory, a very simple document. Brown had grouped the coins into two categories: gold and silver from the United States, and gold and silver from Great Britain and Australia. He listed the number of coins in each category and their approximate value, in British pounds. Then he faxed the invoice to Baker. What Baker did with it, Fenton told Berke, Fenton didn't know. Baker took care of everything so efficiently that Fenton had never had a problem with U.S. Customs—not on this trip nor on any of his previous coin-trading trips to America.

Berke realized that he had to talk to the customs broker, and the sooner the better. He made an appointment with Baker and took along a private investigator, a former employee of the Internal Revenue Service, in case he needed a witness to the interview. He needn't have bothered. Baker was entirely cooperative. No one from the government had even talked to him, he told Berke. If anyone had, he would have explained that the letter in which he described Fenton's coins to the Customs Service—the letter that was the basis of the government's fraud allegations—was boilerplate, a document Baker used whenever he represented a coin dealer. He had first drafted the letter's language back in 1989, in consultation with a coin authority who told him the dates to cite. Fenton probably didn't even know that

Baker's letter included the phrase, "U.S. gold coins minted by the United States government between 1830 and 1932," so he could hardly be accused of fraud because of it.

The Knightsbridge Coins invoice, Baker said, was also innocent. Baker told Berke that the invoice Fenton's assistant had sent to him before the February 1996 trip was the same kind of invoice Knightsbridge Coins always sent—not an attempt by Fenton to hide the 1933 Double Eagle with a deliberately obscure description of the coins he was carrying. It was perfectly adequate for U.S. Customs purposes.

Finally, Berke asked Baker about the value of the coins Fenton had declared. Had Fenton improperly understated the worth of the coins he was importing? Baker told Berke no, that the invoice reflected what Fenton had paid for the coins, not the price for which he intended to sell them.

Berke returned to his office and called Fenton. "Well, we figured this out," Berke reported. "It's black and white." The customs broker had completely exonerated him, Berke said. There was no way prosecutors were going to win possession of the 1933 Double Eagle based on the U.S. Customs allegations, and they would have known it themselves if they had bothered to interview Lawrence Baker. To Fenton's consternation, the government kept the customs argument alive in court papers throughout the case, even after Baker was deposed on January 9, 1997, and swore under oath to the version of events that cleared Fenton. But Berke was right: Prosecutors knew the U.S. Customs issue was a loser. Possession of the 1933 Double Eagle would be determined by the coin's history—the only fitting grounds, Berke believed, for an object with such a strange and eventful past.

BEGINNING THE day that *Coin World* first identified Berke as Fenton's lawyer, Berke's assistant, Olivette Taylor, had fielded dozens of telephone calls from people interested in the 1933 Double Eagle. Some were coin luminaries outraged at Fenton's arrest and the seizure of the coin. Some were collectors reporting rumors of other 1933 Saints. Some were crazies with stories about Nazi gold or their grandmother's long-lost coin albums. The coin world, Berke quickly learned, is founded on towering heaps of arcana and filled with people who happily spend their days sifting through it all. Berke had neither the time nor the desire to join their ranks, but to advocate effectively for Fenton, he needed to know everything about the 1933 Double Eagle—and quite a lot about other controversial coins. The trick for him would be to figure out how to research the case without suffocating in an avalanche of obscure and irrelevant coin history.

On the advice of David Krassner, the Connecticut lawyer and coin collector who had represented Jay Parrino in the criminal case, Berke hired Q. David Bowers to be his lead coin expert.[2] Bowers was one of the most renowned numismatists in the country, the head of a prominent coin auction house and the author of dozens of coin books. Just having him attached to the case lent Fenton credibility with the rest of the coin world. Bowers attacked the 1933 Double Eagle assignment with characteristic alacrity, supplementing his encyclopedic memory with research in his library of old coin books, magazines, and catalogues. He sent Berke a sheaf of material on the 1933 Double Eagle, including a reference in *The Numismatist* to F. C. C. Boyd's display of a 1933 Saint at the American Numismatic Association convention in 1939. Bowers had a libertarian sensibility on the subject of the 1933 Double Eagle: If the coin had been owned openly in the 1930s and 1940s, then the Secret Service had no business going after it—in 1944 or 1996.

More significantly for Fenton's case, Bowers also came to believe that 1933 Double Eagles could actually have left the Philadelphia Mint legitimately. A second researcher advising Berke, a numismatic historian and Mint archival expert named Robert Julian, traveled to the National Archives in College Park, Maryland, to dig up original documents related to the coin. Among the materials Julian unearthed was a March 15, 1933, letter from the director of the Mint to one Lewis Froman of Buffalo. The letter informed Froman that despite the gold embargo, the Mints were permitted to receive and pay out gold, as long as the net gold supply didn't change.[3] Julian concluded, based on this letter, that in the confusion over gold policy in March and April of 1933—after the first 1933 Double Eagles were coined and transferred to the Mint cashier's office—newly minted Double Eagles might have been exchanged legally across the cashier's counter. Perhaps Israel Swirt and Ed Silver hadn't trafficked in stolen coins at all, but rather traded for 1933 Double Eagles during that lacuna of legitimacy.

The rickety platform of hypotheticals that Bowers and Julian constructed had possibilities, Berke thought, but the government's case for possession of the coin rested on a much sturdier foundation of legal precedent. In the 1947 Barnard case, Judge Marion Boyd had decided what he called "the decisive question" of whether *any* 1933 Double Eagles had been issued or legally circulated by the Philadelphia Mint— and he had decided it in a way that didn't help Fenton and Berke. After that trial in Memphis in the summer of 1947, Judge Boyd evaluated the government's evidence of how 1933 Saints were handled by the Mint, from their coining to their destruction. He concluded that Barnard's 1933 Double Eagle "did not leave the mint as regularly and lawfully issued money," but instead "was stolen or through fraudulent breach of trust taken from the Philadelphia Mint."[4]

Boyd's opinion was a serious obstacle for Berke and Fenton, but Berke thought he saw a way around it. The government had proved a negative in the Barnard suit, persuading Judge Boyd that because no 1933 Double Eagle had left the Mint legally, Barnard's coin had been stolen. Berke wanted to twist the syllogism. His plan was to demand the almost-impossible, challenging prosecutors to prove affirmatively that one *particular* coin—the 1933 Double Eagle seized from Stephen Fenton—had been stolen from the Mint. If the government couldn't establish the singular history of Fenton's coin from the moment it left the Mint, Berke reasoned, he could present a judge and jury with an alternate explanation for how some small number of 1933 Double Eagles might have legitimately entered circulation—the theory Julian and Bowers posited, for instance—and argue that Fenton's coin was one of them.

Berke's first request to the government for names and documents, filed on September 6, 1996, was designed with that strategy in mind. The heart of every civil case, this one included, is the process called *discovery*, in which the two sides exchange information according to a set of procedural rules. The evidence that emerges in discovery decides most cases; for lawyers, part of the art of civil litigation is in writing discovery requests that will compel the other side to reveal its most uncomfortable secrets, while at the same time interpreting the other side's discovery requests as narrowly as possible under the rules of civil procedure. Berke wanted to find out everything the government could prove about the minting, storing, testing, and destruction of 1933 Double Eagles, so he requested all manner of Mint, Assay Commission, and Treasury Department documents. He demanded the names of everyone still living who had worked at the Philadelphia Mint in 1933. He asked for all the Secret Service records that formed the basis of the government's assertion that 1933 Double Eagles had been stolen from the Mint.[5] And, in a subtle signal of his plan to force the government to prove that Fenton's particular coin was stolen, Berke also asked the government to produce any evidence in its files that Fenton's 1933 Double Eagle could not have left the Mint legally.

Berke knew that both Fenton and the Secret Service believed Fenton's coin was the King Farouk specimen, the 1933 Double Eagle that had disappeared after the 1954 Palace Collections sale and the only 1933 Saint known to have eluded the Secret Service in its mid-century investigation. To test the strength of the government's evidence, Berke demanded in his September 1996 discovery request everything in government files relating to "a 1933 Double Eagle gold coin allegedly offered as part of a 1954 Sotheby's auction in Cairo, Egypt." He wanted documents that reflected the government's knowledge of the Farouk coin, as well as evidence of any previous attempts by the United States to recover it, before and after the Palace Collections auction.

SEVERAL MONTHS after Berke submitted his discovery demands, prosecutor Evan Barr sent several cartons of paper uptown to Kramer Levin. Berke watched eagerly as messengers stacked the boxes against a wall in his office. Within these cartons, he knew, were the government documents that told the real story of the 1933 Double Eagle—the true historical record, not just newspaper accounts and coin-world rumors.

Finally the messengers left and Berke tore in. Every piece of paper was interesting to him, and every one required calculation. Berke pulled out copies of the original Secret Service reports from 1944, submitted by Harry Strang, who closed each with his showy, oversize signature. How strong, Berke needed to know, was Strang's case against Israel Switt and George McCann? He read through telegrams and letters exchanged among Treasury officials in March and April 1933. Were they consistent with Bowers's theory? Berke studied the records of the sting at the Waldorf. How much did the Secret Service know about the coin's history when Haas and Ensminger seized Fenton's 1933 Double Eagle? The lawyer made notes and created files.

Then he came across the document that would decide the future of Stephen Fenton's coin, just as it had once decided the coin's past. It was Mint Director Nellie Tayloe Ross's February 25, 1944, letter to Smithsonian curator Theodore Belote, requesting Belote's opinion on the matter of an export license for King Farouk's 1933 Double Eagle. Typed on the bottom of the letter was Belote's approval for the license, which was subsequently issued by the Treasury Department to the Egyptian Legation on February 29, 1944. Berke read and reread the document. This letter, he realized, meant that the U.S. government had sanctioned Farouk's ownership of a 1933 Double Eagle. The Mint had even held Farouk's 1933 Double Eagle in its possession for ten days and then had willingly released it to Egypt.

Well, well, well, Berke thought, already imagining himself waving the letter in front of a jury. Our case is suddenly looking a lot better.[6]

FOR PROSECUTORS in the Asset Forfeiture Division of the U.S. Attorney's office, the Farouk export license was the biggest—but not the only—complication in the case of the 1933 Double Eagle. They were plowing unfamiliar land: These were lawyers more accustomed to seizing sports cars from drug dealers than to researching a sixty-five-year-old gold coin. Even the Mint's head lawyer, who worked with the U.S. Attorney's office on the case, knew little about the coin's history. When Secret Service agents first called to ask Kenneth Gubin what background he could provide on the 1933 Double Eagle, Gubin replied, "None. I'm not a numismatist. I'm an attorney. I've never even heard of this coin."[7]

And few coin experts—none of the first rank—were willing to help the government. Gubin and his deputy, Gregory Weinman, thought the coin world might welcome the Mint's effort in the 1933 Double Eagle case to demand legitimacy for numismatic rarities, appreciating what Gubin and Weinman regarded as a shining opportunity to affirm the Mint's exclusive right to issue coinage. They were completely wrong. When Weinman tried to find a coin expert to assist prosecutors and provide a counterweight to the eminent numismatic consultants Berke had hired, no one even returned his phone calls. The coin press was full of letters and editorials decrying the government's pursuit of the 1933 Double Eagle, an endeavor that threw a shadow over the most celebrated and valuable rarities in American coin collecting. Almost all of these coins had questionable provenance. If the government prevailed in the 1933 Double Eagle case, would prosecutors next seize 1913 Liberty Head nickels? 1804 silver dollars? 1885 trade dollars? Pattern coins? "The case put us in a difficult position," Weinman admitted. "Numismatists are our customers, our constituents."

With no outside experts willing to help, Weinman and Gubin did their own archival research to support the U.S. Attorney's office. Weinman walked over to the Library of Congress to find old newspaper articles about gold policy in March 1933, and he traveled to the National Archives in Maryland to look through files of official Mint correspondence. Both he and Gubin were convinced that the documentary evidence stacked up persuasively against Barry Berke's theory of a Mint worker legitimately trading 1933 Double Eagles across the cashier's counter. "It was inconceivable," Gubin said. "There was no one at the Philadelphia Mint who was alive and breathing who was not aware that Roosevelt had prohibited trade in gold. The idea that they nonetheless innocently went on trading was remote in my mind."

But proving the history of 1933 Double Eagles through the documents was going to be a huge problem for the government—one that left the entire case in doubt, despite the precedent of the Barnard decision. In the 1947 Barnard case, the Memphis prosecutor had had a witness list full of officials from the Philadelphia Mint: men and women who had worked there in 1933 and could testify to every detail of the coinage, storage, and destruction of 1933 Saints, vouching for the documents that chronicled the coins' handling. Those documents still existed, but the Mint officials who had created them were all dead. (Prosecutors located one still-living former Mint employee from the 1930s, but when they called him, his son said that he'd had a stroke and his memory was too unreliable for him to be interviewed.) To keep hearsay evidence from reaching jurors, trial procedure requires that documents be introduced through the testimony of live witnesses. There were a few exceptions to the hearsay rule that prosecutors could assert in the 1933 Double Eagle case—most notably an exception that permits the introduction, under some circumstances, of documents more than twenty years old—but the case law wasn't consistent. The government lawyers couldn't be sure, no matter how convincing a case their documents made, that they'd be able to persuade a judge to admit them as evidence. "The lack of living witnesses," Weinman said, "was a fundamental challenge."

No famous numismatists. No Mint witnesses. No Secret Service old-timers from the 1944 investigation. The government's prospective witness list was short indeed. There were, of course, the Secret Service agents who'd conducted the 1996 sting. And there was Jack Moore, the confidential informant. Moore called himself a coin expert. He could testify for the government that the 1933 Double Eagle's illegitimacy was common knowledge in the coin trade, and that Stephen Fenton knew it as well as anyone. Moore had gotten Fenton to admit as much in his brilliant performance at the Waldorf. The government had relied on Jack Moore in its operation to seize Fenton's 1933 Double Eagle. Could prosecutors continue to count on him in the fight to maintain possession of the coin?

Chapter Fifteen

Jack Moore's Last Stand

In Amarillo at the end of 1997, when Barry Berke formally questioned Jack Moore in the presence of a government lawyer, it became painfully clear that the prosecutors could not rely on their onetime star operative. It had taken almost a year to arrange Moore's deposition in the 1933 Double Eagle case, but then Moore had been a busy man in 1997. John Groendyke, the trucking magnate for whom Moore and his coin-trading partner, Kent Remmel, had built the complete Saints set, had asked Moore to sell his collection, then worth almost $2 million. Groendyke sent the coins to Amarillo to be stored under Moore's care in one of the safe-deposit boxes Moore and Remmel shared at Stout Safe Storage. Within months, Moore reported that he was working on a deal. In a breezy August 8, 1997, birthday note to Groendyke, Moore wrote: "Everything is going along just fine to get the Set sold. It will take a little more time, but I know you want it done right. . . . The sale price will be $1,750,000.00."[1]

Moore told Groendyke and Remmel that he was negotiating with Dwight Manley, a prominent coin dealer who also acted as a business manager for basketball player Dennis Rodman.[2] Manley, with his sports and Hollywood connections, was one of the most glamorous people in the coin trade, and Groendyke and Remmel were flattered that he was interested in the Saints set. Moore told them that Manley had proposed a complicated deal involving a trade of Groendyke's double eagles for some other gold coins that Moore would then sell off. Negotiating the details, Moore said, was going to take a while. In the meantime, Moore told Remmel, Manley wanted Groendyke's coins to be held in escrow at a bank in Lubbock. With Remmel's approval, Moore withdrew Groendyke's set from Stout Safe Storage.

But he didn't take the gold coins to any bank in Lubbock. Moore wasn't really negotiating with Dwight Manley. He didn't even know how to spell Manley's name correctly—a mistake that would surface years later, when lawyers discovered forged e-mails, purporting to be from Manley, that Moore had sent to Groendyke. In fact, in May and June 1997, Moore had completed negotiations to sell Groendyke's entire Saints set to New Mexico coin dealer Jay Cammack for about $850,000—half the value he'd touted to Groendyke and less than Groendyke had paid for his coins. Groendyke knew nothing about the deal. Moore didn't tell him, and he gave Groendyke none of the money. Instead, in July 1997, a month before he wrote that cheery birthday note to Groendyke, Moore opened two new checking accounts at Amarillo National Bank. One was in the name of Spike's Place, an exotic bird store he'd opened for his wife, Marty; the other was in his and Marty's names. Moore deposited $142,000 in the two accounts, all of it from Jay Cammack. On August 8—the very day that he informed Groendyke that all was well with Groendyke's coins—Moore and Marty signed a contract to buy a house in Amarillo for $138,000, to be paid in cash. Through the entire second half of 1997, as Barry Berke's investigator tried to pin him to a date for his deposition in the 1933 Double Eagle case, Moore continued depositing money from Cammack into his new accounts at Amarillo National Bank—all the while assuring Groendyke and Remmel that he was still negotiating the details of the sale of Groendyke's Saints to Dwight Manley.

Moore finally appeared at the offices of Amarillo Court Reporting to be deposed by Berke on the morning of December 16, 1997. He marched into the session with confidence, even cockiness. He was the man who had tricked Jay Parrino into paying him $150,000 in the 1933 Double Eagle deal and who had just pocketed hundreds of thousands from John Groendyke's Saints set. Surely he could charm his way through a few questions about his heroic work as a Secret Service informant. A half-hour into the session, after answering with aplomb a series of questions about his roots in the coin trade, Moore even teased Berke: "You seem like too nice of a person to be an attorney."[3]

"Don't be fooled," warned Jonathan Etra, the latest assistant U.S. Attorney to be assigned to the 1933 Double Eagle case. "Don't be fooled."

Etra's admonition was prescient. In retrospect, Moore's deposition in the 1933 Double Eagle case marked the beginning of his downfall. Through Berke's questioning that day, Moore learned that he hadn't deceived everyone as successfully as he'd thought. For the first time, Jack Moore realized that he wasn't going to get away with everything after all.

Berke was gentle for the first couple of hours. He questioned Moore about his acquaintance with Jay Parrino, the call to Dave Freriks that initiated the Secret Service's 1933 Double Eagle investigation, the long negotiations that led to the sting at the Waldorf. Berke seemed understanding, even sympathetic, when Moore testified about receiving threatening phone calls after Parrino was arrested. Moore, for his part, was so unflappable that even when Berke asked if he had talked to John Groendyke about selling Groendyke's Saints set—the set Moore had secretly sold earlier that year—Moore didn't slip. "[Groendyke] would sell his complete collection," he replied, "if, you know, the price was right."

After lunch, everything changed. Berke dropped any pretense of friendliness and showed Moore and Etra what would happen if the government ever called Moore to testify at trial: Berke would destroy him. The lawyer bullied Moore about his early discussions with Parrino. Hadn't Moore really been the one pushing Parrino to sell him a 1933 Double Eagle? And hadn't Moore misled the Secret Service about how many of these conversations he had had with Parrino?

Launching most of his questions with the dreaded cross-examiner's phrase—"Isn't it a fact, sir"—Berke bombarded Moore with evidence of inconsistencies in his stories: his contacts with FBI Agent Colin Scott, his untaped conversations with Parrino, his references to packages mailed to him by the Kansas City dealer.

When Berke began asking questions about the $150,000 payment from Jay Parrino to Moore, Moore knew for sure that he'd been found out. Through the discovery process, Berke had obtained Dave Freriks's reports on the 1933 Double Eagle sting operation, including the report in which Freriks noted his warning to Moore about taking money from Parrino and the report in which Freriks recounted Moore's story of his supposed side deal with Parrino. "Agent Freriks told you to keep the money?" Berke asked.

"That's what he said," Moore replied. "He said it was a separate deal, had nothing to do with this case."

Berke knew Moore was lying. He'd had a long talk with one of Jay Parrino's lawyers about the money Parrino had given Moore. There was no side deal. Parrino paid Moore $150,000 as a commission on the 1933 Double Eagle sale, and Berke was going to make sure that Moore knew the scheme was blown. Wasn't the money, the lawyer demanded, really part of Moore's plan to trick Parrino out of a commission because the government wouldn't pay him a $75,000 informant fee?

Berke laid document after incriminating document in front of Moore, barraging him with questions. Moore became so rattled that his personal lawyer called for a break to permit Moore to calm down, but Berke wasn't finished. There was the matter of the high-relief 1907 Saint, the coin that Moore handed to Jay Parrino on his visit to Parrino's office in January 1996. "Isn't it the case," Berke asked, "that Mr. Parrino required, as insurance in case the [1933 Double Eagle] deal didn't go through, didn't he require that you leave a coin with him that was of substantial value?"

"I left a coin with him to sell," Moore said. "It had nothing to do with that, or I didn't think it did. Maybe he thought it did."

Berke ignored Moore's attempt to extricate himself. Hadn't Parrino returned the 1907 Saint to Moore at the Waldorf because he thought they had completed the 1933 Double Eagle deal? "He gave it back to you because he no longer needed it as collateral," Berke said to Moore. "Isn't that true?"

"I don't know," Moore said.

As Berke continued stabbing at him, asking questions about Moore's tax filings, Moore finally admitted defeat. "There's so much stuff took place," he pleaded. "I've, you know, I've been sick a lot since then. I can't help it that I got sick."

IN TRIUMPH, Berke flew back to New York—on the same plane as prosecutor Jonathan Etra. "So much for Jack Moore," Berke said. "He was not a well-controlled informant," Etra conceded.[4] As always, when he got back to his office, Berke called Fenton with a report. He'd taken care of Moore, Berke told his client. Prosecutors would never dare to put him on the stand. If anyone featured Moore at trial, it would be Berke, playing the videotape of Moore's deposition to show the jury that Jack Moore was a liar.

The government washed its hands of Moore after his disastrous deposition. In 1998, Jay Parrino sued him to recover the $150,000 commission Parrino had paid in the 1933 Double Eagle deal. Moore called Freriks, who had since retired from the Secret Service. "You told me to do whatever it took to get the deal done," Moore said. "That's what I did." Freriks told him that he couldn't help, that Moore should check with the U.S. Attorney's office in New York. Moore did, and he was told the government would do nothing for him. Moore was on his own. He hardly put up a defense against Parrino. Marty was in and out of the hospital with an array of heart and lung problems, and Moore had lost any desire to fight with Parrino over the legality of the 1933 Double Eagle—his only hope of justifying the money he'd accepted from the Kansas City dealer. Moore consented to a judgment against him of $140,000, although he never paid it.

By the time the Parrino suit ended, Moore had even worse problems. He was running out of excuses to feed John Groendyke. In the early spring of 1999, Moore scheduled a series of meetings with Remmel, each time promising they would close the sale of

Groendyke's Saints set to Dwight Manley. Moore broke every appointment. Remmel finally confronted him at his house in Amarillo on May 16. "If the set is back in Lubbock, tell me the banker's name," Remmel demanded. "Mr. Groendyke wants us to go and physically inventory the coins that are there. We are going to go down there and count them."[5]

Moore promised he'd drive to Lubbock with Remmel to retrieve Groendyke's coins. Then he canceled. Marty was in the hospital, he told Remmel. "We're going next Saturday, and that's that," Remmel said. "No more excuses." When Moore canceled yet again, offering an absurd story about being in the custody of the U.S. Marshals Service, Remmel drove to Moore's house. The place looked abandoned. Moore and Marty, it seemed, had skipped town.

Remmel called Groendyke in Oklahoma. "You're not going to believe this," he said. "Moore canceled again."

"Go to Lubbock," Groendyke replied. "Get the coins."

Remmel drove to the bank in Lubbock where the coins were supposed to be stored, presented himself as Moore's business partner, and asked for the safe-deposit-box key. There was no safe-deposit box. Remmel checked with all the other banks in Lubbock. No safe-deposit box, no coins. He got back into his truck and called Groendyke: "We've been duped."

Groendyke and Remmel sued Moore in June 1999. While their lawyers tried to locate Moore—who wasn't in Amarillo and wasn't answering his pager—Remmel did some checking on his own. He called Jay Cammack, the New Mexico dealer to whom, unbeknownst to Remmel, Moore had secretly sold Groendyke's coins. Did Cammack by any chance know, Remmel asked, what had become of Groendyke's Saints set? Cammack told Remmel that he had bought the coins in 1997 and had since sold them all through a dealer in Lubbock. The coins were long gone. Groendyke's set was dispersed, never to be recovered. Remmel seethed—and even more so when he discovered that Moore had also cleared out their jointly held safe-deposit boxes at Stout Safe Storage, selling off the coins that Remmel considered to be his future retirement money.

When Groendyke's lawyers managed to track down Moore in Colorado, Moore claimed that Remmel was the true villain of the affair. Remmel, he said, had been fleecing Groendyke for years, brazenly overcharging his cousin on construction projects as well as coin deals. All along, Moore said, he had been covering for Remmel, helping his friend hide assets from his estranged wife and writing fake e-mails to prevent Groendyke from finding out that Remmel had stolen the Saints set. It was Remmel who kept most of the money from the sale of the Groendyke set, Moore said. Moore got only $300,000.

Groendyke never believed Moore's story of Remmel's perfidy, and he remained loyal to his cousin. There was also no documentary evidence to support Moore's account, and there was plenty of evidence that Moore had secretly sold Groendyke's coins. Groendyke and Remmel won their suit against Moore, who had to turn over to them the title to his house in Amarillo and his two trucks. There was talk of criminal prosecution, but Moore was never charged with the theft.

Moore told me in March 2004 that he wouldn't have cared if he had been arrested. "If they'd have come and got me and prosecuted me and sent me away, I could have cared less," Moore said. Marty was slowly dying, and all of Moore's time and money were consumed by her illness. When she died in the beginning of 2004, he was a ruined man. He had nothing left—no money, no house, no cars, no wife. All that remained were his parrots, which had been his and Marty's last shared pleasure. "I finally got to where I didn't care what happened to me," Moore said. "If I woke up in the morning, I didn't care."

Looking back, Moore blamed it all on the 1933 Double Eagle. "Marty always said about the 1933 deal, 'Don't do it,'" Moore told me. "I wish I'd have took her advice. Then none of this stuff would have happened. It seemed like after the 1933 deal, Parrino and everything—things just fell down a well. If I'd just have took Marty's advice, none of it would have ever happened."

Chapter Sixteen

Splitting the Baby

THE FIGHT FOR THE 1933 Double Eagle continued without Jack Moore. A case as complicated and protracted as this one proceeds simultaneously down two different tracks. There is the uncovering of facts—the depositions and documents that comprise evidence. And there is legal strategy, analyzing the nuances of relevant precedents. Lawyers build their cases where the two tracks intersect—where the facts can be shaped to fit the law or the law can be interpreted to fit the facts. They pick over the evidence, always remembering, if they're any good, what they need to prove under the law. They may magnify the significance of facts that make their arguments seem more compelling and ignore or explain away the evidence that doesn't fit. Truth, in the Platonic sense, is not the point. A lawsuit is not a search for truth. It's a storytelling contest with a highly particular protocol. The lawyer who constructs a better story, using selected evidence to satisfy the requirements of the law, wins.

In 1999, a new assistant U.S. Attorney joined the 1933 Double Eagle case, with a new legal theory that she believed would improve the government's story. Jane Levine would spend the next three years battling Barry Berke for possession of the coin. She was Berke's physical opposite—tiny, wire-haired, and intense instead of tall and relaxed: a hummingbird to Berke's hawk. But the two were more alike than their superficies implied. They were both mavericks, at least within the straitjacketed world of New York litigators, with similar streaks of stubborn independence. Berke's showed in his insistence on working as a public defender after law school, Levine's in her affection for the odd cases of the U.S. Attorney's Asset Forfeiture Division.

Levine is a New Yorker. She was raised on Long Island, educated at New York University Law School, and mentored by a New York state court judge during a postgraduate clerkship. She spent several years bouncing from one large New York law firm to another, each switch deepening her conviction that she didn't belong in private practice. Finally she applied for a job as a federal prosecutor in Manhattan. By then, she was older and more experienced than most of the lawyers in the U.S. Attorney's office, which is considered one of the country's best training grounds for litigators. Young lawyers who join the office as a prelude to careers in private practice seek out high-profile, reputation-making criminal cases. Not Levine. She didn't want to return to a law firm anytime soon, so she was happy to work in the relative obscurity of the forfeiture unit. Levine liked burrowing deep into an investigation, deciphering the intricacies of an overseas money-laundering operation, for instance, or figuring out where an embezzler was hiding his assets.

Her real specialty, though, was art and antiquities forfeiture, an arcane and little-known practice in an office famous for its criminal prosecutions. With so many art deals taking place in New York, the U.S. Attorney would occasionally receive calls from foreign embassies complaining that someone was selling looted or smuggled art. Levine was the assistant most often called upon to investigate, and if the facts warranted, to file suit to recover the piece on behalf of the foreign government. She once handled the forfeiture of a wall panel looted from the tomb of a tenth-century Chinese soldier. Another time she went after a medieval wood panel stolen from the Great Mosque, a UNESCO World Heritage site in northeastern

Turkey. In a third case, she recovered a rare Egyptian stela. The history of the objects appealed to Levine, who had majored in history as an undergraduate at Brown University. History, she believed, demanded reverence.[1]

Levine was the perfect prosecutor for the 1933 Double Eagle case. Old documents came to life in her imagination. She read executive orders banning gold and pictured Franklin Roosevelt delivering fireside chats and Americans lining up to return their coins to the Federal Reserve. Mint records evoked a black-and-white newsreel of gaunt-faced men carting gold around the cavernous old building. Levine noticed the fountain-pen flourish of Agent Harry Strang's signature on his reports to his chief, and she thought of a proud young man in a fedora, tracking 1933 Double Eagles with humorless resolve.

The story she wanted to tell about the 1933 Double Eagle was of a fair and just government determined in 1933 to save the nation's economy, and for sixty-five years thereafter to preserve the integrity of its money supply. So Levine recast the 1933 Double Eagle case slightly, amending the civil complaint that prosecutor Evan Barr had first filed in 1997. Barr had fashioned the case as a forfeiture action, which rested on the theory that Fenton's 1933 Double Eagle represented the proceeds of a crime. To win title, the government would have to prove not only the crime but also Fenton's knowledge of it. Levine added a declaratory-judgment claim to the case, asserting that the government was the legal owner of the 1933 Double Eagle, regardless of how the piece got out of the Mint and what Fenton knew about it. She never doubted that Fenton knew the coin was illegal, but her argument was cleaner: The federal government has the sole right to issue currency, and it never issued 1933 Double Eagles. Therefore, all 1933 Double Eagles belonged to the government, then and now.

Even the export license that Berke kept touting could be explained into irrelevance, Levine believed, under her declaratory-judgment theory. The license had been approved by Theodore Belote, the Smithsonian curator, but only because Belote didn't realize that 1933 Double Eagles had never been issued, and all but the two pieces in the Smithsonian's National Numismatic Collection were supposed to have been locked into Mint vaults. The curator made a mistake,

Levine was willing to concede, but his mistake didn't mitigate the government's fundamental right to the coin.

WITH A raised eyebrow, Berke read Levine's motion to amend the complaint. He understood her strategy and admired her ingenuity, but he didn't change his own plans. Berke didn't intend to fight the government about what Fenton knew. He'd succeeded once with that backdoor approach—when he persuaded Mei Lin Kwan-Gett to drop the criminal charges—but in the struggle for possession of the coin, he wanted to give jurors a better reason to award the 1933 Double Eagle to Fenton. Thanks to King Farouk and the export license, Berke believed he had a better story to tell than Levine.

The man on whom that story depended most heavily, aside from Fenton himself, was Andre de Clermont, the British coin dealer who was to be the last witness deposed in this long-running litigation. De Clermont was the sole link between Fenton's coin and King Farouk; Fenton, after all, had not ever met Khalid Hassan, the Egyptian jeweler who sold him the 1933 Double Eagle. Only de Clermont could testify to Hassan's account of the Egyptian Army officer with a cache of Farouk coins—and even, for that matter, to Hassan's very existence. Without convincing testimony from de Clermont, Berke would never be able to prove that Fenton's coin was the Farouk specimen.

De Clermont's deposition was scheduled to take place on January 18, 2000. Berke flew to London two days beforehand, right after celebrating his thirty-sixth birthday. When he'd started on the 1933 Double Eagle case, he'd been single and newly hired at Kramer Levin. Now he was married, a father, a Kramer Levin partner—and still Stephen Fenton's lawyer in the coin case. Four years of litigation over an ounce of gold, he thought. No wonder his partners teased him.

Berke spent the day before the deposition at de Clermont's London office with the coin dealer and his brother, who kept de Clermont's books. The records were a mess. The three men spent hours pulling papers out of files, looking for anything that documented de Clermont's purchases from Khalid Hassan or his partnership with Fenton. When they'd located all of the invoices and lists, de Clermont sat down with Berke and his hardcover copy of the Palace Collections auction catalogue. With the invoices spread out in front of them, de Clermont showed Berke the comparisons he'd made between coins he bought from Hassan and auction-lot descriptions in the Farouk catalogue. The book, he told Berke, proved that all the Hassan coins had come from Farouk's collection—including the 1933 Double Eagle. There was no other possible source.

Berke, congenitally sanguine, left de Clermont's office more confident than ever. The proof of the Farouk connection was complicated—more complicated than Berke would have liked—but undeniable. Berke told de Clermont to take his auction catalogue to the deposition. He wanted Jane Levine to see the coin dealer paging through the book, pointing to all of the Farouk coins he had purchased from Hassan.

Fenton accompanied Berke to the U.S. Embassy the next day to watch de Clermont testify. De Clermont was an excellent witness, polite and clear-spoken. Under Levine's questioning, he explained how he'd bought that first batch of extraordinary coins from Mohammed Ezzadin, the Egyptian trader, and how he'd dealt thereafter with Hassan. He told how Hassan had eventually revealed the story of the coin-collecting officer in Nasser's army. De Clermont opened his Palace Collections catalogue, showing Levine the listings of unique pieces that he'd purchased from Hassan. It was obvious, even to Levine, that de Clermont had, indeed, acquired a cache of Farouk coins. The auction catalogue, for instance, listed a "probably unique" pattern half-eagle made of gilded copper, a coin that had belonged to Colonel E. H. R. Green before Farouk bought it. In December 1994, de Clermont bought that very coin from Hassan, along with a piece of documentation reading, "ex. Colonel Green." In May 1995, de Clermont bought from Hassan a one-of-a-kind platinum medal of Franklin Roosevelt—a medal listed as part of lot 1565 in the Palace Collections catalogue. The same lot included a platinum United Nations medal, also unique and also purchased by de Clermont from Hassan in May 1995. "There [was] no doubt in my mind whatsoever," de Clermont told Levine at the deposition. "They [were] all from Farouk."[2]

Airtight, Berke thought to himself. Jane can't challenge this. The rules of decorum prevented any show of emotion when the deposition ended, but Berke and Fenton both shook de Clermont's hand. "You were great, Andre," Berke said. "Thank you." De Clermont promised that if the case went to trial, he'd go to New York to testify in person.

JANE LEVINE, experienced prosecutor that she is, was unruffled by de Clermont's deposition. She'd been irritated at the start, when Berke dumped a load of paper from de Clermont's files on her, and surprised in the middle, when she learned for the first time about Khalid Hassan and the mysterious Egyptian Army officer. She had to admit that she'd been fascinated to hear de Clermont account for what had been a glaring gap in her knowledge of the history of the 1933 Double Eagle. But in Levine's view, de Clermont's story raised almost as many questions as it answered. The pile of papers she received at the start of the session documented every purchase de Clermont and Fenton made from Hassan—except for the purchase of the 1933 Double Eagle. Why was there no specific mention of the coin in de Clermont's records? Was it because Fenton and de Clermont knew the coin was illegal? Or was it because it didn't come from Hassan at all? There was still no documentary proof that Fenton's 1933 Double Eagle had been Farouk's—and thus the subject of the export license–even if jurors believed de Clermont's story about Hassan. And who was Hassan, anyway, this supposedly crucial player known only to Andre de Clermont? Levine considered dispatching an investigator to Egypt to search for the jeweler, but then she decided she was probably better off showing jurors that de Clermont's story was shadowy, unsupported by his own documents, and quite convenient for a man who expected to share in the profits from Fenton's sale of the 1933 Double Eagle. Levine believed that if de Clermont testified at trial, she had the facts to neutralize him.

As the trial date approached, both Levine and Berke were counting on Judge Alvin Hellerstein to clarify the case's myriad legal uncertainties. Berke had filed a motion for summary judgment, which asked the judge to decide whether the law alone compelled victory for Fenton.

Berke knew his motion was a long shot—summary-judgment motions are supposed to present the judge with indisputable facts, of which there were surpassingly few in this case—but he and Levine hoped that their briefs and oral arguments before Judge Hellerstein would lead to rulings on such questions as the admissibility of the old Mint and Secret Service documents.

Berke's summary-judgment brief was a fifty-six-page textbook on sculpting evidence to suit a chosen narrative. He described the historical context of FDR's Gold Reserve Act of 1934, taking care to note William Woodin's special carve-out for gold coins of special value to collectors. He discussed Farouk's well-documented application for an export license, the U.S. government's approval of the license, and the subsequent release of Farouk's 1933 Double Eagle from the Mint to the Egyptian Legation. Berke then laid out the evidence that Fenton's coin was the Farouk specimen, relying on testimony from de Clermont's deposition. Such facts, he argued in his brief, could mean only that Fenton's coin—the Farouk coin—was not stolen property. "It is beyond dispute that the government issued a license authorizing the export and possession of the 1933 Double Eagle," Berke wrote. "The government had regained possession of the allegedly 'stolen' 1933 Double Eagle long before Mr. Fenton obtained it, which under well-established law means the coin was not 'stolen property' at the time it was imported by Mr. Fenton."[3]

Levine's reply to Berke's brief offered Judge Hellerstein an entirely different 1933 Double Eagle story, this one about a coin never issued to the public but stolen by a trio of conspirators whose scheme was only later exposed by the dogged work of the Secret Service. Levine's brief was full of unsavory details about George McCann and Israel Switt—a pair whose names never even appeared in Berke's selective history of the coin. Stephen Fenton, as he was depicted in Levine's brief, was a man of similar ilk, conspiring to sell what he knew to be stolen property and tripped up by a Secret Service sting. The Barnard case of 1947, Levine argued, had already established that 1933 Double Eagles could not have left the Mint lawfully. Berke's export-license theory was a red herring, supported only by "the multi-layered inadmissible hearsay testimony of [Fenton's] business partner," Levine wrote. "[The argument] may have simplistic, surface appeal but [is] based on a profound distortion of the facts and misapplication of the law and should be rejected."[4]

For both lawyers, the argument before Judge Hellerstein on March 23, 2000, was a chance to try out their stories. Levine, whom the judge commended for "a fantastic job," succeeded in raising doubts about Fenton's good faith, leading Hellerstein to question whether the high price Parrino was willing to pay for the coin "should suggest something that is not so kosher." Berke's test of the export-license theory, meanwhile, was a flop. "I am a little troubled by the provenance," Hellerstein told the lawyer. "The evidence that [you] presented is not so convincing."

But Hellerstein's ruling, issued from the bench without a formal, written opinion, frustrated both lawyers equally. As expected, he denied Berke's motion for summary judgment. There were too many questions of fact, too many evidentiary holes, for him to decide the case based only on the law. The judge also, however, declined to answer questions of law. "I would have to reflect very hard in terms of how I would rule on various of the important issues," he told Berke and Levine. "I think there are important arguments that both of you make that could persuade me one way or the other, and I would not know how I would rule at this particular point."[5] The two lawyers would have to prepare for trial, scheduled for the beginning of 2001, without knowing what evidence would be admitted.

IN DECEMBER 2000, Mint lawyer Ken Gubin arranged to meet Jane Levine at the National Archives in College Park, Maryland, just to make sure they hadn't somehow overlooked any important documents. For Levine, the onetime history major, the trip was a treat. The National Archives building wasn't the dusty hall of records she'd imagined—it's actually an airy, sunlit facility with a soothing forest view—but she found a windfall in one of the boxes the archivist located for her. It was a file of documents belonging to the Treasury Department lawyer who had assisted on the Barnard case back in 1947. Levine held her breath as she opened the file. The first thing she read was a

memo the Treasury lawyer had written, explaining how the government could prove the disposition of 1933 Double Eagles. He'd actually studied the handwritten Mint ledger books and re-created the
route of the coins as they moved around the Mint. All of the 1933
Double Eagles were accounted for in the Mint records cited by the
long-ago lawyer. None had been innocently exchanged across the
cashier's counter.

Levine paged through the file. There was the Barnard case exhibit
list, along with the two dozen documents the government planned to
introduce as evidence at the Barnard trial. Levine realized that what
she was reading was probably a copy of the materials that prosecutors
had presented to Barnard's lawyers before that trial in 1947. It was
the true story of the short life and fiery death of some 445,500 1933
Double Eagles, compiled with the help of Mint officials who had
been there to witness the events in question. "Here it is," Levine said
to Gubin. "This is a great find. I've got to make copies and really
analyze this."

But when she returned to New York with the file, Levine's flush of
excitement faded. Here she had a record—a documentary, historical
record—that proved 1933 Double Eagles could only have left the
Mint by theft. But she, unlike the Treasury Department lawyer who
had created the file in 1947, had no witnesses to testify about the
record. Without a ruling from Judge Hellerstein on whether he'd admit
hearsay evidence, Levine still didn't know if she'd ever be able to show
jurors what her long-ago predecessor had so painstakingly proved.

BARRY BERKE, meanwhile, was in the midst of a similar dash to find
overlooked evidence before the trial started. He particularly wanted to
shore up the theory favored by his numismatic experts: In the chaos of
gold policy in March 1933, some number of newly minted 1933 Double Eagles might have been legitimately exchanged across the Mint
cashier's counter. In January 2001, a month before the trial was to
begin, Stephen Fenton flew to New York and set up camp at the Lombardy Hotel. (Ever since the sting in 1996, he had avoided both the
Hilton and the Waldorf.) Each morning Fenton would meet Berke at

the Kramer Levin offices and volunteer for paralegal duty. When Berke sent his associate, Justine Harris, and paralegal, Sam Tepperman-Gelfant, to the National Archives in College Park, Fenton accompanied them.

Unlike the government lawyers, who had the benefit of an archivist to help them figure out which sketchily described boxes of documents to examine, the team from Kramer Levin simply waded into paper. It was an exasperating process. They would read a description of a box of documents in the Archives index, fill out a request form, wait for Archives assistants to retrieve the box and bring it to the reading room, and finally open it—sometimes only to find that its contents didn't match the index description at all. But near the end of the day, Tepperman-Gelfant discovered a trove of letters to and from Mint officials. There was a 1933 note, for instance, from M. M. Reilly, acting director of the Mint, to G. B. Thomas, Jr., advising him that the Mint in Philadelphia was "authorized to exchange gold for gold."[6] Another letter, dated March 14, 1933, stated that the Federal Reserve was permitted to deliver gold to banks despite the gold recall. Tepperman-Gelfant turned to Fenton and Harris excitedly. "No one thought there was anything special about these coins at the time," he whispered. "They could have gotten out."[7]

But his epiphany at the National Archives ended up being as short-lived as Levine's. While Fenton and Harris returned to New York, Tepperman-Gelfant stayed an extra day in Maryland, then made plans to go to the regional archives in Philadelphia, where some of the records of the Philadelphia Mint are stored. In Philadelphia, he requested the cashier's record books from 1933, when the Double Eagles were being minted and stored. Studying the books was tedious—accounts were recorded in dollar amounts, rather than numbers of coins—and ultimately discouraging. The longer Tepperman-Gelfant studied the ledgers, the less plausible it seemed to him that a 1933 Double Eagle might have been exchanged innocently across the cashier's counter. He called Berke from Philadelphia to report the bad news.

With only a few weeks remaining before jury selection was to begin, Berke was practically living at the office, returning home only to say hello to his wife and baby daughter and fall into bed. Levine had sent him her proposed exhibit list—193 documents, from Mint records of 1933 and Secret Service reports of 1944 to the transcripts of Jack Moore's taped conversations with Jay Parrino in 1996. Berke drafted objections to 169 of the proposed exhibits, writing challenges to every document except those relating to the export license and Fenton's U.S. Customs paperwork. His legal research ranged far and wide. He studied the Coinage Act of 1965, in which Congress authorized the ownership of gold coins, regardless of when they were minted. He wrote a brief on the Egyptian "thieves market" law, contemplating an assertion that because the coin was held for so long in Egypt, Egyptian law should govern its ownership. In a huge omnibus of a brief, he argued against every exception to the hearsay rules that would permit Levine to introduce Secret Service reports from the 1940s. He sent letter after letter to Levine: Who would present first? Who had the burden of proof under the forfeiture laws as most recently amended by Congress? Which issues were for the jury to decide and which for Judge Hellerstein?

Downtown at the U.S. Attorney's office, Levine and Steven Cobry, the assistant prosecutor she'd roped in to help with trial preparation, matched Berke letter for letter, brief for brief, hour for hour. Levine was on the phone to Berke at least once a day. The two lawyers had become friends, each appreciating the other's passion for the coin case. By now, each knew the other's arguments intimately; each knew the strengths and deficiencies of the story the other planned to tell the jury. They'd fight in court, but on the phone they commiserated.

"Working on that hearsay brief, Jane?" Berke might say.

"Yeah," she might answer. "You too?"

Late in the day on Friday, January 19, 2001, with a snowstorm threatening the city, Levine called Berke to discuss document production. She complained about the crushing burden of getting this case ready for trial. "You know, Jane," Berke teased, "you could just agree to settle and we could all go home and have a good weekend."

To his surprise, Levine replied, "Let me call you back."

•   •   •

BERKE HAD floated settlement offers to Levine before. They all began with Fenton keeping the 1933 Double Eagle, a condition Levine rejected reflexively. The whole point of the litigation for Levine was to ensure the federal government's unqualified right to determine the legitimacy of its currency. There was no way she would ever cede title to the 1933 Double Eagle to Fenton. Even Judge Hellerstein's intervention couldn't nudge Berke and Levine closer to a deal. After his summary-judgment ruling, the judge ordered Fenton and the Mint lawyers working with Levine to attend a formal settlement conference. It accomplished nothing.

But now, with trial imminent, Levine and the Mint lawyers were worried. So much of their case was uncertain. What if Judge Hellerstein sustained Berke's objections to documents they tried to introduce? Would Levine be left standing in front of a jury with nothing to say? And what if they lost at trial? The disposition of one coin wasn't really important, but the principle of government autonomy was. Losing title to the 1933 Double Eagle might set a dangerous precedent.

Then Levine had an idea, based on one of Berke's settlement proposals. Berke had suggested selling the 1933 Double Eagle and splitting the proceeds between Fenton and the government. What if, Levine asked Mint lawyers, Fenton agreed to concede the government's ownership of the 1933 Double Eagle before they sold the coin? He'd still get his share of the profits but just wouldn't be called an owner. The government wouldn't get to keep the coin, Levine said, but it would preserve the principle of its ownership rights. "It's palatable," said Mint lawyer Greg Weinman. "We just have to structure it in a way that gives us title and certainty."

On the snowy Friday afternoon of January 19, Levine called Berke back. "Remember how you raised the possibility of selling the coin and splitting the profits? Would you still be interested in that?"

"I didn't think that was something you would agree to," Berke said.

"We might, if you drop the claim that the coin belongs to Fenton," Levine said. "We need you to concede that the coin was never issued and belongs to us."

"I'll check with Stephen," said Berke.

Fenton had already left the office and was back in his room at the

Lombardy. Berke called him. "The government wants to talk about a deal," the lawyer said. "They'll sell the coin and we'll split the profits."

"How's it going to be done?" Fenton asked. "Are they going to pay back half of what I've already paid for the coin?"

"We'll have to work that all out," Berke said. "Should I talk to them? Do you want me to settle the case?"

Fenton hesitated. He'd paid a small fortune for the 1933 Double Eagle in 1995, and it had brought him nothing but trouble. The arrest at the Waldorf. His reputation tarnished. Another small fortune gone to pay legal fees in this years-long fight to recover the coin. Fenton cared about principles, too. He believed he was the legitimate owner of the 1933 Double Eagle, and he resented the U.S. government's accusations about his conduct. But at heart Fenton was a businessman. He knew the 1933 Double Eagle would be worth more than ever if it were sold with the government's sanction, especially with all the publicity the case had received.

"Let's go for it," Fenton told Berke. "Let's settle."

Chapter Seventeen

Second Chances

ON THE MORNING OF Monday, April 30, 2001, Barry Berke and Stephen Fenton met for breakfast at a cafe in the lobby of Washington, DC's Willard Hotel. It was a quick and happy affair, the two men laughing at the irony of Fenton's changed circumstances. Stephen Fenton, onetime criminal defendant, had become the United States government's business partner, with an equal say, under the agreement Berke had negotiated with Jane Levine, in how the 1933 Double Eagle would be sold. During the litigation, Berke had had to go to court for permission just to check on the coin's condition in the Secret Service vault at Seven World Trade Center. After the January 25 settlement was signed, his paralegal, Sam Tepperman-Gelfant, was welcomed at Secret Service headquarters for the 1933 Double Eagle's official photo session.

Now the coin was in the custody of the U.S. Mint—an armed escort of Mint police officers had transported it to Fort Knox, Kentucky—and Berke and Fenton were in Washington to attend presentations by four eminent auction houses vying to sell the 1993 Double

Eagle. That was how Fenton and the Mint lawyers had decided to proceed: Despite offers to buy the 1933 Double Eagle privately—including one from Mark Raffety, a California coin dealer who said he had a client willing to pay $4 million—they had opted to auction the coin publicly. The Double Eagle, they had reasoned, would probably bring more money at auction than in a private deal. Besides, an auction seemed more appropriate. The 1933 Double Eagle epic deserved a triumphant finale, not the quiet offstage disappearance of its main character.

In early April, a five-person Mint selection committee, following government procurement procedures, had invited thirteen auction houses to submit proposals to sell the coin. Among them were Sotheby's and Christie's (the latter invited through Spink, at the time its rare-coin arm); Guernsey's, a New York auction house known for big-money memorabilia sales; and a plethora of coin specialists, including Dave Bowers's company, Bowers and Merena Galleries. Six houses responded by the April 25 deadline. Mint officials selected three finalists—Bowers and Merena, Sotheby's, and Guernsey's—to come to Washington for in-person presentations. Fenton, exercising his equal-partner prerogatives, insisted that Heritage Rare Coin Galleries, whose principals were his friends, also be considered a finalist.[1]

April 30 was presentation day. After their jolly breakfast at the Willard, Fenton and Berke headed for the Mint's office building on Ninth Street, where they met up with the five officials on the Mint selection team. At nine, they all took their seats in the amphitheater-style auditorium on the second floor—Fenton and Berke sat on the left side of the room, the Mint people in the center—and asked the first presenters to come in.

DAVID REDDEN and Larry Stack had had only days to prepare for this performance, but they believed nevertheless that they were destined to sell this coin. They represented, after all, both of the auction houses that had previously attempted to sell 1933 Double Eagles. Redden was the vice-chairman of Sotheby's, which had lost the chance to sell Farouk's 1933 Saint in 1954, when the American

Embassy in Egypt insisted on the coin's withdrawal from the Palace Collections auction. And Larry Stack was the grandson of Morton Stack, one of the brothers from whom Agent Harry Strang seized Colonel James Flanagan's 1933 Double Eagle during the fateful Stack's auction in 1944. Big-boned, abundantly bearded, and gruff, Stack was the third generation of his family to head the eponymous coin house on 57th Street in New York.

When Redden first received the Mint's request for a proposal to sell the 1933 Double Eagle, he and Stack were in the midst of another joint pitch, this one to sell the collection of a Texas oilman named H. Jeff Browning. Browning had died suddenly in 1978, leaving an astonishing collection of 600 gold coins. His family had held onto the set, known as the Dallas Bank Collection, for more than twenty years, but had finally decided to sell it in 2001. Browning's executor invited auction houses to make proposals to run the auction. Redden asked Stack, an old friend, to join his bid, and Sotheby's marketing office put together a written presentation that explained why Stack's coin expertise and Sotheby's international reach made them the best choice to sell the collection.[2] For their initial submission to the Mint on the 1933 Double Eagle sale, Redden and Stack recycled much of the material from the Dallas Bank pitch.

It was an effective piece of marketing. When Redden and Stack found out that they had been named one of the four finalists to make an in-person presentation to Fenton and the Mint selection committee, they were in Dallas, fresh from a meeting with the Browning family in which they had been awarded the Dallas Bank sale. With only a weekend to fly home from Texas and plan the 1933 Double Eagle presentation, they decided to keep their presentation simple and direct. That approach had worked with the Browning family. With luck, it would work at the Mint as well.

As THEY walked into the auditorium on the morning of April 30, Stack wondered if they had miscalculated. He, Redden, and Sotheby's coin consultant David Tripp were empty-handed; they had already sent sample catalogues to the selection committee to show the kind of attention they would bestow on the 1933 Double Eagle. But the competition, Stack noticed, had brought laptops and overhead projectors. "Uh-oh," he said to Tripp and Redden, "they're going electronic on us."

Redden needed no electronic enhancement. He is supremely effective as a Sotheby's pitchman not because he's charming, urbane, and British-accented, although he is all of those things with a Hugh Grant–like flop to his hair, to boot. It's because he is passionate about interesting objects—whether the textiles he and his wife have collected, the rare books that were his first area of expertise at Sotheby's, or the *Tyrannosaurus rex* skeleton he auctioned for more than $8 million in 1997. In the way he talks about *things*, Redden broadcasts his own in-the-bones affinity with the people who covet them. He told Berke, Fenton, and the Mint selection committee that he didn't regard the 1933 Double Eagle as simply a rare coin. It was a treasure, a work of art, a unique piece of history, and that was how Sotheby's and Stack's would sell it. "If this coin isn't the most famous coin in the world right now, it will be when we're through," Redden promised. And not just in the coin world. "This coin has such a good story, it could attract buyers outside of the numismatic community," he said. "To bring a really fantastic price we need to reach those buyers." Between them, Redden assured his small audience, Sotheby's and Stack's would bring in both kinds of collectors—coin lovers as well as those with a passion to possess extraordinary objects of all sorts.

When Stack spoke, he was more blunt. "We deserve this," he said, at one point addressing Fenton directly. "Sotheby's had one confiscated in 1954, Stack's in 1944. You guys owe it to us now."

There were still three more auction houses waiting to make presentations, as well as a round of post-presentation written submissions to consider, but by the time they left the Mint auditorium on April 30, Redden and Stack had already won over Fenton and the Mint officials. Redden was irresistible, and Larry Stack's appeal for fairness had some resonance even with Mint bureaucrats who had to justify their choice with a matrix of rankings in four different categories. The official announcement finally came from the Mint on February 7, 2002: Sotheby's and Stack's had been chosen to auction the 1933

Double Eagle. On July 30, the day the coin would be sold, the two auction houses would have their chance, with the government's wholehearted backing, to avenge the aborted 1933 Double Eagle sales of the past.

THE DATE had been Larry Stack's idea. High summer isn't usually auction season, but the American Numismatic Association's annual convention was scheduled to be held in New York City in 2002, beginning on July 31. If Sotheby's and Stack's held the 1933 Saint sale the night before, they'd be assured of a huge audience of coin dealers and collectors. In the meantime, the auction houses had about seven months to whip up Double Eagle frenzy.

Sotheby's arranged for the coin's debut. On March 19, Mint Director Henrietta Holsman Fore, trailing an entourage of U.S. Mint and New York City police officers, arrived at the Rockefeller Center studios of the *Today* show.[3] Fore carried the 1933 Double Eagle in an antique oak box once used to transport gold bars, and she played up the theatricality of its unveiling in her interview with host Matt Lauer. Fore, the head of an operation that contributes billions to the federal treasury through the sale of collectible coins, was a shrewd marketer. The 1933 Double Eagle, she told Lauer, was "the Mona Lisa of coins."

The manufactured drama continued when the coin went on the road. David Pickens, the Mint's associate director of marketing, wanted to be sure that his constituency, coin collectors, had a chance to see the 1933 Double Eagle on both coasts. Sotheby's placed it on heavily guarded display in New York in April; then in early June, Larry Stack and David Tripp accompanied the 1933 Double Eagle to the Long Beach Coin and Stamp Expo. There the coin was treated like a holy artifact. Every morning of the three-day show, William Daddio, the head of Mint security, would pull up to the convention center in an eight-car motorcade. He would march onto the bourse floor with the coin and a contingent of armed officers, who would stand as solemn as a palace guard detail through the daylong viewing. Stack once teased Daddio about the guns-drawn ceremony of the display. "Get out of the way, Larry," Daddio teased back, "or else if I have to shoot someone it will hit you first." No one understood better than Daddio the real point of the security ritual: The more attention the Mint lavished on the coin, the higher the price it would fetch when it was auctioned at the end of July.

Fenton, at the Long Beach show on ordinary coin business, watched the fuss over the 1933 Double Eagle at first with bemusement, then with irritation. "I carried it around in my pocket," he grumbled. All day people kept running up to him with copies of David Tripp's lush, fifty-six-page 1933 Double Eagle catalogue, asking Fenton to autograph what was sure to become a collectible in its own right.

From the bourse floor, Fenton called his girlfriend in London: "It's driving me crazy. The coin has *bodyguards*."

"Just enjoy it," she advised.

Fenton couldn't forget, though, that he'd once been arrested for owning the Double Eagle that was now receiving royal treatment. He called Berke. "You should see the armed guard," he told his lawyer. "The coin's half mine, right? Could I just go up and take it and walk around with it?"

"I guess you could, Stephen," said Berke, "but I wouldn't suggest it."

DAVID REDDEN was a wreck as summer passed and the auction date loomed. He had promised Fenton and the Mint that Sotheby's would be able to bring in bidders from outside the universe of wealthy coin collectors—"people who never collected coins, never had a clue they'd be interested in a coin until our marketing onslaught," he had said. Redden had to keep assuring government officials who wanted to see a timeline and paperwork that in the auction business you have to count on serendipity. But even for him, waiting for these elusive would-be collectors to emerge was nerve-racking.

To be sure, some bidders—a handful of coin dealers and collectors—had already surfaced. Mark Raffety, the California coin dealer who had already offered to buy the 1933 Double Eagle for $4 million represented a collector named Philip Morse. Morse had secretly amassed one of the two or three finest sets of Saint-Gaudens double eagles in the country, and he badly wanted to cap his collection with the 1933 Saint. As soon as the coin went on display at Sotheby's in April, Raffety went to see it. He had been the first bidder to pass Sotheby's vetting process (a confirmation that he had the liquid assets to pay for the coin), receiving paddle 100.[4] Another premier Saints collector—a man whose name was known only in the highest echelons of the trade—had contacted Larry Stack when the auction was announced. Even before the litigation over ownership of the 1933 Double Eagle was resolved, he and his usual dealer, Todd Imhof of Pinnacle Rarities, Inc., had attempted to strike a private deal with Fenton, offering to buy Fenton's stake in the case. Imhof had met with Barry Berke at a coin show in Philadelphia the summer before the case was settled, but Fenton wanted more than Imhof's client was willing to pay.[5] Now that the coin was up for auction, Imhof's client asked Larry Stack to represent him at the sale.

Most of the collectors and dealers cleared by Sotheby's kept quiet about it, but Barry Goldwater, Jr., of the National Collector's Mint, issued an announcement that he would be bidding on the 1933 Double Eagle. Larry Stack considered him to be interested primarily in the publicity—the National Collector's Mint was selling replicas of the 1933 Double Eagle—but Goldwater took some of the pressure off Redden when he said he was willing to pay the reserve that Sotheby's had set on the coin. That reserve, the minimum price for which the Mint and Fenton were willing to sell the piece, had been set strategically by Stack and Redden. Though the estimate on the coin was $4 to $6 million, the reserve was much less: only $2.5 million. And, contrary to standard auction procedure, Redden published the reserve amount. He didn't want to scare away any qualified bidders who might balk at the estimate. Luring them across the threshold, onto the auction floor with paddles in their hands, was crucial.

THE DAY before the 1933 Double Eagle auction, Redden was still fretting. Thanks to Goldwater, he knew the coin would sell for at least the reserve price of $2.5 million, but if the bidding stopped there, the sale would be a terrible disappointment, hardly justifying the hoopla

Redden had orchestrated. As of July 29, fewer than a dozen bidders had been cleared, and only one, a young Bahamian financier,[6] was the kind of wild card Redden had been hoping for—someone who had never heard of the 1933 Double Eagle until the Sotheby's publicity offensive. The rest were all coin people.

That afternoon, Redden's assistant paged him to the telephone. A man was calling to ask about the coin. The auctioneer picked up. When the caller introduced himself, Redden didn't recognize the name. The man wasn't a coin collector and had never bought anything at Sotheby's. He'd never even been to an auction, he told Redden. But he was interested, he said, in unusual pieces of history, one-of-a-kind objects like the 1933 Double Eagle. He wanted to bid on the coin the next day.

Redden was polite; if there was one thing he had learned in his years in the auction business, it was that you have to take every prospective buyer seriously. The man said he wanted to remain anonymous. He didn't want his name to be disclosed, didn't even want anyone to see him bidding. "We can be discreet," Redden said. "We can put you in a skybox." The man said that he wanted to meet with Redden at Sotheby's the next morning, to have the process explained to him. Redden said that would be fine. He'd be busy, but he always had time for a bidder.

Chapter Eighteen

"Fair Warning"

AT LAST IT WAS Tuesday, July 30, 2002, the most important day in the strange, fateful, and inanimate life of the 1933 Double Eagle. Just after six o'clock that night, a handful of bidders would decide—in an auction grander than any the numismatic world had ever seen—how much that extraordinary coin was worth. When it was over, one of them would be the only person in the world to own a legal 1933 Double Eagle.

A hot, wet curtain of humidity hung over the city that morning. It was going to be a brutal day. David Redden, wearing a dark suit and his favorite good-luck tie, arrived at Sotheby's early, before the heat became unbearable. There was so much to do on the day of a big sale, so many details to consider. How many chairs should be set up on the enormous auction floor? Not too many, Redden instructed the Sotheby's staff; he wanted standing-room-only drama. Where should Henrietta Holsman Fore and her Mint delegation sit? Near the front,

Redden decided, in the center section. More critically, what should be done about last-minute bidders who hadn't been vetted? Larry Stack, who turned up at Sotheby's just after lunchtime, vouched for two of them, a banker and a coin collector. Another bidder, a man named Stephen Tebo, called Sotheby's from an airplane above the Caribbean. Tebo was a onetime coin dealer who'd made millions in Colorado real estate. He believed that at the right price, the 1933 Double Eagle was a smart investment, and so he was cutting short his vacation and flying into New York for the auction. Tebo wanted to confirm that Sotheby's had a paddle waiting for him. There'd been a glitch in checking his financials, Tebo learned, but Sotheby's promised that by the time he landed in New York, he'd be cleared.[1]

The prospective bidder who'd called Redden the previous day arrived at Sotheby's and asked to see the auctioneer. Redden dropped what he was doing to escort the anonymous man to a skybox overlooking the auction floor. "How will this work?" the man asked. Redden spent ten minutes explaining. There was a phone in the skybox. The man would telephone down to a desk in the phone bank on the auction floor, just to the right of Redden's podium. Redden had asked Selby Kiffer, the head of Sotheby's Rare Books Department, to handle the man's call. The man would instruct Kiffer when he wanted to bid, and Kiffer would signal his bids to Redden. The auction would move quickly, Redden told the man. Bidding would begin with Barry Goldwater's $2.5 million opener and would move up in hundred-thousand-dollar increments. "Okay," the man said. "Thanks." Redden left him in the box and hurried off.

The heat built all afternoon. Outside the Sotheby's granite-and-glass box of a building, limousine drivers sat behind their smoked windows, cars idling with the air-conditioning on. Cameramen, not so lucky, climbed out of television news vans, sweat beads popping across their foreheads as they swung equipment onto their shoulders and lugged it inside. News was going to be made at Sotheby's that night, heat or no.

Inside, it was cooler, but not much. The cavernous seventh-floor auction room was filling quickly. Just as Larry Stack had predicted, the entire coin world seemed to have turned out—and in unaccustomed finery—for the 1933 Double Eagle auction. And just as David Redden had hoped, the crowd expected to witness history. Only a few coins had sold for more than a million dollars since Jay Parrino had first broken the barrier in 1996. The highest price any coin had fetched at auction was $4.1 million—David Akers's bid for an 1804 silver dollar at a 1999 Bowers and Merena auction.[2] The 1933 Double Eagle would become the second-most-valuable coin in the world the instant Barry Goldwater raised his paddle with his opening bid of $2.5 million. And if the gossip buzzing through Sotheby's that afternoon was right, the 1933 Double Eagle would go on to break the 1804 silver dollar's record.

The anticipation was electric, as if the crowd of coin collectors was waiting for a rock concert to begin—except, of course, that the star of this particular show was inert. Huge projected images of the 1933 Double Eagle filled the screens flanking Redden's podium. The coin itself stood on display toward the back of the enormous room, protected in a special lit-from-within case atop a velvet-draped stand. People swarmed to get a look.

When Fenton and Berke arrived at Sotheby's at around four forty-five, they were mobbed by autograph seekers who wanted not only the British coin dealer but even his lawyer to sign their catalogues. Fenton had been in New York for several days, keeping up with gossip on the bidders and their plans. He heard some of the crazier talk—that Bill Gates was bidding, that $20 million was within reach—but steeled himself to dismiss it. "Until the thing is sold and I get paid," he had told Berke on the way over to Sotheby's, "I'm not believing any of it." The crowd at Sotheby's shocked him. Fenton had attended countless coin auctions; he'd never seen anything like this.

Mark Raffety got to the auction house at about five and grabbed his seat in the front row. Redden had offered him a skybox—Raffety had the feeling that the auctioneer was providing special treatment because Redden expected his client, Philip Morse, to win the coin—but Raffety wanted to be on the floor, close to the action. Sotheby's had set up a phone line at his seat so he could receive instructions from Morse, who was in New York City but had elected not to attend the sale. Raffety picked up the phone to test it. He felt a rush of panic: There was no dial tone. He couldn't get the Sotheby's phone to work. The coin dealer took out his cell phone, turned it on, and called Morse. When he got through, he decided to use his phone during the bidding. He didn't want to take a chance with the Sotheby's equipment.

Six o'clock approached. Mint police officers moved the 1933 Double Eagle to the front of the room, near Redden's podium. Fenton and Berke, along with Fenton's girlfriend and a contingent from Kramer Levin, went up to the skybox that Sotheby's had reserved for them. Prosecutor Jane Levine, in attendance with the assistant U.S. Attorney who would have helped her try the Double Eagle case, sat down near the Mint lawyers in their reserved seats. Amid the commotion, Levine felt a pang of regret. She was glad the coin's story had been told in David Tripp's catalogue, glad that a ceremony after the sale of the 1933 Double Eagle would affirm the all-important principle of the Mint's exclusive right to issue coins. But Levine was enough of a competitor to wonder if she should have brought the case to trial after all. Now that she was here, waiting for the auction to begin, she realized how unsatisfying a resolution the settlement had been.

Larry Stack sat down at the long wooden desk that separated the phone bank to the right of the podium from the main selling floor. He'd be bidding on behalf of Todd Imhof's client, the Saints collector. Larry's father, Harvey Stack, stood behind his son. Next to Harvey was another Stack's client, a collector who hadn't planned to bid on the 1933 Double Eagle but was now reconsidering. Selby Kiffer sat farther to the back of the phone bank, receiver in hand, waiting for instructions from the anonymous man in the skybox.

At precisely six o'clock, David Redden walked up three steps to the auctioneer's podium at the front of the room. He'd been a Sotheby's impresario for twenty-five years, but he never ceased to wonder at the simultaneous thrill and terror of running a sale like this. Redden had succeeded in raising hopes for the 1933 Double Eagle sale to giddy heights. If one of the bidders didn't come up with the cash to meet those towering expectations, Redden would be left standing before a deflated audience, humiliated. The coin wasn't his, but the spectacle was.

"My name is David Redden," he said when he reached the

podium.[3] As if the crowd didn't know. Redden quickly explained the terms of the sale—a fifteen percent buyer's premium would be added to the hammer price, as well as a one-of-a-kind $20 payment to make the coin legal. There would be no sales tax because the United States government was the seller. To the audience, Redden seemed his usual self, but in fact he'd already shifted into auction mode. His eyes darted around the crowd, picking out bidders. His ears registered the hum on the floor. He made instantaneous decisions about the tone of voice to use, the pace to set.

Then it started. "I need to begin the bidding with two million five hundred thousand dollars," Redden said, looking to his right for Barry Goldwater, Jr. Seated on the outer edge of the second row, Goldwater raised his blue plastic paddle. The bidding was underway. Redden breezed through two million six hundred thousand, two million seven hundred, two million eight hundred thousand dollars. Bids were coming from all over the floor: the phone bank, the right side of the audience, the center. Three million. Three million one hundred thousand from Goldwater. Three million two. Redden was speaking quickly, pointing at bidders, maintaining momentum. Three million three hundred thousand on the telephone in the back. Three million four. Three million five hundred thousand.

Larry Stack's phone bidder told Stack he was out. Seated in the crowd, Todd Imhof sighed. He and his client had talked about when to stop bidding—there were so many unanswered questions about the 1933 Double Eagle—but it was still a disappointment.

Larry Stack wasn't quite done though. Harvey's client, the Stack's collector, stepped up. He wanted Larry to bid for him. Larry raised his hand. Three million six. Three million seven. Barry Goldwater jiggled his left leg and craned his neck to see who was still in. Three million eight hundred thousand. Goldwater raised his paddle again. Three million nine in the second row. Larry Stack's second bidder was out. He'd lasted less than a minute.

Redden slowed the pace incrementally, lowering his voice as he called for a bidder to cross the momentous four-million-dollar mark. For the first time, Selby Kiffer raised his hand from the phone bank. Redden silently took note: The mysterious man in the skybox was in.

"Four million dollars on the telephone," Redden said, gesturing at Kiffer with his left hand.

Now it was Goldwater again at four million one hundred thousand. The bids were coming a little more slowly. Redden had to work for them. He pumped up the drama, rolling out numbers syllable by syllable. Four million two hundred thousand dollars. Kiffer on the phone again.

A new bidder caught Redden's eye. A shabbily dressed young man, tall and sweaty, standing toward the back of the room with a cell phone pressed to his ear, raised a blue plastic paddle. Heads turned. A murmur spread. This guy was bidding millions? Redden didn't pause. The man had a paddle, so he—or the person on the other end of his cell phone—had money. "In a new place, standing in the back, at four million three hundred thousand," Redden said.

Kiffer raised his hand. Four million four hundred thousand. Goldwater bid at four million five. That was it, Goldwater's limit. He was out. Stephen Tebo, the Colorado real-estate developer seated on the center aisle in the fifth row, was out, too. He tucked away his blue plastic paddle. I'm holding onto this, he thought to himself. I'll always be able to say I was here, bidding on the 1933 Double Eagle.

ON HIS cell phone in the front row, Mark Raffety heard Philip Morse say he was done bidding. Raffety whispered urgently into the phone, reminding Morse that this was his only chance to make his Saints set complete. Morse was torn but wouldn't budge. Raffety twirled his paddle disconsolately. He was out. The auction was now down to two bidders: Selby Kiffer on the phone and the tall man standing in the back. The Double Eagle had already surpassed the 1804 silver dollar's price. It was the most valuable coin in the world. Now the question was just what the new record would be.

Four million six hundred thousand on the phone. Four million seven in the back. The bidders seesawed. Four million eight from Kiffer. Four million nine from the man with the cell phone. The next bid would be five million dollars, a wondrous barrier for a coin to break. Redden paused. "At four million nine hundred thousand," he said, gesturing at the cell-phone bidder and repeating, "Four million nine hundred thousand."

Kiffer raised his hand: "At five million dollars on the phone," Redden announced. "At five *million* dollars on the telephone now, five million dollars." The crowd broke into applause. On his feet to watch the bidding from up in their skybox, Fenton looked over at Berke standing next to him. He grinned. This was not a scene he could possibly have imagined six and a half years earlier. "The first time you stood next to me," Fenton said to his lawyer, "we were at a bail hearing."

But the auction still wasn't over. The cell-phone bidder raised his paddle. Five million one hundred thousand. Back to Kiffer. Five million two. A pause. Five million three. Five million four. Redden's left arm was sweeping like a pendulum from Kiffer on his left to the tall man in the center. Five million five hundred thousand. Five million six. Five million seven. Eight from Kiffer. Nine from the man with the cell phone.

Kiffer immediately raised his hand again. "Six. *Million*. Dollars," Redden proclaimed. A burst of clapping drowned out his next words. Six million dollars was the high end of the published estimate for the 1933 Double Eagle. Could Redden coax any more from the two bidders? The next move was the cell-phone bidder's, and Redden had sensed hesitation from him. Would he go higher?

He would. "Six million one hundred thousand dollars," Redden said, slowly. Kiffer's bidder came right back with six million two hundred thousand. A brief pause. The cell-phone bidder at six million three. Kiffer at six million four. Cell phone at six five. Kiffer at six six.

Redden looked at the man with the cell phone. The man shook his head slightly. He was out. Redden glanced around the room. No one moved. "Six million six hundred thousand dollars," he repeated, slowly now. "Fair warning, on my left, on the telephone, fair warning at six million six hundred thousand dollars."

It was over. Redden banged the gavel. The 1933 Double Eagle was sold. Its total price, including the fifteen percent buyer's premium, was $7,590,000. The 1933 Double Eagle's story had made it the most valuable coin in the world. And now that story had a happy ending.

Chapter Nineteen

Only One Coin

OF COURSE, IT WASN'T really quite over. As the audience whooped and cheered, a few coin dealers rushed toward the tall young man on the cell phone—the losing bidder—pushing business cards at him. It was to no avail. The cell-phone bidder was a friend of the Bahamian financier who had taken a fancy to the 1933 Double Eagle's story,[1] and neither of them were interested in any other coins. The tall man left Sotheby's that night and was never seen again in the coin world.

Reporters, meanwhile, surrounded David Redden and Selby Kiffer, asking them to identify the winning bidder. The men from Sotheby's stayed mum; Kiffer didn't know and Redden wouldn't say. Speculation on the floor was that Bill Gates, a sometime client of Kiffer's, was the mystery bidder, but the gossips were wrong. The anonymous bidder had come down from his skybox after the sale and was actually on the floor, recognized by no one except David Redden. The coin's new owner watched the ceremony in which Henrietta Holsman Fore signed the documents that made the 1933 Double Eagle legal to own, and then the press conference that followed. Afterward, he asked

Redden how the auctioneer had known that he would be the bidder who won the 1933 Double Eagle.

"I didn't know," Redden said.

"You mean you spent all that time with me before the auction and you didn't know I'd buy it?" the man asked.

"You never know," Redden replied.

By the time the press conference was over, Redden was wrung out. Larry and Harvey Stack and their contingent were going out to celebrate at a nearby Italian restaurant, but Redden declined. He'd done what he promised, spreading excitement about the 1933 Double Eagle far afield of the coin world. Both of the last two bidders, he congratulated himself, had been men whom no ordinary coin house would have attracted to the auction floor.

Jane Levine watched the hullabaloo wistfully. Her onetime colleagues from the Mint were overjoyed at the record-setting price the coin had brought, half of which would become Mint revenue. Levine stood apart. She didn't feel like celebrating, so she just went home.

Stephen Fenton, Barry Berke, Fenton's girlfriend, and Berke's wife went across town to Jean-Georges on Central Park West. Thanks to the 1933 Double Eagle, Fenton was a newly minted millionaire, but Berke insisted that dinner was on him. He called for a bottle of Veuve Clicquot champagne and pressed Fenton, a teetotaler except on airplanes, to accept a glass. "A lesser person would have folded," he toasted the coin dealer. "A person with a lesser lawyer," Fenton countered.

With the coin safely sold, Fenton abandoned his customary caution and began celebrating his association with the 1933 Double Eagle as he never had before. He took to handing out gold-foil–wrapped chocolate 1933 Double Eagles at coin shows, and he no longer objected when people called him "Mr. 1933." He even stayed at the Waldorf-Astoria from time to time on trips to New York. When he was in the city in January 2005, Fenton paid a visit to the 1933 Double Eagle, which was on display in the vaulted lobby of the New York Federal Reserve Bank. The coin had just been returned to its place of honor in the American Numismatic Society's "History of Money" exhibit at the Fed, after a hiatus in storage during a terrorist alert. Fenton was standing before the 1933 Double Eagle when a tour group came through. "I once owned it, you know," Fenton remarked to the tour guide. "Sir, you must be mistaken," she said. "This is the 1933 Double Eagle, the most valuable coin in the world."

Fenton smiled. "I'm the British coin dealer," he said, pointing to the exhibit's display text. "That was my part in the story." He walked off, thoroughly enjoying the stares that followed him.[2]

IT HAD been David Redden's idea to display the 1933 Double Eagle at the Fed. After the auction, the coin's new owner made complicated arrangements to pay Sotheby's while maintaining his anonymity. Redden kept the buyer's secret faithfully; even Larry Stack, Sotheby's partner in the 1933 Double Eagle auction, was not apprised of the new owner's identity. The buyer, who never took physical possession of the coin, asked Redden to serve as the Double Eagle's guardian. "I'd like to have others see it," he told Redden, who immediately thought of the American Numismatic Society, a New York–based group widely reckoned to have the second-best coin collection in the country, after the Smithsonian. Part of the ANS collection was on display at the Federal Reserve. If the 1933 Double Eagle joined the display there, it would be better guarded than it would be anywhere else on public view. The new owner agreed to make a long-term loan of the coin to the ANS.

A couple of years after the 1933 Double Eagle auction, Redden was commissioned to sell a rare ultra-high-relief 1907 double eagle, one of the dozen or so spectacular, sculptural coins minted at Theodore Roosevelt's insistence from Augustus Saint-Gaudens's original design. It was a magnificent piece, Redden thought, and a fitting companion to the 1933 Double Eagle. Redden called the 1933's owner, with whom he spoke occasionally, to offer him the 1907 coin.[3]

The man declined. "I told you, David," he said, "I don't collect coins. Only one coin."

Only one coin, indeed.

Epilogue

Roy Langbord never asked for notoriety. He never even asked for notice. Slight and gray-haired, with droopy eyes and a hangdog tilt to his head, Langbord is about as flashy as a vacuum cleaner. He and his wife both keep glamorous company—she is the executive assistant to a celebrity Manhattan restaurateur and he is a television executive—but Langbord prefers to blend into the background. He always has. When his grandfather gave him his first watch, a child-sized antique Rolex, Langbord was disappointed; he'd wanted the same clunky model that all of his friends wore. One of the reasons he went to New York to attend Columbia University in the 1970s was to leave behind his prominent family and its spider web of connections in his hometown of Philadelphia.

In August 2005, the 1933 Double Eagle ended Langbord's carefully cultivated obscurity. Langbord could not care less about rare coins; his devotions are model-yacht racing, his family, and his two Maine coon cats. He first heard of Stephen Fenton's 1933 Double Eagle in the summer of 2002, on a plane to Las Vegas, where he was headed for a Showtime boxing match. An advertisement in *The New York Times* for the upcoming Sotheby's auction caught his attention. Langbord skimmed the ad's breathless account of the 1933 Double Eagle's history. He stopped to read—and then to reread—one particular line. Langbord tore the advertisement out of the newspaper, and when the plane landed he phoned his mother in Philadelphia. "Mom," he said, "You need to search the store."[1]

Roy Langbord was soon to join the long and unlikely list of people whose lives were changed irretrievably by the 1933 Double Eagle.

BUT I'VE jumped ahead. To tell Langbord's story properly, I must instead look back, to 1995, when Andre de Clermont first told Stephen Fenton that a 1933 Double Eagle had surfaced. Fenton hesitated before buying it. One of the risks he foresaw—presciently, as it turned out—was the coin's questionable legality. The other was its true rarity. Rumors of 1933 Double Eagle sightings had circulated in the coin world for years. Fenton didn't want to overpay for a coin that might turn out to be one of a handful, not one of a kind.

In the end that question didn't matter for Fenton's coin. Jane Levine and the U.S. Mint lawyers never formally conceded that Fenton's coin had belonged to Farouk, but they made sure that no one else could cite Farouk's export license to claim the legitimacy of a 1933 Double Eagle. The piece of paper signed by Mint Director Henrietta Holsman Fore at the end of the 2002 auction at Sotheby's transformed Fenton's 1933 Double Eagle into official U.S. currency—and promised its new owner that it would be the only 1933 Saint to hold that status. If any other 1933 Double Eagles surfaced, the Mint warned, they would be seized as government property, just as Fenton's coin had been in 1996.

The Mint's promise didn't mean, however, that Fenton's was the only 1933 Double Eagle outside of the Smithsonian. Most of the coin world, in fact, believed at the time of the auction that it wasn't, that there was at least one 1933 Double Eagle that the government hadn't discovered—not in 1944 and not since. As I began researching this book I resolved to find proof of the long-rumored secret coin, or else to say definitively that it didn't exist.

Looking for the missing double eagle was like trying to catch a big fish barehanded; I'd glimpse glittery flashes, but they'd disappear before I could grab hold of anything solid. I started in Philadelphia, where every 1933 Double Eagle was born and most of them died. If there were other 1933 Saints floating around, they would have originated in Philadelphia. Besides, it was obvious from the old Secret Service reports that Israel Switt and Ira Reed knew more than they had admitted in 1944, especially about the number of 1933 Double Eagles that Switt had obtained. James Macallister, the Philadelphia dealer who'd bought five coins from Switt, told agents that Switt claimed to have owned twenty-five 1933 Saints. Moreover, Louis Eliasberg's 1933 Double Eagle—the coin that Harry Strang didn't find out about until Eliasberg surrendered it to the Mint in 1952—proved that the Secret Service wasn't all-knowing. Even the agency admitted it. The last Secret Service discussion of the 1933 Double Eagle prior to Jack Moore's call to Dave Freriks in 1995 was a 1969 memo prepared by an agent named S. A. Carnes. Apparently while doing research for an agent writing a history of the Secret Service, Carnes retrieved the service's two-folder 1933 Double Eagle file from the archives. "Oddly enough," he noted after looking through the folders, "I don't see that it was ever definitely established as to how many coins were involved."[2]

Two Philadelphia old-timers had told me that Switt and Reed offered them 1933 Double Eagles long after the Secret Service's 1944 investigation fizzled to an end. The first account came from Harry Forman, a longtime coin dealer who as a young man sold gold coins to Switt. "One day, [Switt] said to me, 'Do you have a buyer for a thirty-three twenty?'" Forman said. "This was in the nineteen sixties. I knew the coin was extremely radioactive. [Switt] said, 'If you have a customer overseas, I can get you a thirty-three twenty.'" (Forman, worried about the legal complications, told Switt he wasn't interested.)

Philadelphia antiques dealer Charlie Steinberg, who ran errands for Ira Reed back in the 1950s, offered a similar story about Reed. According to Steinberg, at the end of his career Reed bought a resort in New Hampshire, where he planned to spend his retirement. When Reed's heart condition worsened, however, he returned to Philadelphia, dispatching Steinberg to New Hampshire to retrieve two bags of gold coins he'd stored at his bank up there. "He told me later," Steinberg said, "that there was a 1933 Double Eagle in those bags."

In February 2004, I met up with Steinberg at his antiques shop in the Philadelphia suburbs. He drove me downtown, pointing out Ira Reed's house, telling stories, and securing introductions to people who had known Switt. Steinberg told me that Reed was survived by a wife and daughter, but neither he nor I could discover their whereabouts. Reed, unfortunately, was not going to be my route to any missing 1933 Double Eagles.

Israel Switt's daughter was easier to find than Reed's descendants. Since her father's death in 1990, she has run I. Switt and Ed. Silver, Switt's four-story shop on Jewelers' Row in Philadelphia. I had called Switt's daughter twice and written to her once, requesting an interview. She declined. When I told her I was coming to Philadelphia in February 2004, she informed me that her shop would be closed that week. I took a chance and walked up to I. Switt's locked shop door anyway.

I looked inside, through the jumbled storefront window that seemed to have been last cleaned and rearranged in the 1940s. There was Switt's daughter—a tiny, frail woman standing behind the counter. I rang the bell. Mistaking me for a customer, she buzzed me into the fusty old shop, which looks more like an overgrown flea-market booth or an office cubicle run amok than a store famous for selling the best estate jewelry on the mid-Atlantic seaboard. When I introduced myself, she was not happy to learn whom she'd just admitted to this peculiar sanctuary. "Not today," she said, cutting me off even before I asked whether she had time to talk. She shrugged when I requested permission to walk around the store. Grudgingly, she conceded that the uniformed young man pictured in a photograph hanging on the wall was her father. But that was the extent of our conversation. She seemed almost relieved when three young women, browsers, rang the doorbell. Her father's daughter, she dispatched them without the slightest hint of courtesy. Then she went behind the counter, put on her coat, and scurried out into the February cold, leaving me behind in her shop to be scolded by her business partner. I might have a hundred questions about Israel Switt and the 1933 Double Eagle. Switt's daughter would answer none of them.

AFTER THAT emphatic brush-off, I had to conclude that I wasn't going to be able to trace any missing 1933 Double Eagles through Switt or Reed. In the meantime, I looked for alternative routes a coin might have traveled. Might one or two 1933 Double Eagles, for instance, have accidentally slipped into a government shipment of gold to Europe in the late 1930s, before the gold coins in the vaults of the Philadelphia Mint were melted? Even after Roosevelt issued the gold recall in 1933, the United States continued to use gold coins to satisfy foreign obligations. Beginning in the late 1940s and early 1950s, enterprising American coin dealers traveled to Europe to buy bags of double eagles that had been stored in bank vaults in France and Switzerland.[3] At least one great rarity, an 1861 double eagle of which only one other specimen was known, was discovered in Europe, as well as quantities of other scarce coins. Before dealers' European excursions, the 1924 double eagle from the San Francisco Mint had been considered the rarest of the Saint-Gaudens run. European hoards turned up dozens, if not hundreds, of mint-state examples. The value of such previously hard-to-find Saints as the 1924-D, the 1925-S, and the 1931-D dropped drastically in the 1960s as long-hidden coins returned from Europe. But according to both gold-coin authority David Akers[4] and Q. David Bowers, who published a 2004 guidebook to double eagles, the European hoards included no 1933 Double Eagles.

Nor had any 1933 Saints surfaced via the innocent-exchange theory championed by Bowers and amateur Mint historian Robert Julian in the Fenton litigation. Bowers had speculated that in the confusing days at the beginning of the Roosevelt administration, a customer might have arrived at the cashier's window at the Philadelphia Mint and, in a time-honored tradition of coin collecting, asked to trade a double eagle of an earlier vintage for a 1933 specimen. "While at the time the Treasury might not have been actively paying out twenty-dollar pieces or other coins for paper money," Bowers wrote in his

2004 guidebook, "it seems quite certain (at least to me!) that someone trading like for like could have obtained such pieces."[5] But Bowers's certainty aside, no collector has ever come forth with a story of having obtained a 1933 Double Eagle in an exchange at the Mint—not before 1944, when the coins were openly trading among dealers and collectors, and not since.

In other words, the means by which any missing 1933 Double Eagles might have escaped from the Mint proved impossible for me to confirm. That only meant, however, that I couldn't figure out *how* any unknown 1933 Double Eagles had gotten out, not *whether* they had. On that question—the existence of a 1933 Double Eagle other than the Fenton coin and the two in the Smithsonian—I accumulated an anthology of stories from coin dealers. When, for instance, I interviewed Dave Bowers in August 2003 at his home on an island in New Hampshire's Lake Winnipesaukee, he told me that he'd once been offered the chance to buy a 1933 Double Eagle. He expanded the account in his 2004 guidebook: A now-deceased Texas dealer named Mike Brownlee, he wrote, had made the offer in the 1980s. Bowers said he turned it down, sight unseen.[6]

Larry Stack, however, told me that he actually saw a 1933 Double Eagle—one he later determined was not the Farouk coin—in California, at around the same time Bowers was offered Brownlee's coin. (Like Bowers, Stack declined to purchase the coin.) And Robert Julian told me that a friend of his, a Stack's researcher and coin photographer named Carl Carlson, was hired to photograph a 1933 Double Eagle in the late 1970s or early 1980s. The coin, Julian said, was delivered to Carlson's studio by a courier who had flown it from Europe. After the shoot, the courier took the coin straight back to the airport. Julian said that he later tried to find his friend's photographs which never surfaced.[7]

When I talked to Tony Terranova, a highly respected New York dealer, I realized why the rumored 1933 Double Eagle always seemed to lurk just out of sight. Terranova told me that in the early 1980s, a West Coast dealer invited Terranova to his office to discuss the possible sale of a major coin he wouldn't identify on the phone. Terranova went to see him. The dealer said that he had a 1933 Double Eagle—

not Farouk's coin, Terranova said, but another specimen—that he would sell to Terranova for two hundred thousand dollars. Terranova said no. "How could you pass it up?" I asked him. "Weren't you tempted?"

"It wasn't my cup of tea," Terranova said. "You can't sell it. What do you do with it?"[8]

FINALLY, IN November 2004, I got lucky. Back in the 1970s, an enterprising coin collector and lawyer had filed a Freedom of Information Act request to obtain the government's records on the 1933 Double Eagle. I tracked him down. He suggested that I call one particular dealer, a man noted in the coin business for his integrity. This dealer—he asked me not to reveal his name, so I'll call him Ted—told me a remarkable story that at last made sense of everything I'd heard from others.

In 1975, Ted said, he and Mike Brownlee (the Texas dealer cited by Dave Bowers), were working together to build a world-class gold-coin collection for H. Jeff Browning, the Texas oilman whose collection was jointly auctioned by Sotheby's and Stack's in 2001. Brownlee and Ted located a longtime collector who owned an outstanding set of double eagles—both the early twenty-dollar pieces known as Liberties and the later Saint-Gaudens coins. Among this collector's Saints was a 1933 Double Eagle.

"We'd heard he had it," Ted told me. "It wasn't like we just walked in and there it was." The collector didn't reveal how he'd obtained the 1933 Double Eagle, but Ted said that Abe Kosoff, a good friend of the collector, had probably sold him the coin.

Brownlee and Ted bought the 1933 Double Eagle for Jeff Browning, who paid $250,000 for the coin. "Jeff had not one second of hesitation about buying it," Ted said. Nor, he added, did he and Mike Brownlee have any qualms about selling it. They actually showed the coin to some other dealers—"We thought people would enjoy seeing it," Ted told me—but they didn't disclose that they had purchased it for Browning.

After Browning died in 1978, his family, according to Ted, gave the

1933 Double Eagle to one of Browning's friends, the man who had actually started him in coin collecting.[9] In an attempt to confirm Ted's story, I called the attorney for the Browning estate, Jack Klein, and asked whether Browning had once owned a 1933 Double Eagle. "I don't think my client would ever be involved in an illegal deal," Klein said.

"That's not really an answer," I replied. "Did Mr. Browning ever have a 1933 Double Eagle in his collection?"

"We don't answer that question," Klein said. "There's no reason for us to talk about it."

So be it. According to Ted, the man to whom the Browning family gave the 1933 Double Eagle asked Mike Brownlee to sell the coin on his behalf. Brownlee ended up trading the 1933 Double Eagle to a West Coast dealer for a rare Liberty twenty-dollar piece. "When the coin was being offered around, people were hesitant," Ted said. "They were scared of handling it, even though nothing had been done about it [by the Secret Service] for their whole careers. They just didn't have the same excitement we did."

The West Coast dealer, Ted said, also tried to sell the 1933 Double Eagle, which explained the stories Larry Stack and Tony Terranova had told of being offered the coin in California. Ted told me that he had had one last brush with the secret 1933 Double Eagle. While the West Coast dealer was trying to sell the coin, Ted was helping a client build a set of Saints. He asked the West Coast dealer if he could show the 1933 Double Eagle to his client, and the West Coast dealer agreed. Ted flew thousands of miles to pick up the 1933 Double Eagle and take it to his client.

The collector was interested enough in the coin to offer Ted a trade: a twenty-five-carat yellow diamond, supposedly worth between three and five hundred thousand dollars, in exchange for the 1933 Double Eagle. The deal fell apart when the diamond turned out to have been irradiated, and thus not worth what the collector had said. Ted returned the 1933 Double Eagle to the West Coast, he said, and never saw the coin again.

Then he told me one more thing: "I still have a photograph of it. My client's daughter was a professional photographer. She took the photographs of the coin."

I felt lightheaded, like Stephen Fenton when he first saw the Farouk coin. Was this the evidence of an unknown 1933 Double Eagle that I'd been looking for? "It's only the face," he continued.

I interrupted: "Could you send me a copy of the picture?"

"Sure," he promised. And he did, electronically, within the hour. I clicked open the e-mail file. I stared. I had spent so much time looking at images of Stephen Fenton's 1933 Double Eagle. I had seen the coin itself at Sotheby's before the auction in 2002 and had visited it twice in its place of honor at the Federal Reserve Bank in New York. This photo was obviously not of that coin; the tiny nicks and scratches on its face were different. Yet the year—1933—was the same.

I was looking at a photograph of a fourth 1933 Double Eagle. It exists, I said to myself. Someone owns it. There really is another 1933 Saint.

Ted had told me that he didn't know for sure who now possessed the fourth 1933 Double Eagle, but he had a guess. I asked around, and kept hearing about one collector—a Connecticut man who made a fortune in the entertainment industry and is very secretive about his set of Saint-Gaudens gold pieces. I knew that Jack Moore had given this collector's name to the Secret Service in 1996, and I knew that the collector had bid, through a dealer, on Fenton's coin at the 2002 auction at Sotheby's. I wrote to him, enclosing a photocopy of the picture Ted had sent me and requesting an interview. I followed up with several phone calls, but he never replied.

I still had one last hope of finding the missing 1933 Double Eagle—or so I believed. It was Barry Berke, as I discovered quite by accident at the beginning of 2005. The previous month I had attended a luncheon meeting with a lawyer tangentially involved in Stephen Fenton's case. At the end of the meeting we'd chatted offhandedly about the coin. "You know, there's something going on with the case," the lawyer told me. "Something about some other coin." I'd asked for details, but the lawyer claimed not to know any more. I assumed that Jane Levine or someone else in the government had, like me, tracked down information about Jeff Browning's phantom 1933 Double Eagle.

I could hardly wait to share my speculation with Berke and Fenton, whom I was scheduled to see a couple of weeks later at Berke's Kramer Levin office. I unveiled my big surprise—a printout of Ted's photo of the missing 1933 Double Eagle—and told Berke and Fenton what I'd heard from the lawyer at the lunch meeting. "What do you think [the lawyer] was talking about?" I asked Berke.

"I can't comment," Berke said. This was not the answer I'd expected from Berke, who usually loved to trade 1933 Double Eagle speculation.

"What do you mean?" I asked.

"I can't say anything now," he replied. "But if there is news, I promise I'll tell you."

Fenton looked as baffled as I felt. Then I figured it out: "You have another client with a 1933 Double Eagle!" I said to Berke. "That's it! You're representing someone who's trying to keep the coin."

Berke remained expressionless. "I think there will be news before your book comes out," he said. "That's all I can say."

I surmised that the owner of the Browning coin—whoever he was—had hired Berke to lobby lawyers at the Mint and the U.S. Attorney's office. Over the next several months I pestered Berke occasionally, baiting him about the photo Ted had sent me and dropping the name of the collector whom I believe owns the coin. "Is he the client?" I kept asking. Berke gave nothing away. "When I can, I'll tell you," he would say. I expected the news, when he was able to reveal it, to be that the owner of the Browning coin was, with Berke's counsel, filing a suit or seeking federal legislation to have his 1933 Double Eagle declared legal.

I was staggeringly—and thrillingly—wrong. Berke's news was much bigger, much stranger, and much more appropriate to the story of the 1933 Double Eagle.

IN EARLY August 2005 Berke called me. "I promised I'd tell you when I could," he said. "The Mint is about to make an announcement."

"Another coin," I said smugly.

"Ten."

Ten? I stared at the phone. *Ten* more 1933 Double Eagles? My assiduous tracking of *one* missing coin suddenly felt silly, and my guess that Berke represented the Browning coin owner was obviously wrong.

"Who's your client?" I asked.

"Israel Switt's daughter and grandsons," he said. "The Langbord family."

I laughed and laughed. Of course it was the Langbords—the most satisfying possible candidates, at least from a narrative perspective. Now I understood why Switt's daughter, Joan Langbord, had run out of her store when I visited in 2004: She owned ten secret 1933 Double Eagles. Cranky, crusty old Izzy Switt had stumped the government back in the 1940s. If his descendants do as well, there will someday be a lot more 1933 Double Eagles on the market.

THAT DAY, however, remains a long way off. Mint officials announced in August 2005 that the government considers the Langbord coins to be the proceeds of a crime and thus the rightful property of the United States. "We do not intend to monetize, issue, or auction the recovered Double Eagles," said acting Mint director David Lebryk in a press release. Berke countered with a declaration, in a front-page *Coin World* article, that the Langbords would sue, if necessary, for ownership rights to the ten newly discovered 1933 Double Eagles. It will probably be years before the courts unknot a tangle of procedural issues—even the particular forfeiture statute that covers the Langbord coins is in dispute—and reach the facts of the new double eagle case. Jane Levine, as is only fitting, is expected to represent the government in this rematch with Berke.

In the meantime, Berke arranged for me to meet Roy Langbord, Israel Switt's grandson. On October 25, 2005, the three of us had lunch at a small Italian restaurant in Manhattan. Berke wanted to be sure that Langbord didn't say anything that would compromise the soon-to-follow litigation, but Langbord told me what Berke permitted of his story.

After Roy read the ad in *The New York Times* and called his mother from Las Vegas in 2002, Joan Langbord dithered about searching the store for stray 1933 Double Eagles. It was a monumental undertaking; the store is so crammed with stuff Israel Switt bought at estate sales that the family seriously considered simply chucking all of the old, flaking silver-plated trays and tea sets that fill one floor. Joan Langbord also wasn't eager to deepen the Switt family's involvement with the 1933 Double Eagle. The family has been pained by unflattering portrayals of Israel Switt, a man they regard as a generous father and grandfather, a hard-working entrepreneur who shared his wealth and his time with Philadelphia Hospital and the city's Home for the Jewish Aged. The man portrayed by the Secret Service in the investigation of the 1933 Double Eagle—the "gold coin bootlegger" with a criminal conviction—was not their Israel Switt. His family, Roy Langbord told me, preferred to remember how Switt would give away cases of salamis all year long and bottles of kosher wine at Passover. Switt distributed pumpkins decorated with costume jewelry to police officers and firefighters for Halloween. He had an African American business partner when such relationships were rare in Philadelphia. Switt made pickles in the basement at home, and was famous in the family for his "ipsy-pipsy" fruit punch. He bought stock in McDonald's when the company first went public, not because he was a brilliant investor but because he loved the hamburgers at the McDonald's drive-through on the turnpike between Philadelphia and Atlantic City, where the Switt and Silver families shared a house. "There was no hidden agenda with my grandfather," Langbord said. "He was very straightforward. If he didn't like you he'd throw you out, and if you were his friend there was nothing he wouldn't do to help you. He loved his family, the store, and his charities. You'd never have known he was wealthy. To buy a Cadillac would never even cross his mind."

Nevertheless, Langbord kept after his mother to look around the store for hidden 1933 Double Eagles. "Just check and see what else is there," he would say. When the coins were finally located—Berke advised Langbord not to provide me with specifics—"I was there," Langbord told me. "I saw the original wrapping they came in. I thought, 'Holy *shit!*'"

Langbord was well aware that the 1933 Double Eagle sold at

Sotheby's in 2002 had brought $7.59 million. He realized that the ten coins he and his mother had found could be worth millions as well, but a quick check of the coins' history on the Internet persuaded him that he needed a lawyer's advice. Langbord called Berke. Through him, the Langbord family contacted Mint lawyers, disclosed their discovery of Switt's 1933 Double Eagles, and agreed to have the authenticity of the ten coins tested by the Smithsonian. "What else could we do?" Roy Langbord said. "Really. What else could we do?"

Berke negotiated with Mint lawyers for several months, insisting that the newly discovered coins belonged to the Langbords. The Mint, predictably, argued otherwise. As of November 2005, while Berke and the Langbords awaited the government's response to their formal request for the return of the coins, Berke was once again examining old Mint ledgers, looking for evidence that Israel Switt obtained his 1933 Double Eagles legitimately.

"He was at the Mint three times a day every day," said Langbord, toward the end of our lunch in October 2005. "It could have been like going to a shoe store to buy a pair of shoes when the clerk says, 'Oh, we just got a new brand in.' Who would have been in a better position than my grandfather?"

I don't know if the Langbords will ever recover their coins, though without the Farouk export license they have a tougher case to win than Fenton's. Berke believes that the Langbords' good faith, demonstrated in their forthright disclosure of the coins' discovery, will ultimately help them in the litigation, but even he can't know for sure what will happen. The story of the Langbord 1933 Double Eagles is just beginning.

And that's why their discovery is the best conclusion I could imagine for this book. The tale of one extraordinary coin ends, but the epic of the 1933 Double Eagle continues.

Acknowledgments

I'VE BEEN A REPORTER for twenty years, but researching this book made me appreciate the miracle of journalism as I never had before. People permitted me into their lives with no motive but to help me tell the extraordinary story of the 1933 Double Eagle as it deserved to be told. I didn't know anything about rare coins when I (like Roy Langbord) first read an advertisement for the Sotheby's sale in *The New York Times* in July 2002. Only through the generosity of all the people to whom I've talked over the last four years—many of whose names don't even appear in the text—was I able to learn about the 1933 Double Eagle and its place in history.

My largest debt is to the people who lived the story. Stephen Fenton made time during his trips to New York to spend many hours with me. Jay Parrino, who does not particularly enjoy reliving his experience with the 1933 Double Eagle, was good-humored enough to sit for an interview after I ambushed him at a coin show in 2004. Jack Moore invited me to Amarillo for two meals and a long, sometimes painful session of remembering his involvement with the coin. (I'm happy to report that Moore's situation has improved since our interview; he has a new girlfriend and is, he says, happy again.) Jane

Levine answered all of my questions—even the dumb ones—with patience, thoughtfulness, and candor. After the Double Eagle case, Levine received an appointment to a newly created federal art-fraud squad. They're lucky to have her.

Barry Berke was the first person I ever interviewed about the 1933 Double Eagle—the afternoon before the Sotheby's auction in July 2002—and his delight in the coin case was infectious. Without his help, I truly could not have written this book. He opened his files from *U.S. v. A $20 Gold Coin* (within the limits of attorney-client privilege, of course), permitting me free rein in what amounts to an archive of 1933 Double Eagle documents. And every one of the dozens of times I called or e-mailed him with yet another "one last question," he made me believe he was glad I'd asked. I don't know if the Langbords will prevail in their efforts to regain possession of the ten newly discovered 1933 Double Eagles, but I do know that they couldn't have picked a better or kinder lawyer to represent them. I hope the government, as expected, asks Jane Levine to handle the new coin case so that she and Berke will have a chance to revive their friendly rivalry—and perhaps at last test the case of the 1933 Double Eagle before a jury.

Jay Brahin, who earned entry into the fraternity of Saint-Gaudens double eagle collectors with his keen eye and his self-diagnosed case of mild obsessive-compulsive disorder, taught me how the coin world really works and allowed me to share the excitement of building his brilliant Saints set. Without Jay's friendship, I would never have understood the passion and drive of coin collectors. If I could, I'd buy Brahin an MS-66 1927-D—that's the magnitude of my debt to him. Other collectors to whom I owe particular thanks are: Steve Duckor, owner of one of the world's best Saints sets, who obliged me with a lovely afternoon at the Long Beach show in June 2004; Dan Hamelberg, the country's foremost collector of numismatic literature, whom I got to watch in action at the most exciting numismatic-literature auction in history; David Ganz, a lawyer, collector, and writer, and the "father" of the state quarters program; James Swan; Tom Mendenhall; Dan Bespalko; Charlie Robbins; Bob Shippee; Steve Heller; Bruce Morelan; and finally, Ron Zevin, who helped persuade my family that

I wasn't a lunatic for wanting to write about a coin and showed my children their first Saint-Gaudens double eagles.

Coin dealers were equally generous with their time and insight. Q. David Bowers, the closest thing numismatics has to an official historian, was gracious enough to invite my entire family to his marvelous home on a Lake Winnipesaukee island. He was the first coin expert I interviewed, and I can't thank him enough for his patience with a rank novice. George Kolbe, a dealer of rare numismatic books, allowed me to interview him at his glorious house in Crestline, California. Larry and Harvey Stack not only submitted to multiple interviews at Stack's but also welcomed my presence at a number of Stack's auctions. Watching generations of Stack men and women running an auction is a testament to the enduring power of both family and numismatics. Thanks also to David Akers, David Hall, Tony Terranova, Steve Contursi, Greg Rohan, John Hamrick, Mark Raffety, Todd Imhof, Ruth Bauer, and Harry Forman for helping me understand the coin business and its history. Charlie Steinberg spent a day driving me around Philadelphia. I hope he remembers it as fondly as I do. And I am especially grateful to the dealer I identify in the epilogue as "Ted." I won't disclose his name, but I'll offer him profound thanks for his photo of the still-hidden 1933 Saint.

My deep thanks are also due to Dave Freriks, David Krassner, John Groendyke, Kent Remmel, and David Redden. Their contributions to the story of the 1933 Double Eagle were crucial. Alan Mansfield, Greg Weinman, Dan Shaver, David Pickens, Ken Gubin, Andrew Moore, Mei Lin Kwan-Gett, Sam Tepperman-Gelfant, Jonathan Etra, William Daddio, and Gil Hunter all gave me interviews that enriched the story. Bryan Christy served me a hearty and healthy dose of skepticism. Tim Payne offered his home for my interview with Moore. Barry Berke's assistant, Olivette Taylor, not only was incredibly helpful, she was also always friendly, no matter how many additional documents I asked her to retrieve from storage.

Librarians and archivists were unfailingly courteous and cooperative. I've come to believe that they have the best jobs in the world, able to share the thrill of every researcher's project. I'd like in particular to thank the folks at Dartmouth College's Rauner Rare Books

Library, home of Augustus Saint-Gaudens's papers, who early on fired my imagination by sending me some of the letters exchanged by Saint-Gaudens and Theodore Roosevelt. The staff there has been nothing but helpful since. The general library collection at Dartmouth, my alma mater, turned out to be a trove of information for me, particularly because the unparalleled numismatic library of the American Numismatic Society in New York was moving to its new location and thus unavailable during much of my research. I never would have guessed in my undergraduate days that Dartmouth owned a complete collection of *The Numismatist*, but indeed it did.

The curator at the Saint-Gaudens National Historic Site in Cornish took the time to walk me through the artist's studios; anyone who cares at all about coins, art, or gardens should spend a day at this magical place. The librarians at the American Numismatic Association packed up untold shipments of books for me. The devoted readers of *E-sylum*, the indispensable weekly electronic newsletter of the Numismatic Bibliomania Society, offered leads and encouragement. What an unexpected treat it was to run into Roger Burdette, a tireless numismatic researcher, at the National Archives in College Park! Thanks also to Pete Smith, a collector of William Woodin memorabilia, and to Len Augsburger, a whiz at ancestry research. The staff at my hometown library in Sea Cliff, New York, filed requests for book after book from libraries across Nassau County. My bad handwriting stumped them only occasionally.

My bosses and friends at *The American Lawyer* not only indulged my peculiar interest in the 1933 Double Eagle in 2003, when they found space in our magazine for a story about a rare coin, they also granted me time to research the book in 2004 and cheered me on throughout the project. My deep thanks to Aric Press, Dirk Olin, Mark Obbie, and all of my colleagues in the pit who endured my incessant chatter about rare coins.

My agent, Robert Lescher, gave me confidence that I could actually write a book and seemed to know just the editors who would be most excited about my proposal. There is no wiser agent in the business. And it was a privilege to be edited by Starling Lawrence, a man who has published some of my very favorite books. Thanks also to

Lawrence's assistant, Morgen Van Vorst, whose cheerfulness persisted in the face of occasionally extreme authorial crabbiness.

Finally, to my friends, family, and cats, who tolerated this project every day for four years: thank you, thank you, thank you. My book club read early, messy drafts. My parents, Howie and Judy Frankel, and my sister, novelist Valerie Frankel, read and advised throughout. My amazing daughters, Anna and Lily, learned to make their own damn dinners, and my husband, Dan Fagin, a newspaper reporter and journalism professor, shared every reporting triumph and writing conundrum along the way. Dan, Anna, and Lily are my biggest cheerleaders and my personal publicity department. Whenever anyone asked what my book was about, they'd take over and do a brilliant job. I only hope I've managed to produce a work that measures up to their loving hype.

Notes

Chapter One
"Give Us a Coinage That Has Some Beauty!"

1. The program from the dinner is contained in the Augustus Saint-Gaudens Collection of the sculptor's papers at Dartmouth College, Hanover, New Hampshire.
2. Louise Hall Tharp, *Saint-Gaudens and the Gilded Era*. Saint-Gaudens's first biographer, Tharp paid special attention to Saint-Gaudens's letters to Augusta.
3. Burke Wilkinson, *Uncommon Clay: The Life and Works of Augustus Saint Gaudens*. Wilkinson's is the definitive Saint-Gaudens biography.
4. Wilkinson.
5. Henry Adams, *The Education of Henry Adams*.
6. Tharp, citing a letter of January 12, 1907.
7. August 3, 1903, letter from Theodore Roosevelt to Augustus Saint-Gaudens, contained in the archives at Dartmouth.
8. August 9, 1903, letter in Dartmouth archives.
9. Though there's no direct evidence in Saint-Gaudens's papers that Roosevelt made the request at the American Academy dinner, Wilkinson concluded that the president asked Saint-Gaudens at the banquet to redesign the inaugural medal.
10. Wilkinson, citing a letter that John LaFarge wrote to Henry Cabot Lodge about the dinner party. (Note: Wilkinson spells Saint-Gaudens's name without a hyphen, because he says that was the sculptor's preference. The standard spelling, however, includes the hyphen.)
11. Paul Gilkes, "Pledge for Liberty," *Coin World*, December 8, 2003.

12. Don Taxay, *The U.S. Mint and Coinage*, pp. 287–94. Taxay's book is the definitive history of U.S. coinage, based on his extensive archival research.

13. Cornelius Vermeule, *Numismatic Art in America*, pp. 94–95.

14. David L. Ganz, *The World of Coins and Coin Collecting*, pp. 7–9. Ganz's book is a good introduction to coins, combining basic coin history with collecting advice.

15. Bruce McNall, *Fun While It Lasted: My Rise and Fall in the Land of Fame and Fortune*, p. 5. Also, Ganz, *The World of Coins*, pp. 14–16.

16. Don Taxay, *Counterfeit, Mis-Struck, and Unofficial U.S. Coins*, p. 4.

17. Ganz, *The World of Coins*, p. 14.

18. Ganz, *The World of Coins*, p. 16.

19. McNall, p. 2.

20. Ganz, *The World of Coins*, pp. 124–25

21. Taxay, *Counterfeit*, p. 21.

22. Jeff Garrett and Ron Guth, *100 Greatest U.S. Coins*, coin number 12.

23. Taxay, *U.S. Mint*, p. 7.

24. Robert Van Ryzin, *Twisted Tails: Sifted Fact, Fantasy and Fiction from U.S. Coin History*. Van Ryzin discusses the legend in chapter 6.

25. Edgar H. Adams and William H. Woodin, *United States Pattern, Trial, and Experimental Pieces*, p. 1.

26. Garrett and Guth, coin number 15.

27. Walter Breen, *Early United States Half-Eagles 1795–1838*, p. 4.

28. Ibid., p. 41.

29. Taxay, *U.S. Mint*, pp. 205–7.

30. Roosevelt's letter is cited in Q. David Bowers, *American Gold and Gold Coinage*, p. 280

31. Most of the correspondence between Saint-Gaudens and Roosevelt is contained in the archives at Dartmouth. The letters were first published in an article written by Saint-Gaudens's son, Homer, in *Century Magazine*.

32. Wilkinson, p. 129.

33. Wilkinson, p. 156.

34. Tharp, p. 202.

35. A typescript of a chapter from Fraser's autobiography—the chapter on his years with Saint-Gaudens—is part of the Saint-Gaudens archives at Dartmouth.

36. Frances Grimes's short memoir of her time in the Saint-Gaudens studio is part of the Saint-Gaudens archives at Dartmouth.

37. Grimes.

38. John H. Dryfrout, *The 1907 United States Gold Coinage*, includes an essay by William E. Hagans about his distant relative, Hettie Anderson, and her work as a model for Saint-Gaudens. Van Ryzin writes about the controversy over Saint-Gaudens's models for Liberty in *Twisted Tails*, chapter 8.

39. Wilkinson, p. 359.

40. Wilkinson, p. 310.

41. Tharp, p. 354.

42. Wilkinson, p. 347.

43. Wilkinson, p. 364.

44. May 29, 1906, letter, reproduced in Taxay, *U.S. Mint*, p. 311.

45. Henry Hering, "History of the $10 and $20 Gold Coins of 1907 issue," *The Numismatist*, August 1949.

46. Ibid.

47. Ibid.

48. David Akers, *A Handbook of 20th-Century United States Gold Coins 1907–1933*, p. 97.

49. Akers.

50. Hering's letter is in the archives at Dartmouth. Saint-Gaudens biographer Wilkinson attributes the unsigned letter to poet Witter Bynner, another regular at Aspet. Dartmouth cataloguers attribute it to Hering, though the language is unusually flowery for him.

51. Roosevelt's letter is quoted in its entirety in Taxay, *U.S. Mint*, p. 315.

52. Ibid., pp. 317–18.

53. Frank A. Leach, *Recollections of a Mint Director*, p. 102.

54. Ibid., p. 103.

55. January 10, 1908, letter from Roosevelt to William Sturgis Bigelow, cited in Taxay, *U.S. Mint*, p. 325.

56. "Art and Artists," *Philadelphia Press*, November 17, 1907.

57. "The Women Who Served as Models for the Coins," *The New York Times*, Sunday, December 15, 1907. Hettie Anderson's role in modeling Liberty remained a secret for years, until one of the model's descendants found the letters that suggested it. Homer Saint-Gaudens, who edited his father's memoirs, noted the Mary Cunningham controversy with amusement, considering Anderson's African heritage. "As a matter of fact, the so-called features of the Irish lass appear scarcely the size of a pinhead upon the full-length Liberty, the body of which was posed for by a Swede. Also, the modern American blue blood may delight in the discovery that the profile head [on the $10 piece] was modeled from a woman supposed to have negro blood in her veins."

58. Leach, p. 104.

59. Ibid., p. 105.

60. Ibid., p. 104.

Chapter Two
"All Persons Are Hereby Required to Deliver All Gold Coin Now Owned by Them"

1. Adams and Woodin, *United States Pattern, Trial, and Experimental Pieces.*

2. Raymond Moley, *After Seven Years*, p. 139. The book is Moley's insider account of the tumultuous early months of the Roosevelt administration.

3. Moley, pp. 140–41.

4. Moley, p. 121.

5. "Woodin Succeeded in Many Fields," *The New York Times,* May 5, 1934.

6. Ibid.

7. "Woodin and Mills Hold Conference," *The New York Times,* February 24, 1933.

8. "Gov. Miller Makes William H. Woodin State Coal Head," *The New York Times,* September 6, 1922.

9. "Now the Penthouse Palace Is Evolving," *The New York Times,* March 23, 1930.

10. "Woodin Withdraws from 2 Companies," *The New York Times,* June 7, 1924.

11. "W. H. Woodin Is Revealed as a Composer," *The New York Times,* February 19, 1930.

12. Elvira Eliza Clain-Stefanelli, *Numismatics: An Ancient Science: A Survey of its History,* p. 9.

13. Ibid.

14. Q. David Bowers, *The Rare Silver Dollars Dated 1804,* pp. 51–53.

15. Sketch of Stickney from Bowers, *The Rare Silver Dollars,* pp. 348–50.

16. Ibid., p. 422.

17. Bowers, *The Rare Silver Dollars,* pp. 411–13.

18. Ibid. Bower's book includes wonderful scholarship on early collectors and dealers.

19. "The Commercial Element in Numismatics," *The Numismatist.* Cited in Bowers, *American Gold,* p. 144.

20. The coin, subsequently owned by famed collectors Louis Eliasberg and Harry Bass, is described on the Harry Bass Foundation website: www.harrybass foundation.org.

21. Letters that recount the negotiations, written mainly by Woodin's lawyer, Henry W. Jessup, are excerpted in the John J. Ford, Jr., Numismatic Library auction catalogue, pp. 288–89.

22. Part of Woodin's negotiations with the Mint concerned the future disposition of pattern pieces from the Mint. To the irritation of thirty-six-year-old reformist Mint Director Abram Piatt Andrew, there had been no uniformly enforced policy about these illicit coins. Before he gave up his coins, Woodin wanted an assurance of the end of the longtime (if surreptitious) practice by Mint employees of striking unauthorized pattern coins. Andrew went a step beyond the guarantee. In May 1910, according to numismatic researcher Roger Burdette, Andrew invited Woodin to Washington for a historic mission of ruin at the Philadelphia Mint. With Woodin in attendance, Andrew swept through the Mint, ordering the destruction of hundreds of dies for experimental and obsolete coins. Charles Barber—Saint Gaudens's old nemesis and part of the group that toured the Mint with Andrew and Woodin—undoubtedly was devastated to witness the melting of dies cut by him and his father, but Andrew and his boss, Treasury Secretary MacVeagh,

regarded the project as a success. Andrew was promoted to assistant secretary of the treasury and continued a warm correspondence with Woodin through the summer of 1910, with Woodin once urging Andrew to join him for dinner in New York. Of course, Woodin had reason to be grateful to Andrew: The destruction of the old dies meant that the pattern coins Woodin obtained in exchange for his $50 pieces would remain rare, if not unique.

23. "Roosevelt Will Go to Capitol Today for Inauguration," *The New York Times*, March 2, 1933.

24. Helen M. Burns, *The American Banking Community*, p. 33.

25. Moley, p. 144.

26. Burns, p. 35; Moley, p. 146.

27. Moley, p. 147.

28. Burns, pp. 38–40.

29. "The Presidency," *Time*, March 13, 1933.

30. "The Presidency," *Time*, March 20, 1933.

31. Moley, p. 151.

32. Moley, p. 152.

33. "Woodin Still Can Pun," *The New York Times*, March 10, 1933. *Newsweek* reported that the exchange actually took place at daybreak outside the White House after Woodin showed the bill to Roosevelt.

34. "The Presidency," *Time*, March 20, 1933.

35. Moley, p. 155.

36. April 19, 1933, telegram from T. W. Lamont to the president, containing the statement of J. P. Morgan. From the holdings at the Franklin D. Roosevelt Library.

37. From the holdings at the Franklin D. Roosevelt Library: January 12, 1934, letter from Attorney General Homer Cummings to the president; January 12, 1934, letter from Henry Morgenthau to the president; January 19, 1934, letter from Louis Howe to Henry Morgenthau.

38. "Mint Not Affected by Banking Holiday; Busy Making Money," *The Philadelphia Inquirer*, March 7, 1933.

Chapter Three
The Mysterious Man at the Money Factory

1. The date comes from a September 26, 1945, memo from the coining department superintendent, which was part of the court record in *United States of America v. A $20 Gold Coin, known as a 1933 "Double Eagle" Minted at the United States Mint in Philadelphia*, U.S. District Court for the Southern District of New York, 96 Civ. 2527. (Hereafter *U.S. v. A $20 Gold Coin.*)

2. See the Philadelphia newspaper articles listed in the bibliography.

3. The Mint produced a sheaf of documents in *U.S. v. A $20 Gold Coin*, including the telegrams and letters cited here. Research by Fenton's lawyers at Kramer

Levin Naftalis & Frankel turned up additional correspondence from Mint officials in the National Archives in College Park, Maryland, which contains Philadelphia Mint records from the 1930s.

4. November 2003 interview with Dr. William Daddio, director of Mint security.

5. November 2003 interview with Dr. Gil Hunter, former Mint quality-control officer.

6. Leach, *Recollections of a Mint Director*, pp. 25–34. Also, documents regarding the Adams case, including Leach's correspondence, are located in the National Archives in College Park, Maryland.

7. Eric P. Newman and Kenneth E. Bressett, *The Fantastic 1804 Dollar*, p. 113. The Newman and Bressett book is considered the definitive account of the much-chronicled 1804 dollar. Other details of this discussion come from Bowers, *The Rare Silver Dollars Dated 1804*, and from Taxay, *The U.S. Mint and Coinage* and *Counterfeit*.

8. Bowers, *The Rare Silver Dollars*, p. 2.

9. Taxay, *Counterfeit*, p. 82.

10. Newman and Bressett, p. 79.

11. Newman and Bressett (pp. 80–81), referring to correspondence from Du Bois reproduced in the *American Journal of Numismatics* in 1878.

12. Taxay, *Counterfeit*, p. 87.

13. Newman and Bressett, pp. 88, 114.

14. Both Bowers, *The Rare Silver Dollars*, and Taxay, *The U.S. Mint*, discuss Linderman's activities.

15. Taxay, *Counterfeit*, p. 115.

16. Garrett and Guth, *100 Greatest U.S. Coins*, coin number 2.

17. Thaddeus Herrick, "Big Money: When 5 Cents Is Worth $3 Million," *The Wall Street Journal*, May 21, 2004.

18. Treasury Department press release of June 12, 1934, in the Treasury Department files at the National Archives, College Park, Maryland.

19. March 31, 1934, letter from Secret Service Chief W. H. Moran to Philadelphia field office. The letter is in the Secret Service files at the National Archives.

20. April 14, 1934, report from Houghton to Secret Service Chief W. H. Moran. The report is in the Secret Service files at the National Archives.

21. October 26, 1934, report from Houghton to Secret Service Chief W. H. Moran. The report is in the Secret Service files at the National Archives.

Chapter Four
The "Gold Coin Bootlegger" and the Coin Dealers

1. Secret Service investigation of Israel Switt in 1944.

2. I spoke to more than a half-dozen people about Switt—including a former longtime employee who asked not to be identified, a devoted customer, two

Philadelphia coin dealers who traded with him, and a longtime Switt acquaintance, antiques dealer Charles Steinberg. I attempted several times—by telephone and letter and in person—to interview his only child, Joan Langbord, but she declined to speak to me.

3. Charles Steinberg told me the story of the widow. It actually turned out to be a rare defeat for Switt. The widow was so insulted by his behavior that she declined his offer and asked Steinberg and his father to sell her pieces on consignment instead.

4. March 29, 1944, Secret Service report.

5. Macallister's account is contained in the March 29, 1944, Secret Service report. All of the Secret Service reports cited below are part of the case file in *U.S. v. A $20 Gold Coin.*

6. Although the official catalogue from the Sotheby's/Stack's sale of the 1933 Double Eagle places the date of the sale to Kosoff in 1939, Kosoff, according to the Secret Service report of April 24, 1944, told the Secret Service that the sale occurred in 1937. To the Secret Service Kosoff admitted buying only one 1933 Double Eagle from Switt; in a *Coin World* column published many years later, he mentioned selling "two or three or four" coins.

7. Reed was evasive in questioning by the Secret Service. Agents based estimates of his purchases on the records of those to whom Reed sold the coins.

8. Q. David Bowers, *Abe Kosoff: Dean of Numismatics*, p. 41.

9. Interview with Charles Steinberg in February 2004.

10. Secret Service Agents Harry Strang and George Drescher interviewed Willard Boyce, George McCann's successor as Mint cashier, about Reed. They reported Boyce's recollections on April 21, 1944.

11. Abe Kosoff, *Abe Kosoff Remembers*, p. 23. The book is a collection of columns Kosoff wrote for *Coin World* magazine.

12. Kosoff recounts his autobiography in a series of columns included in *Abe Kosoff Remembers.*

13. Bowers, *Abe Kosoff*, p. 30

14. Interview with Dr. Stephen Duckor, a double eagle collector, in June 2004.

15. Bowers, *Abe Kosoff*, pp. 32–36.

16. Macallister opened his records on the 1933 Double Eagle to the Secret Service in 1944.

17. Bowers, *Abe Kosoff*, p. 73–74.

18. Boyd's address is cited in Bowers, *The Rare Silver Dollars*, pp. 376–77.

19. *The Numismatist*, April 1937.

20. *The Numismatist*, November 1939.

21. Kosoff, p. 31.

22. B. Max Mehl, "Proof of Proven Success: A Partial List of the More Important Collections Handled by Me in Recent Years."

23. Bowers, *The Rare Silver Dollars*, p. 414.

24. Mehl, "Proof of Proven Success."

25. Wilfred Weiss.

26. Bowers, *The Rare Silver Dollars*, p. 415.

27. *The Numismatist*, October 1948.

28. Mehl.

29. Tom LaMarre, "B. Max Mehl: The 1913 Nickel Man," www.bowersand merena.com.

30. Peter J. Molyneaux, "A Texas Master of Coins." Originally published in *The Numismatist*, March 1929.

31. Kosoff, p. 267.

32. Bowers, *Abe Kosoff*, p. 67.

33. Bowers, *The Rare Silver Dollars*, p. 417.

34. Kosoff, p. 274.

35. Secret Service report of April 7, 1944.

36. The ownership chain of this coin is contained in Secret Service reports from the 1944 investigation and summarized in the catalogue from the Sotheby's/Stack's sale.

37. February 25, 1944, letter from Nellie Tayloe Ross to Theodore Belote.

38. Stack's paperback history of the firm, published in 1995 to celebrate its sixty years in the auction business.

39. Mark Van Winkle, "An Interview with John J. Ford, Jr., Part I." *LEGACY*, April 1990.

40. Sotheby's/Stack's catalogue, p. 22.

Chapter Five
The First Investigation

1. Howard's telegram is part of the court record in *U.S. v. A $20 Gold Coin*.

2. March 21, 1944, letter from the Mint superintendent to Mint Director Nellie Tayloe Ross.

3. Agent Harry Strang described the beginning of the investigation in his March 27, 1944 report. All of the Secret Service reports relating to the 1944 investigation of the 1933 Double Eagle case are part of the court record in *U.S. v. A $20 Gold Coin*. Harvey Stack, who was present during some of Strang's visits to Stack's, told me in an interview how Morton and Joseph Stack responded.

4. David R. Johnson, *Illegal Tender: Counterfeiting and the Secret Service in Nineteenth-Century America*, p. 37. Most of my account of early Secret Service history is from Johnson's book. It may be of interest to numismatists that, according to Johnson, coins were cheaper to fake than paper money, but less profitable. Counterfeiters would make molds from real coins, then produce fakes of base metal plated with gold or silver. Since every counterfeit coin had to be filed individually, however, production was limited; only one or two percent of the coins in circulation in 1862 were counterfeit.

5. Johnson, p. 66.

6. Ibid., pp. 21–22.

7. Ibid., pp. 75–76.

8. Ibid., pp. 137–39.

9. Ibid., p. 177.

10. Frank J. Wilson and Beth Day, *Special Agent: A Quarter Century with the Treasury Department and the Secret Service*, p. 4.

11. Ibid., p. 25.

12. "Frank J. Wilson, 83, Famed Chief of U.S. Secret Service," *Washington Post*, June 23, 1970.

13. Wilson and Day, p. 93.

14. Ibid., p. 96–97.

15. August 30, 1937, report of John Fitzgerald, in the Secret Service files, National Archives, College Park, Maryland.

16. April 26, 1937, report of Austin Sutterfield, in the Secret Service files in the National Archives.

17. Not much is known about Harry W. Strang. The Secret Service could not locate records of his tenure, which indicates that he never served on the White House detail, since agents who protected presidents tend to turn up in the service's photo archives. Neither the association of retired agents nor the union that administers the pensions of Secret Service employees has records of his service or his whereabouts. Social Security records do not indicate when or if he died. Harvey Stack, a teenager working at his father's coin store at the time of the Secret Service's investigation of the 1933 Double Eagle, saw Strang a few times and remembers him as "a nice guy, a government official following his orders in a gentlemanly way." My description of his cases as "inconsequential" comes from the few Strang case reports I found in the National Archives.

18. March 16, 1942, letter from Wilson to Strang, with letter from Edgar Olivere attached.

19. The two agents went first to see Stephen K. Nagy, a Philadelphia coin dealer who'd once worked with Captain John Haseltine, the source of some of the most valuable (and suspect) coins in American numismatics. Nagy had never handled 1933 Double Eagles, but he had an intriguing story for the agents. He claimed that while William Woodin was still secretary of the treasury, he'd invited Nagy, a coin-collecting friend, to visit him in Washington. "During this visit," Strang reported in his March 29, 1944, memo, "Secretary Woodin exhibited to Nagy five 1933 Double Eagle gold coins, making an offer to let Nagy have one if he so desired. Mr. Nagy declined this offer but discussed the coins with Mr. Woodin to the extent of asking him whether he had more than the five, to which Mr. Woodin replied with a knowing wink of his eye." In the early part of the investigation, however, Strang and Drescher ruled out Woodin as a suspect in the 1933 Double Eagle case. Woodin died long before any of the 1933 Double Eagles sur-

faced, and none of the coins the Secret Service knew about could be traced back to him.

20. March 29, 1944, report of Harry Strang and George Drescher.

21. April 21, 1944, report of Harry Strang and George Drescher.

22. I contacted Edward Silver's daughter, Judith S. Cohen, by telephone and by letter for comment. In my letter I enclosed Secret Service reports naming Silver. Mrs. Cohen responded by letter on March 10, 2004: "My father, Edward Silver, was a kind and generous man, well liked and respected in his business. He was also a very quiet and very private person who kept his business and his home life strictly separate. I had no knowledge of this 'Affair of the Double Eagle' until you contacted me. I therefore do not have the knowledge to confirm or refute any of this information, and since my father obviously is not here to speak for himself, I am very uncomfortable with your use of materials which may contain unproved allegations, especially since no charges were ever brought against my father."

23. May 19, 1944, report of Harry Strang and George Drescher.

24. October 20, 1944, report of Harry Strang and Charles Rich.

Chapter Six
Seizure

1. May 31, 1945, letter from F. C. C. Boyd to Herbert Gaston, assistant secretary of the treasury.

2. June 8, 1946, report of A. G. Sutterfield.

3. The story is recounted, among other places, in George Kolbe's June 1, 2004, catalogue of the sale of John J. Ford's reference library. See Kolbe, p. 255.

4. Kosoff, *Abe Kosoff Remembers.*

Chapter Seven
Farouk of Egypt

1. "A King's Home," *Time*, September 8, 1952.

2. Hugh McLeave, *The Last Pharaoh: Farouk, of Egypt, 1920–1965*, p. 40.

3. William Stadiem, *Too Rich: The High Life and Tragic Death of King Farouk*, p. 114. Stadiem's is the most recent and best biography of Farouk.

4. Stadiem, p. 125.

5. McLeave, p. 5.

6. Stadiem, p. 128.

7. McLeave, p. 58.

8. Stadiem, p. 173.

9. Philipp Blom, *To Have and To Hold: An Intimate History of Collectors and Collecting*, p. 134.

10. Werner Muensterberger, *Collecting: An Unruly Passion*, p. 173. His chapter

on Phillipps appears on pp. 73–100. The letter from Phillipps's wife is quoted on p. 99.

11. Muensterberger, p. 3.

12. Stadiem, p. 74.

13. Ibid., pp. 63–64.

14. Hans Schulman was quoted in *The Repository*, vol. IV, no. 1, January-February 1986.

15. Kosoff, *Abe Kosoff Remembers*, p. 68.

16. Ibid., p. 77.

17. Stadiem, p. 212.

18. McLeave, p. 165.

19. January 7, 1949, telegram from the U.S. chargé-d'affaires in the United Kingdom to the U.S. secretary of state.

20. October 12, 1949, telegram from Caffery to the secretary of state.

21. Stadiem, p. 314.

22. Schulman, quoted in *The Repository*, vol. IV, no. 1.

23. November 26, 1951, telegram from Caffery to the State Department.

24. Stadiem, pp. 21–22.

25. Ibid., p. 22.

Chapter Eight
Disappearing

1. Kosoff, *Abe Kosoff Remembers,* reprints on pp. 93–94 a November 16, 1977, *Coin World* column by Hans Schulman in which Schulman recounts his experiences with Farouk and at the Palace Collections auction.

2. Schulman saw Farouk in 1956, when the ex-king was still hoping the French and the Israelis would overthrow the Nasser government and install his young son as king. Schulman stayed in touch with Farouk's secretary until just before Farouk's death in 1965.

3. Bowers, *Abe Kosoff*, p. 171.

4. Frank Hermann, *Sotheby's: Portrait of an Auction House*, p. 343.

5. "Supply and Demand in Paperweights," *The Times of London*, November 9, 1953.

6. Hermann, pp. 340–45, offers a vivid account of Sotheby's involvement in the Palace Collections sale, which is the basis of this account.

7. Kosoff, p. 63.

8. Van Winkle, "An Interview with John J. Ford, Jr., Part I." Ford also said that he had to send Baldwin a copy of the Adams-Woodin book on patterns. "He was trying to catalogue one of the greatest collections of patterns ever put together with no book. The whole thing was just a fiasco."

9. Kosoff, pp. 93–95.

10. Undated letter from secretary of treasury to secretary of state. The letter, part of the court file in *U.S.* v. *A $20 Gold Coin,* is also unsigned.

11. "Serag ed-Din Sentenced," *The Times of London,* February 1, 1954.

12. Kosoff, p. 89.

13. Mark Van Winkle,"An Interview with John Pittman," *LEGACY,* November 1988.

14. Hermann, p. 344.

15. "The Fond Collector," *Time,* February 22, 1954.

16. Ibid.

17. Kosoff, p. 62.

18. Van Winkle, "An Interview with John Pittman."

19. Ibid. "We also had a 1933 $20 gold piece removed from the auction," Pittman asserted. "I did that." Also, Kosoff, p. 65.

20. The embassy reported to the State Department that the lot had been purchased by an American citizen, but I consider Kosoff, who made notes on purchasers and prices in his catalogue, to be a more reliable source on this point.

Chapter Nine
Surfacing

1. This account of de Clermont's story, including all direct quotations and dialogue, is derived from de Clermont's January 18, 2000, deposition testimony in *U.S.* v. *A $20 Gold Coin.* De Clermont did not respond to my letter request for an interview. He has never spoken publicly about the 1933 Double Eagle except at his deposition. De Clermont did agree to speak to one journalist—Bryan Christy of *Playboy* magazine—about the coin, but then, according to Christy, abruptly cut the interview short. "You've been to Cairo?" Christy quoted de Clermont as saying in the April 2004 issue of *Playboy.* "Remember, people construct all sorts of stories. People put out versions of what they want to say. You know what I mean?"

2. This is Fenton's recollection of the encounter, from my three-hour interview with him on January 19, 2004. De Clermont, in his deposition, remembered the incident a bit differently. He did not recall telling Fenton at the convention that he thought the coins came from Farouk, nor did he remember showing the coins to Fenton. Fenton's memory seemed more specific, so I relied upon it.

3. De Clermont asked in his deposition that the true name of the Egyptian jeweler be treated as a trade secret and kept confidential. Although the jeweler's name also appears in another document from the litigation, to respect de Clermont's wish I have used a pseudonym.

4. De Clermont produced financial records as part of the litigation in *U.S.* v. *A $20 Gold Coin.* Though the records aren't always definitive, and de Clermont's memory wasn't perfect, this account of his dealings with Hassan and with Fen-

ton is based on his records, his deposition testimony, and my interview with Fenton.

Chapter Ten
The Deal

1. Fenton described the conversation to me in an interview on January 19, 2004. Mark Emory did not respond to an e-mail request to discuss his role in the sale of the 1933 Double Eagle.

2. "We Interview: Jay Parrino, The Mint L.L.C.," *The Rosen Numismatic Advisory*, October/November 1996. I located Parrino's onetime partner, Ed Wirth, at a nursing home in Missouri. Wirth, whom I interviewed by telephone on December 21, 2004, said he never had more than a few shops but didn't know how big Parrino's operation was after they split.

3. *The Rosen Numismatic Advisory*.

4. Parrino told me that Moore initiated the first and all subsequent conversations about the 1933 Double Eagle before December 1995. "He started all this crap with the '33," Parrino said. "I never once—except when I found out the coin was there—I never approached him. I don't have the time to babysit a guy like Jack." Remmel did confirm, however, in my interview with him on February 6, 2004, that Parrino asked Moore at the 1993 Baltimore show if Groendyke was interested in obtaining a 1933 Double Eagle.

5. Moore made the statement in his December 16, 1997, deposition in *U.S. v. A $20 Gold Coin*.

Chapter Eleven
"It's Not Okay Over Here"

1. Moore's biography comes from my interview with him in Amarillo on March 2, 2004.

2. The dialogue is as reported by Jack Moore during my interview in Amarillo. The basic facts were confirmed by John Groendyke in a telephone interview on February 2, 2004, and by Kent Remmel in a telephone interview on February 6, 2004. Other sources for the relationship among Groendyke, Remmel, and Moore are the court records in *John D. Groendyke, Kent Remmel, Remmel Enterprises, Inc., and R&M Rare Coins v. Jack R. Moore a/k/a Jackie Roy Moore and Martha L. Moore*, case 86274-E in the 108th District Court, Potter County, Texas. (Hereafter *Groendyke v. Moore*.)

3. Moore gave this account of buying the gold coins in a September 1, 1999, deposition in the case of *Groendyke v. Moore*. Remmel and Groendyke have denied giving Moore cash to trade for gold coins.

4. Moore asserted in his September 1, 1999, deposition that Remmel also skimmed money from Groendyke in this fashion. Both Groendyke and Remmel

have denied under oath that Remmel took money from his cousin without Groendyke's knowledge.

5. According to Moore's 1999 deposition in *Groendyke* v. *Moore*, the Texas dealer obtained a judgment against him for $16,500 in 1982. Moore testified about the gold deal gone bad in his 1997 deposition in *U.S.* v. *A $20 Gold Coin*.

6. Groendyke told me that he had no particular opinion of Parrino, whom he met at a coin show in Baltimore but with whom he never did business directly. "He has very high-end, good coins," Groendyke said.

7. Parrino told me that he never initiated a conversation with Moore about a 1933 Double Eagle until Fenton's coin surfaced. "Jack Moore is a liar," he said. "This guy is a piece of scum. He double-crossed everyone."

8. In taped conversations with Moore, Parrino confirmed that he was undergoing an IRS audit. "Auditing me for three and a half years," he complained on one tape. "They can't find anything, except the upgrading of coins [obtained at] market value and inventoried at the moment the coin becomes upgraded."

9. Moore told me this story in our interview in 2004. He also testified about it in his 1997 deposition in *U.S.* v. *A $20 Gold Coin*.

10. Moore telephoned the retired agent (who asked that his name not be revealed) during our interview, after I asked him how I could confirm his stories of law enforcement cooperation. I spoke to his friend on the phone.

11. I interviewed Freriks by telephone on February 12, 2004.

12. Freriks noted his speculation in a Secret Service synopsis report dated January 10, 1996. Records of the second Secret Service investigation—including transcripts of Moore's conversations with Parrino—were produced by the government in *U.S.* v. *A $20 Gold Coin*.

13. The Secret Service Public Information Office denied my requests to interview Ensminger and the other still-active agents involved in the 1933 Double Eagle investigation. This account of Ensminger's involvement comes from Freriks, whom I interviewed by telephone on February 12, 2004.

14. January 15, 1996, report from Freriks to Agent Don Dillard in New York.

15. January 26, 1996, report from Freriks to Agent Don Dillard in New York.

Chapter Twelve
The Sting

1. This account of why Ensminger approved the initial investigation comes from Freriks. (The Secret Service Public Information Office would not permit interviews with active agents, including Ensminger.) Freriks and two other agents, Don Dillard and William Whiteside, were deposed in *U.S.* v. *A $20 Gold Coin*. Additional details of the Secret Service's plans for the sting at the Waldorf come from those depositions, as well as from Secret Service reports produced by the government in that lawsuit.

Chapter Thirteen
"I Was Just Selling a Coin"

1. This account of the interrogation comes from my interview with Parrino at the coin show in Orlando in January 2004. The Secret Service Public Information Office declined my request to interview agents still on active duty.

2. This account comes from Fenton.

3. The final purchase price negotiated between Parrino and Moore at their final meeting in Missouri, according to Freriks's reports, was actually $1.65 million. Moore told Freriks that the extra $150,000 was a sweetener for the seller, but he probably presented it to Parrino as justification for his commission.

4. I interviewed Berke several times. His biography comes from our discussion on September 12, 2003.

5. I interviewed Alan Mansfield on January 22, 2004.

6. I interviewed Mei Lin Kwan-Gett on January 20, 2004.

7. This information comes from Don Dillard's May 29, 1997, deposition in *U.S. v. A $20 Gold Coin.*

Chapter Fourteen
"All Right, Then. Let's Fight"

1. June 4, 1996, message from Ensminger to Flanagan, part of the record in *U.S. v. A $20 Gold Coin.* "Evidently, the Mint was no more willing to push the arguement [sic] that this coin was unlawfully struck and never legitimately released from the Mint than we were," Ensminger noted. "They did not confiscate the nickel and it was sold at auction."

2. Michael Hodder, a historian and cataloguer who frequently works for Stack's, also did a limited amount of research for Berke and Fenton.

3. The entire text of the letter is: "Receipt is acknowledged of your letter of March 13th. The Mints are allowed to receive gold and to pay out for it an equivalent amount of gold; that is, if a depositor presents gold scrap in the form of jewelry or dental scrap and asks to have the equivalent in gold returned this would be done. Such a transaction neither increases nor depletes the stock of gold in the Treasury."

4. *United States v. Barnard*, decided on July 22, 1947.

5. "Fenton's first set of document requests and first set of interrogatories," part of the court record in *U.S. v. A $20 Gold Coin.*

6. Journalist Bryan Christy, who conducted extensive research on the 1933 Double Eagle, continues to question whether Fenton's coin is the Farouk specimen. "Farouk was Fenton's courtroom defense," he wrote in his April 2004 *Playboy* article, asserting that "one of the oldest, most respected names in numismatics" told Christy that the Fenton coin was not Farouk's. Having studied Andre de Cler-

mont's deposition and the documentary evidence—as well as having interviewed Fenton and Berke at length—I believe the Fenton coin was Farouk's. It simply begs credulity that de Clermont and Fenton could have acquired and carefully documented so many unique Farouk pieces from de Clermont's Egyptian jeweler source, then conspired to use him to provide a tenuous provenance for a 1933 Double Eagle they acquired elsewhere. A more reasonable explanation of the vagueness of the invoice by which Fenton purchased the 1933 Double Eagle is that Fenton knew he was buying a coin of dubious legality and wanted to keep it quiet.

7. I interviewed Kenneth Gubin by telephone on January 21, 2004. I interviewed his then-deputy Gregory Weinman at the Mint offices in Washington, DC, on January 15, 2004.

Chapter Fifteen
Jack Moore's Last Stand

1. The note and the other documents referenced in this section—an affidavit from the custodian of records at the Amarillo National Bank and a real-estate contract signed by Moore and his wife—are part of the court record in *Groendyke* v. *Moore*.

2. Groendyke's and Remmel's affidavits in *Groendyke* v. *Moore*.

3. Moore's deposition is part of the record in *U.S.* v. *A $20 Gold Coin*.

4. I interviewed Jonathan Etra by telephone on January 22, 2004.

5. I interviewed Kent Remmel by telephone on February 6, 2004.

Chapter Sixteen
Splitting the Baby

1. I have interviewed Jane Levine several times in person and by telephone. She told me about her background in an interview on March 17, 2004, at the U.S. Attorney's office in Manhattan.

2. De Clermont's January 18, 2000, deposition in *U.S.* v. *A $20 Gold Coin*.

3. February 1, 2000, Memorandum of Law in Support of Claimant Stephen C. Fenton's Motion for Summary Judgment, in *U.S.* v. *A $20 Gold Coin*.

4. March 3, 2000, The Government's Opposition to Claimant's Motion for Summary Judgment, in *U.S.* v. *A $20 Gold Coin*.

5. March 23, 2000, hearing transcript in *U.S.* v. *A $20 Gold Coin*.

6. March 8, 1933, letter, copied by Tepperman-Gelfant at the National Archives.

7. I interviewed Tepperman-Gelfant, now a student at Harvard Law School, by telephone on February 4, 2004.

Chapter Seventeen
Second Chances

1. The complete list was, in the order they appeared on the U.S. Mint's "Bidder's Mailing List": Bowers and Merena Galleries; Spink America (a division of Christie's); Butterfields; Heritage Numismatic Auctions (the auction arm of Heritage Rare Coin Galleries); Numismates (a Belgian company); Sotheby's; Phillips New York; Downie's USA; R. M. Smythe; Superior Galleries; David Akers Numismatics; Greg Manning Auctions; Guernsey's. The two houses that submitted proposals but were not invited to make oral presentations were—according to a May 14, 2001, Mint memo entitled, "Summary of Source Selection Activities to Date for the 1933 Double Eagle"—Spink America and Superior Galleries.
2. I interviewed Larry Stack in February 2005 and David Redden in March 2005 about the Mint selection process and the 1933 Double Eagle auction. This account is based on those interviews.
3. Paul Gilkes, "1933 $20 Makes Public Debut During March 19 Today Show," *Coin World*, March 29, 2002.
4. I interviewed Mark Raffety by telephone on May 25, 2005.
5. I interviewed Todd Imhof by telephone on June 2, 2005.
6. David Tripp, *Illegal Tender: Gold, Greed, and the Mystery of the Lost 1933 Double Eagle*, p. 285.

Chapter Eighteen
"Fair Warning"

1. I interviewed Stephen Tebo by telephone in March 2005.
2. Coin experts believe that Akers's client, whom he described at the time as a businessman from the Southwest specializing in early U.S. coins, was Dallas real-estate mogul Mack Pogue, who sat with Akers and his son and fellow collector, Brent, at the auction.
3. *Coin World* has archived a video of the auction. It's available at www.coin world.com/news/081202/MOV01334.mpg.

Chapter Nineteen
Only One Coin

1. Tripp, p. 289–90.
2. Stephen Fenton interview, January 13, 2005.
3. David Redden told me the story when I interviewed him on March 16, 2005. Obviously, I could not confirm the account with the buyer, whose identity remains unknown to everyone except Redden.

Epilogue

1. I interviewed Langbord at a restaurant in Manhattan on October 24, 2005.

2. February 3, 1969, memo from S. A. Carnes to Mr. Warner, produced by the government in *U.S. v. A $20 Gold Coin.*

3. Q. David Bowers, *A Guide Book of Double Eagle Gold Coins*, pp. 22–23. Bowers himself first went to Europe to import gold coins in 1961. "Immense quantities of double eagles were in the vaults [in Swiss banks]," he wrote. "Anyone positioning himself as a serious buyer would likely be ushered into a private room for a conference."

4. I interviewed David Akers about the European hoards by telephone in November 2004.

5. Bowers, *A Guide Book*, p. 278.

6. Ibid., p. 284.

7. I interviewed Julian for a story called "The Coin Chase," which appeared in *The American Lawyer* in March 2003.

8. April 7, 2004, telephone interview with Tony Terranova.

9. Both David Redden and Larry Stack told me there was no 1933 Double Eagle in Browning's Dallas Bank Collection in 2001.

Selected Bibliography

Books, Catalogues, and Pamphlets

Adams, Edgar H., and William H. Woodin. *United States Pattern, Trial, and Experimental Pieces*. New York: The American Numismatic Society, 1913.

Akers, David W. *A Handbook of 20th-Century United States Gold Coins 1907–1933*. Wolfeboro, NH: Bowers and Merena Galleries, Inc., 1988.

———. *United States Gold Patterns*. Racine, WI: Western Publishing, 1975.

Baldwin, Fred. *The Palace Collections of Egypt: Catalogue of the Highly Important and Extremely Valuable Collection of Coins and Medals*. London: Sotheby & Co., 1953.

Blom, Philipp. *To Have and To Hold: An Intimate History of Collectors and Collecting*. Woodstock and New York: Overlook Press, 2003.

Bowers, Q. David. *Abe Kosoff: Dean of Numismatics*. Wolfeboro, NH: Bowers and Merena Galleries, Inc., 1985.

———. *American Gold and Gold Coinage: An Overview*. Los Angeles: Bowers and Ruddy Galleries, Inc., 1982.

———. *A Guide Book of Double Eagle Gold Coins*. Atlanta: Whitman Publishing, 2004.

———. *The Rare Silver Dollars Dated 1804 and the Exciting Adventures of Edmund Roberts*. Wolfeboro, NH: Bowers and Merena Galleries, 1999.

Breen, Walter. *Early United States Half Eagles 1795–1838*. Chicago: Hewitt Brothers, 1966.

———. *United States Eagles*. Chicago: Hewitt Brothers, n.d.

———. *Varieties of United States Half Eagles 1839–1929*. Chicago: Hewitt Brothers, n.d.

Burns, Helen M. *The American Banking Community and New Deal Banking Reforms: 1933–1935*. Westport, CT: Greenwood Press, a division of Williamhouse-Regency Inc., 1974.

Clain-Stefanelli, Elvira. *Numismatics: An Ancient Science: A Survey of its History*. Washington, DC: Government Printing Office, 1965.

Drummond, A. L. *A Curious Thievery at the Philadelphia Mint*. Wolfeboro, NH: Bowers and Merena Galleries, Inc., 1997.

Dryfrout, John H. *The 1907 United States Gold Coinage*. Cornish, NH: Eastern National, 2002.

Ganz, David L. *The World of Coins and Coin Collecting*. New York: Charles Scribner's Sons, 1980.

Garrett, Jeff, and Ron Guth. *100 Greatest U.S. Coins*. Atlanta: H. E. Harris, 2003.

Goodwin, Jason. *Greenback: The Almighty Dollar and the Invention of America*. New York: Henry Holt, 2003.

Hall, David. *A Mercenary's Guide to the Rare Coin Market*. Fort Worth, TX: American Bureau of Economic Research, 1987.

Hermann, Frank. *Sotheby's: Portrait of an Auction House*. New York: W. W. Norton, 1981.

History of the New York Numismatic Club . . . 1908–1961. New York: New York Numismatic Club, 1961.

Houck, Davis W. *FDR and Fear Itself: The First Inaugural Address*. College Station, TX: A&M University Press, 2002.

Johnson, David R. *Illegal Tender: Counterfeiting and the Secret Service in Nineteenth-Century America*. Washington, DC: Smithsonian Institution Press, 1995.

Kobler, John. *Capone: The Life and World of Al Capone*. New York: G. P. Putnam's Sons, 1971.

Kolbe, George. *John J. Ford, Jr. Collection. Reference Library, Part I. June 1, 2004.* Crestline, CA: George Kolbe Fine Numismatic Books, 2004.

Kosoff, Abe. *Abe Kosoff Remembers.* New York: Sanford J. Durst Numismatic Publications, 1981.

Leach, Frank A., and David Q. Bowers. *Recollections of a Mint Director.* Wolfeboro, NH: Bowers and Merena Galleries, Inc., 1987.

McLeave, Hugh. *The Last Pharaoh: Farouk of Egypt, 1920–1965.* New York: McCall Publishing, 1969.

McNall, Bruce, with Michael D'Antonio. *Fun While It Lasted: My Rise and Fall in the Land of Fame and Fortune.* New York: Hyperion, 2003.

Moley, Raymond. *After Seven Years.* New York: Harper & Brothers, 1939.

Muensterberger, Werner. *Collecting: An Unruly Passion. Psychological Perspectives.* New York: Harcourt, Brace, 1995. Originally published by Princeton University Press, 1994.

Newman, Eric P., and Kenneth E. Bressett. *The Fantastic 1804 Dollar.* Racine, WI: Whitman Publishing, 1962.

Smith, A. M. *U.S. Mint and Coins. Coins and Coinage. The United States Mint, Philadelphia, History, Biography, Statistics, Work, Machinery, Products, Officials.* Philadelphia: A. M. Smith, n.d.

Stack's Rare Coins: The Leader in Numismatics Since 1935. New York: Stack's, 2000.

Stadiem, William. *Too Rich: The High Life and Tragic Death of King Farouk.* New York: Carroll & Graf, 1991.

Taxay, Don. *Counterfeit, Mis-Struck, and Unofficial U.S. Coins.* New York: Arco Publishing, 1963.

———. *The U.S. Mint and Coinage.* New York: Arco Publishing, 1966.

Tharp, Louise Hall. *Saint-Gaudens and the Gilded Era.* Boston: Little, Brown, 1969.

Tripp, David. *Illegal Tender: Gold, Greed, and the Mystery of the Lost 1933 Double Eagle.* New York: Free Press, 2004.

———. *The 1933 Double Eagle.* New York: Sotheby's, 2001.

Van Ryzin, Robert R. *Twisted Tails: Sifted Fact, Fantasy and Fiction from U.S. Coin History.* Iola, WI: Krause Publications, 1995.

Vermeule, Cornelius. *Numismatic Art in America: Aesthetics of the United States Coinage*. Cambridge, MA: Belknap Press of Harvard University Press, 1971.

Weinberg, Steve. *Armand Hammer: The Untold Story*. Boston: Little, Brown, 1989.

Weiss, Wilfred. *Want $3750 for a Nickel; B. Max Mehl, the Dean of American Numismatics*. Philadelphia: Curtis Pub. Co., 1949. (Reprinted from the *Saturday Evening Post*.)

Wilkinson, Burke. *Uncommon Clay: The Life and Works of Augustus Saint-Gaudens*. New York: Harcourt Brace Jovanovich, 1985.

Wilson, Frank J., and Beth Day. *Special Agent: A Quarter Century with the Treasury Department and the Secret Service*. New York: Holt, Rinehart and Winston, 1965.

NEWSPAPER, MAGAZINE, AND OTHER ARTICLES

"Art and Artists." *Philadelphia Press*, November 17, 1907.

"Auction of Prince Farouk's Stamps." *The Times of London*, February 13, 1954.

Berliner, Milton. "Farouk's Treasures Going, Going, Gone." *The Washington Daily News*, December 2, 1953.

Burdette, Roger W. "By Hammer and Anvil." *Coin World*, January 12, 2004.

Christy, Bryan. "Curse of the Double Eagle." *Playboy*, April 2004.

Cipriano, Ralph. "Israel Switt, dean of Jewelers' Row." *The Philadelphia Inquirer*, January 19, 1990.

Deisher, Beth. "Smithsonian to Dismantle 'History of Money' Exhibit." *Coin World*, May 3, 2004.

"The Fond Collector." *Time*, February 22, 1954.

"Frank J. Wilson, 83, Famed Chief of U.S. Secret Service." *Washington Post*, June 23, 1970.

Friedus, Dan. "Ford Library Sale Smashes Records." *Coin World*, June 21, 2004.

Ganz, David. "The 1964 Peace Dollar. The Mystery Remains." *The Numismatist*, August 2004.

Gilkes, Paul. "Are Feds Poised to Drop 1933 $20 Criminal Case?" *Coin World*, April 22, 1996.

———. "Authorities Drop Criminal Charges." *Coin World*, April 29, 1996.

———. "Authorities Seek Ownership of 1933 $20 Coin in Civil Case." *Coin World*, April 29, 1996.

———. "A Challenging Series: Assembling Barber Dime Set Tests Collector's Mettle." *Coin World*, September 29, 2003.

———. "1933 $20 Makes Public Debut During March 19 Today Show." *Coin World*, March 29, 2002.

———. "Pledge for Liberty." *Coin World*, December 8, 2003.

"Gold Hoarders Returning Coin to Phila. Banks." *The Evening Bulletin*, March 9, 1933.

"Gold Was Hidden in Long Undies." *The Evening Bulletin*, March 15, 1933.

"Governor Miller Makes William H. Woodin State Coal Head." *The New York Times*, September 6, 1922.

Hering, Henry. "History of the $10 and $20 Gold Coins of 1907 issue." *The Numismatist*, August 1949.

Herrick, Thaddeus. "Big Money: When 5 Cents Is Worth $3 Million," *The Wall Street Journal*, May 21, 2004.

"Inside Farouk's Palaces." *Newsweek*, September 8, 1952.

Julian, R. W. "The 1933 Double Eagle." Draft article, September 2002.

"King Farouk's Abdication and Departure." *The Times of London*, July 28, 1952.

"A King's Home," *Time*, September 8, 1952.

Kolbe, George F. "An Exotic Specialty: Selling Rare Numismatica." *AB Magazine*, December 24–31, 1990.

Korver, Bob. "The Collector King." *Coin World*, June 3, 2002.

Kraljevich, John J., Jr. "Found Money: The duPont Dollar Comes Home." *The Numismatist*, June 2004.

"Legal Action by Prince Farouk." *The Times of London*, February 22, 1954.

Logies, Martin A. "First Buck." *The Numismatist*, May 2004.

Mehl, B. Max. "Proof of Proven Success: A Partial List of the More Important Collections Handled by Me in Recent Years." March 1, 1939.

"Mint Not Affected by Banking Holiday." *The Philadelphia Inquirer*, March 7, 1933.

Molyneaux, Peter J. "A Texas Master of Coins." *The Numismatist*, March 1929.

"Now the Penthouse Palace Is Evolving." *The New York Times*, March 23, 1930.

"On Gold Standard, Woodin Declares." *The New York Times*, March 6, 1933.

"Philadelphia Gold Yield for Day Is $907,000." *The Philadelphia Inquirer*, March 11, 1933.

"The Presidency." *Time*, March 6, 1933.

"The Presidency." *Time*, March 13, 1933.

"The Presidency." *Time*, March 20, 1933.

"Prince Farouk's Art Treasures." *The Times of London*, October 22, 1953.

"Prince Farouk's Coins." *The Times of London*, March 18, 1954.

"Prince Farouk's Collections." *The Times of London*, February 10, 1954.

"Prince Farouk's Stamps." *The Times of London*, August 13, 1953.

"Prompt Action Relieves Financial Tension." *Newsweek*, March 18, 1933.

"Rare Coins Not 'Hoarded.'" *The New York Times*, April 9, 1933

Ray, Cyril. "A King's Treasures." *The New York Times Magazine*. March 14, 1954.

The Repository, vol. IV, no. 1, January–February 1986.

"Roosevelt Will Go to Capitol Today for Inauguration." *The New York Times*, March 2, 1933.

Rosen, Maurice. "We Interview: Jay Parrino, The Mint L.L.C." *The Rosen Numismatic Advisory*, October/November 1996.

"Sale of Prince Farouk's Art Treasures." *The Times of London*, March 17, 1954.

Schofield, Matthew. "$1.5 million and a Nickel Add Up to History." *The Kansas City Star*, May 25, 1996.

"Supply and Demand in Paperweights." *The Times of London*, November 9, 1953.

"The Treasures Farouk Left Behind." *Life*, November 24, 1952.

"Treasures of Former King of Egypt." *The Times of London*, February 9, 1954.

"United States Government to Sell the Famed 1933 Double Eagle." Sotheby's/Stack's press release, February 7, 2002.

Van Winkle, Mark. "An Interview with John J. Ford, Jr., Part I." *LEGACY*, April 1990.

———. "An Interview with John J. Ford, Jr., Part II." *LEGACY*, June 1990.

———. "An Interview with Walter Breen." *LEGACY*, September 1988.

———. "An Interview with John Pittman." *LEGACY*, November 1988.

Von Klinger, Eric. "Fugio Fiasco Ended Federal Contract Coinage." *Coin World*, December 1, 2002.

"W. H. Woodin Is Revealed as a Composer." *The New York Times*, February 19, 1930.

"The Women Who Served as Models for the Coins." *The New York Times*, December 15, 1907.

"Woodin and Mills Hold Conference." *The New York Times*, February 24, 1933.

"Woodin and Others Unable to Reach Inaugural Stand." *The New York Times*, March 5, 1933.

"Woodin Still Can Pun." *The New York Times*, March 10, 1933.

"Woodin Still Shuns 'Asbestos Breeches.'" *The New York Times*, April 9, 1933.

"Woodin Succeeded in Many Fields." *The New York Times*, May 5, 1934.

"Woodin Withdraws from 2 Companies." *The New York Times*. June 7, 1924.

Zerbe, Farran. "Pattern Pieces Seized." *The Numismatist*, July 1910.

———. "Status of Pattern Coins Seems Established." *The Numismatist*, October-November 1910.

Index